# Behavioral Dimensions of Retirement Economics

# Behavioral Dimensions of Retirement Economics

Henry J. Aaron
*Editor*

BROOKINGS INSTITUTION PRESS
*Washington, D.C.*

RUSSELL SAGE FOUNDATION
*New York, N.Y.*

*BNV 1481-5/2*

Copyright © 1999
THE BROOKINGS INSTITUTION
RUSSELL SAGE FOUNDATION

*Behavioral Dimensions of Retirement Economics*
may be ordered from:

Brookings Institution Press
1775 Massachusetts Avenue, N.W.
Washington, D.C. 20036
Tel.: 1-800-275-1447 or (202) 797-6258
Fax: (202) 797-6004
*www.brookings.edu*

*Library of Congress Cataloging-in-Publication data*

Behavioral dimensions of retirement economics / edited by Henry J. Aaron.
    p. cm.
    Includes bibliographical references and index.
    ISBN 0-8157-0064-4 (alk. paper)
    ISBN 0-8157-0063-6 (pbk. : alk. paper)
    1. Retirement—United States—Planning. 2. Retirement—Economic
aspects—United States. 3. Retirement income—United
States—Planning. 4. Finance, Personal—United States. I. Aaron,
Henry J.
    HQ1063.2.U6 B44 1999                                    99-6604
    332.024'01—dc21                                          CIP

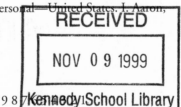

9 8 7 6 5 4 3 2 1

The paper used in this publication meets minimum requirements of the
American National Standard for Information Sciences—Permanence of Paper
for Printed Library Materials: ANSI Z39.48-1984.

Typeset in Adobe Garamond

Composition by Harlowe Typography, Cottage City, Maryland

Printed by R.R. Donnelley and Sons, Harrisonburg, Virginia

# Preface

RETIREMENT STANDS as one of the most important economic, psychological, and social transitions in most people's lives. Furthermore, as life expectancies grow and incomes rise, people are spending an increasing fraction of their lives in retirement. Yet abundant evidence, derived from anecdote and social science, shows that many people plan very imperfectly for this crucial period. The largest programs of the federal government are fashioned to ensure that people have basic retirement income and adequate acute and long-term health care either as a matter of earned right or in the event of destitution. Many of these programs rest on the explicit premise that people will often not voluntarily behave in their own best interests. Yet the prevailing drift in many social sciences has been to appropriate the assumption of rational behavior that has been so productive in economic analysis.

This book applies to retirement research and retirement policy the insights of behavioral economics, an emerging field that blends insights of psychology, sociology, and economics and tries to treat rigorously the fact that behavior frequently falls well short of the rational ideal. It grew out of a seminar held at the Center for the Advanced Study in the Behavioral Sciences in April 1997 and a research conference held in April 1998 at the western offices of the National Bureau of Economic Research. Henry

Aaron thanks the Alfred P. Sloan Foundation, the Russell Sage Foundation, and the National Science Foundation (grant SBR9601236) for support during the year 1996–97 and the Russell Sage Foundation for support in organizing and editing this volume.

In addition to several of the authors of papers in this volume, George Akerlof, David Card, Laura Carstensen, Mark Granovetter, Angela O'Rand, Norbert Schwarz, and Neil Smelser participated in the 1997 seminar, and Kenneth Arrow and Thomas Schelling participated in the 1998 research conference. James Schneider and Tanjam Jacobson edited this volume. Kathleen Elliott Yinug assisted in conference arrangements and in manuscript preparation. Trish Weisman proofread the pages and Sherry L. Smith prepared the index.

HENRY J. AARON

# Contents

# Behavioral Dimensions of Retirement Economics

HENRY J. AARON

# Introduction

R ECENT EVENTS have brought center stage the question of whether public policy should be used to influence retirement behavior. In 1996 a majority of the Advisory Council on Social Security supported an increase in the age at which full social security benefits are paid. Many members of Congress subsequently endorsed this recommendation. Senator John Breaux, cochair of the National Bipartisan Commission on the Future of Medicare, proposed in late 1998 raising the age of eligibility for medicare benefits from 65 to 67. Both proposals would assuredly lower budget costs for social security and medicare. They might cause people to defer retirement and thereby boost lifetime money incomes. They might even be "fair" if one accepts an argument, freighted with unstated assumptions, that working lives should lengthen as life expectancies increase. But would these legislative changes improve the welfare of affected workers? And how could one know?

The innovative analytical methods used in the papers contained in this volume are drawn from the nascent field of behavioral economics, a field that encompasses efforts by some economists, psychologists, sociologists, and legal scholars, working together and separately, to blend research findings from their various disciplines while retaining the logical rigor and statistical precision that characterize standard economic theory and econo-

1

metrics. Behavioral methods have produced important analytical insights in the analysis of financial markets, and they have illuminated various aspects of the law, including the methods used to calculate damages.[1] But they have not been applied systematically to any major question of public policy. This book takes a small step to fill that gap.

The book begins with Gary Burtless's simple explanation of the standard framework economists use for analyzing lifetime labor supply. This framework assumes that people make consistent lifetime plans regarding the timing of work and retirement. As new information becomes available, they modify these plans. Within this framework, one can identify how such public policies as social security and medicare influence the lifetime distribution of income. Burtless presents evidence that changes in rules on when people become entitled to social security have altered behavior gradually. Although the age of initial eligibility for benefits was lowered from 65 to 62 in 1961, the age at which men actually claimed benefits has dropped gradually since the rules changed. This result is difficult to reconcile with the view that people understand the rules completely and are immune to influence from the behavior of peers. Under these assumptions, people should alter their behavior promptly when rules change. The fact that the adjustment is slow and gradual suggests that processes other than response to rules that changed abruptly and have been stable ever since have influenced behavior.

Henry Aaron explains why findings from psychology, sociology, and information theory suggest that traditional economic models are likely to go astray in analyzing the retirement decision and the effects on behavior and welfare of policies to influence the decision. In particular, he contends that, contrary to assumptions of standard economics, people typically do not have clearly defined preferences, they lack information that would be necessary for a full analysis of the implications of various decisions regarding work and saving, they lack the mental capacity to analyze even the data that are available to them, they are heavily influenced by social networks, and they tend retroactively to justify as optimal the course of action that they happened to select.

Annamaria Lusardi tests various predictions of the life-cycle model of decisionmaking with data from the Health and Retirement Study, a longitudinal panel survey carried out by the Survey Research Center of the University of Michigan. The life-cycle model posits that people plan consumption each year based on their best estimates of the income they expect

---

1. Thaler (1994); and Sunstein, Kahneman, and Schrade (1997).

to receive over their lifetimes. This model suggests that the young, whose income is normally lower than it will be in the future, will save little and may go into debt. The middle-aged, who are in their prime earnings years, will save at a relatively high rate to prepare for their last working years, when income normally declines, and for retirement, when earnings cease. The evidence from the Health and Retirement Study indicates that people save much less than the model suggests is optimal and that a large minority of the population saves nothing and does not even think about retirement. These results represent a major challenge to the life-cycle model, which underlies most analyses of retirement decisionmaking. William Gale's comments on Lusardi's findings follow her chapter.

Ted O'Donoghue and Matthew Rabin examine procrastination, a phenomenon that is not considered in standard economic analysis but that seems to be a prominent candidate for explaining the failure of most people to save adequately for retirement. They point out that because people normally save a little bit each period for retirement, many believe that the cost of waiting to start retirement saving is small and that a little bit of extra effort in the future can make up for lost time. In short, they procrastinate. O'Donoghue and Rabin explain formally the mental processes that can cause such temporizing to be repeated period after period, so that the necessary first steps are delayed or indefinitely postponed. The key is people's failure to recognize that today's incentives for delay will be similar to tomorrow's, and that it will be as tempting tomorrow to wait to start saving as it is today. The authors provide a formal explanation for Lusardi's empirical findings regarding retirement saving. The striking finding of their analysis is that small impediments to acting now can have long-run consequences out of all proportion to the size of the initial obstacle. Comments by Peter Diamond follow their paper.

Robert Axtell and Joshua Epstein address the question raised by Gary Burtless: why has the age at which men claim social security benefits changed so slowly following the change in the age of eligibility for benefits? Although many explanations are possible, Axtell and Epstein explore the possibility that most people do not respond specifically to the change of rules but instead to the behavior of peers or to other, random events. To develop this idea, they employ a computer-based model consisting of "software agents," people represented in a computer program by a set of behavioral rules. They find that even if only a few percent of agents respond directly to changed incentives, the population as a whole eventually behaves *as if* everyone were responding to those rules. However, the transition to the new behavioral norm may be protracted. The reason for the delay is that agents who do not respond to these rules may retire randomly, while others, who are part of social networks, retire when a sufficient fraction of agents who belong to their social networks retire. Models based on standard analytical assumptions would infer from the fact that the entire population eventually behaves like those who responded "rationally" to the new rules that the entire population is responding rationally to the policy change, although few members of the population actually are doing so. Axtell and Epstein point out that seemingly rational behavior of large groups may emerge not from actual rationality but from social networks that gradually propagate the rational behavior of only a few people. If most people are behaving imitatively, it is not clear that changes in behavior that occur as rules change mean that welfare has increased for the majority of the population. Comments by Robert Hall follow the chapter by Axtell and Epstein.

David Fetherstonhaugh and Lee Ross present results of an experiment that tests whether people's responses to public policies depend on how public policies are "framed," or presented, and whether the effects of retirement policies are subject to "wealth illusion." Framing refers to the reference point with which some policy is compared. For example, would actual retirement behavior differ depending on whether retirement at age 65 is described as (a) retiring "late," because the "normal" retirement age is 62; (b) retiring at the "normal" age, because the "normal" retirement age is 65; or (c) retiring "early," because the "normal" retirement age is 68? Wealth illusion refers to the tendency of people to prefer lump sums to streams of payments of equal, or greater, present value.

Both issues come into play with respect to the actuarial adjustments provided to social security beneficiaries who claim "early retirement benefits" before age 65 or whose benefits are delayed because they continue to have sizable earnings after age 65. The adjustments in both cases are changes in the monthly benefit that the retiree receives—a reduction for "early" retirement and an increase for "late" retirement. Fetherstonhaugh and Ross find some evidence that behavior would be different if the decision were framed differently—that is, if the "normal" retirement age were higher or lower than age 65, even if the benefits were unchanged. And they find stronger evidence that people would be more willing to defer retirement if they received a lump-sum payment rather than an increase in their monthly retirement benefit, even if the lump sum were worth no more than the present value of the increased annuity. Comments by Daniel Kahneman follow the chapter by Fetherstonhaugh and Ross.

George Loewenstein, Drazen Prelec, and Roberto Weber compare key assumptions of economic analysis with amply replicated findings of psychology. The assumptions are that higher income boosts people's welfare and that their current judgments about the effects of current decisions on their future well-being are reasonably accurate and unbiased. Together with the finding that consumption drops abruptly at retirement, the assumptions suggest that welfare declines at retirement. They also suggest that people who are not yet retired should correctly anticipate the drop in consumption and take steps to prevent it or at least should foresee that their well-being will fall after retirement.

Unfortunately for the standard model, the findings of psychological research contradict all of these implications. Loewenstein, Prelec, and Weber report survey results indicating that a person's sense of well-being does not deteriorate at retirement. Furthermore, the not-yet-retired do not accurately forecast the effect of retirement on their well-being and the retired do not accurately recall what they thought the effect of retirement on their well-being would be. Their findings cast serious doubt on the view that people accurately anticipate or recall the impact of one of life's major passages on their well-being. The findings also call into question the *subjective* impact of income shifts that occur at retirement and of public policies that would change these income shifts. Comments by Matthew Rabin follow the chapter by Loewenstein, Prelec, and Weber.

Shelly Lundberg explores the relevance for the analysis of retirement behavior of the fact that the retirement decisions of married workers are likely to be the result of some form of interaction between spouses. That retirement by one member of a couple involves the interests of both and normally involves joint deliberation may seem obvious, but most empirical and theoretical economic analyses of retirement assume that the decision is made by an individual based on his or her earnings, wealth, health, and selected other variables, such as the spouse's earnings and health or local employment conditions. Lundberg shows that a well-developed part of standard economic analysis—game theory—could be applied to the analysis of retirement decisions. Husbands and wives are seen as "playing a game" in which the decisions of each influence the well-being of both. Each partner adopts some strategy that may be designed to maximize his or her own well-being or they may cooperate to maximize their joint well-being. The rich literature of game theory provides a variety of theorems on how individuals will behave in different objective situations. For example, behavior can change as the "players" age and death threatens to put an end to the "game." Because game theory has not yet been applied to the analysis of retirement decisions, one of Lundberg's contributions is to suggest scope for additional research. B. Douglas Bernheim, whose comments follow Lundberg's chapter, proposes certain modifications of Lundberg's conclusions.

# References

Sunstein, Cass R., Daniel Kahneman, and David Schrade. 1997. "Assessing Punitive Damages (with Notes on Cognition and Valuation in Law)." Law and Economics Working Paper 50. University of Chicago Law School.
Thaler, Richard. 1994. *Quasi-Rational Economics*. Russell Sage.

GARY BURTLESS

# 1 An Economic View of Retirement

RETIREMENT IS an event with profound personal, social, and economic consequences. Economists, not surprisingly, focus on its financial ramifications. When workers withdraw from the labor force in old age, their earnings cease and must be replaced by some other source of income. Nowadays the main alternative sources of income are employer-provided pensions and social security. But these only became important within the past half century. Before that, workers who wished to retire were ordinarily forced to rely on transfers from relatives, their own savings, public aid, or charity.

Economists' interest in retirement has focused on three interrelated phenomena: saving in anticipation of retirement, the timing of retirement, and the impact on the economy of transfers needed to support a large retired population. This chapter focuses on the timing of retirement and its relationship with lifetime consumption.

## Trends in Retirement

When workers retire, they withdraw from their normal occupations and reduce their work effort or stop work altogether. At the turn of the twen-

I gratefully acknowledge the research assistance of J. J. Prescott and Stacy Sneeringer.

7

tieth century, retirement was relatively rare but not unknown; two out of three men past age 65 were employed, but one-third were not.[1] By mid-century retirement was far more common: less than half the men 65 and older held jobs in 1950. By 1990 just 16 percent of men older than 65 were employed or actively seeking a job. The proportion of women past age 65 who were employed also fell during the century, but the reduction was far smaller than among men because the percentage of older women in paid work has always been low.

The decline in labor force participation among older men has not been confined to the United States. It is characteristic of all rich industrialized countries. In some European countries, employment rates among the elderly are now significantly below those in the United States.[2] Along with a shrinking workweek and rising labor force participation among women, earlier retirement among men has been a distinctive feature of economic development in the rich countries.

That older men are increasingly retired is clearly evident in figure 1-1. Each line traces the labor force participation rate of older American men, by age, during a different year of the twentieth century (a person is considered a labor force participant if he or she holds a job or is actively searching for work). The top line shows age-specific participation rates of older men in 1910. There was a clear pattern of labor market withdrawal with advancing age. Even at age 74, however, the participation rate in 1910 was only slightly below 50 percent. Participation rates in 1940, 1970, and 1995–96 also show a characteristic pattern of labor market withdrawal as men grow older, but the fall-off begins at an earlier age and proceeds at a faster pace.

The decline in male participation has been neither smooth nor uniform over the century. Figure 1-2 shows the amount of decline in participation at each year of age, measured as a percentage of the 1910 participation rate at the same age. By far the largest proportionate declines have occurred among men past the age of 66. In 1996, for example, the participation rate among 74-year-olds was nearly 80 percent below the equivalent rate in 1910. The fall-off in participation has been proportionately smaller at younger ages.

The shading scheme in the figure shows how fast participation rates fell in different periods. In general, large declines occurred early in the cen-

---

1. Bureau of the Census (1975, p. 132). Retirement patterns are much more difficult to measure among women because most worked primarily within the home (and without pay) during most of their adult lives.

2. Quinn and Burkhauser (1994, pp. 56–61).

Figure 1-1. *Male Labor Force Participation, by Age, Selected Years, 1910–96*

Percent

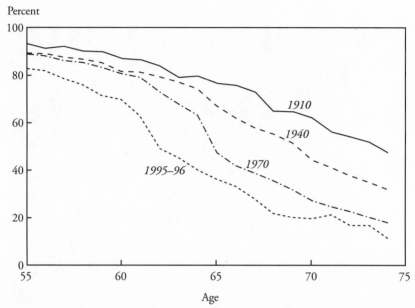

Age

Source: Labor force participation rates for 1910, 1940, and 1970 are based on responses to employment questions in the decennial censuses. See Ransom, Sutch, and Williamson (1991, pp. 45–46); and Munnell (1977, p. 70). Rates for 1995–96 are the arithmetic average participation rates on the March 1995 and March 1996 Current Population Survey (CPS) files.

tury for the oldest age groups; large declines have occurred more recently among younger groups. The largest percentage declines among men older than 70 occurred between 1910 and 1940. The fastest declines among those aged 65 to 69 took place between 1940 and 1970. The biggest declines among men younger than age 65 did not occur until after 1970. As we shall see, this pattern of labor market withdrawal is consistent with the view that the introduction and liberalization of social security was an important factor in pushing down the rates. Social security old-age pensions were first paid in 1940, and they were first made available to men aged 62 to 64 in 1961.

The basic pattern in figures 1-1 and 1-2 is that, although retirement has been present throughout the twentieth century, it is now more prevalent and occurs at a much younger age. Figure 1-3 shows the trend in the "average" retirement age, if that age is defined as the youngest age at which fewer than half the men in the age group remain in the labor force. Under

Figure 1-2. *Reductions in Male Labor Force Participation Rate,*
*by Age, Selected Periods, 1910–96*

Percent of 1910 rate

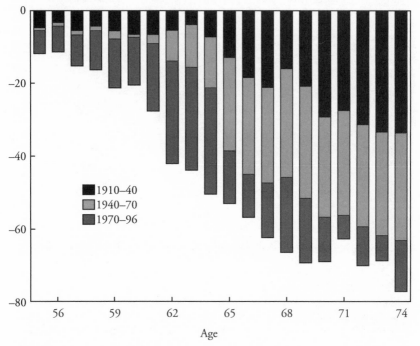

Age

Source: Ransom, Sutch, and Williamson (1991, p. 45); Munnell (1977, p. 70); and author's tabulations of Current Population Survey, March files.

this definition, the average male retirement age fell from 74 to 62 between 1910 and 1996, a drop of about 1.4 years a decade.

The decline in the average retirement age has occurred in an environment of rising life expectancy among older Americans, especially since 1940 (table 1-1). Falling mortality rates among the elderly have added 3 years to the expected life span of a 65-year-old man and 5.5 years to the life expectancy of a 65-year-old woman since 1940. Because expected male life spans increased about 0.6 year a decade during a period in which the retirement age dropped 1.4 years a decade, the amount of the male life span devoted to retirement climbed about 2 years a decade. Retirement now represents a substantial part of a typical worker's life. For many if not most workers, retirement will last longer than the period from birth until full-time entry into the job market.

Figure 1-3. *Average Retirement Age of Men, 1910–96* [a]

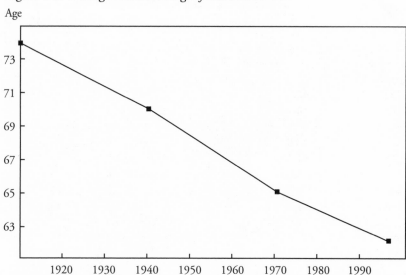

Age

Source: Author's tabulations based on sources for figure 1-2.

a. The average retirement age is the earliest age at which the labor force participation rate of older men drops below 50 percent.

Most of the early U.S. research on retirement trends was conducted by analysts in the Social Security Administration using survey information from retired workers receiving social security benefits or workers who had recently retired. This research, which dates to the mid-1940s, has been summarized by Joseph Quinn, Richard Burkhauser, and Daniel Myers.[3] In the earliest surveys an overwhelming majority of male respondents reported retiring because they were laid off by their latest employer or were in such poor health that further work was unappealing or impossible. In fact, these explanations for retirement dominated the survey responses from the 1940s through the early 1970s. Only a very small percentage of men reported leaving work because they wanted to retire. Quinn quotes an early analyst as suggesting that "most old people work as long as they can and retire only because they are forced to do so. . . . [O]nly a small proportion of old people leave the labor market for good unless they have to."[4]

In more recent surveys of new social security beneficiaries the proportion of workers who say they have retired to enjoy additional leisure or

3. See Quinn, Burkhauser, and Myers (1990, pp. 43–53); and Quinn (1991, pp. 119–23).
4. Quinn (1991, p. 120).

Table 1-1. *Life Expectancy, by Gender and Decade, 1900–2070*[a]

| Year | Life expectancy at birth | | Life expectancy at age 65 | |
|---|---|---|---|---|
| | Male | Female | Male | Female |
| *Actual* | | | | |
| 1900 | 46.4 | 49.0 | 11.4 | 11.7 |
| 1910 | 50.1 | 53.6 | 11.4 | 12.1 |
| 1920 | 54.5 | 56.3 | 11.8 | 12.3 |
| 1930 | 58.0 | 61.3 | 11.8 | 12.9 |
| 1940 | 61.4 | 65.7 | 11.9 | 13.4 |
| 1950 | 65.6 | 71.1 | 12.8 | 15.1 |
| 1960 | 66.7 | 73.2 | 12.9 | 15.9 |
| 1970 | 67.1 | 74.9 | 13.1 | 17.1 |
| 1980 | 69.9 | 77.5 | 14.0 | 18.4 |
| 1990[b] | 71.1 | 78.8 | 14.9 | 18.9 |
| *Projected*[c] | | | | |
| 2000 | 72.6 | 79.7 | 15.4 | 19.4 |
| 2010 | 74.0 | 80.5 | 15.8 | 19.7 |
| 2020 | 74.7 | 81.2 | 16.3 | 20.2 |
| 2030 | 75.3 | 81.8 | 16.7 | 20.6 |
| 2040 | 75.9 | 82.4 | 17.1 | 21.1 |
| 2050 | 76.5 | 82.9 | 17.5 | 21.5 |
| 2060 | 77.0 | 83.5 | 17.9 | 22.0 |
| 2070 | 77.5 | 84.0 | 18.3 | 22.4 |

Source: Office of the Actuary, Social Security Admnistration.

a. Life expectancy for any year is the average number of years of life remaining for a person if that person were to experience the death rates by age observed in, or assumed for, the selected years.

b. Estimated.

c. Based on the intermediate mortality assumptions of the 1993 *Annual Report of the Board of Trustees of the Federal Old-Age and Survivors Insurance and Disability Insurance Trust Funds.*

other purely voluntary reasons is plainly on the increase. Figure 1-4 presents Quinn's summary of survey responses by men aged 65 and older to the question "Why did you retire?" He has divided responses into four broad categories: "Lost last job," "Health reasons," "Wished to retire," and "Other." This classification is not precise, because survey questionnaires were not always consistent in the way they framed the question or the possible responses a retiree might offer.

The growing importance of voluntary retirement is clearly apparent in figure 1-4. In the 1940s and early 1950s fewer than 5 percent of new retirees reported leaving work because of a wish to retire or enjoy more

Figure 1-4. *Reasons for Retirement among Retired Men Aged 65 and Older,
Selected Years, 1940–80*

Percent

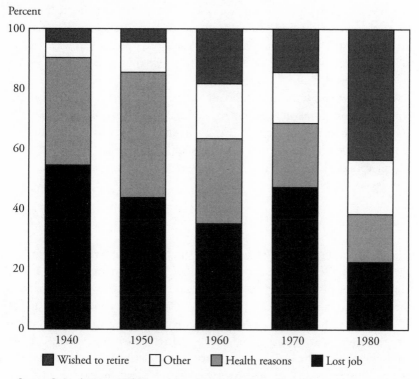

Source: Quinn (1991, p. 123). Years given are approximate year of surveys.

leisure. About 90 percent left because of poor health or a layoff. By the
early 1980s the desire to leave work explained nearly half of all retirements among men aged 65 or older, while poor health accounted for only
a little over a fifth and involuntary layoff about 15 percent.

Many readers might accept these responses at face value, but economists
treat them more skeptically. For example, from 1940 through the early
1970s well over a third of respondents explained their entry into retirement
as the result of involuntary job loss. Although this explanation might seem
reasonable to noneconomists, hard-headed practitioners of the dismal science realize that millions of workers lose their jobs each year without
becoming retired. The overwhelming majority of workers who offer "job
loss" as the explanation for their retirement probably lost several jobs during their careers, but on no previous occasion did a layoff cause them to
withdraw permanently from the work force. When forced into unem-

ployment at a younger age, they looked for another job and eventually found one. It is natural to ask why job loss pushed them into retirement on this one occasion but not on the others. Even the health explanation arouses skepticism among some economists. Social security beneficiaries may justify their retirement with the excuse that poor health leaves them no alternative, but many economists wonder whether their decision would have been any different if social security were not available.

Economist and noneconomist can both agree, however, that the persistent trend toward earlier retirement has an important voluntary component. The survey responses plainly show it, and the responses are consistent with what we know about increasing wealth, wider eligibility for public and private pensions, and the increasing generosity of pensions.

## Retirement and Consumption

The downward drift in the labor force participation of older men has had a significant effect on the growth in aggregate labor supply, both in the United States and in other industrialized countries. The long-term trend in the retirement age did not attract much notice from economists until the 1970s. Curiously, the first aspect of retirement to command their attention was the effect—or hypothesized effect—of retirement on individual and national saving. The classic statement of this relationship is contained in articles written or coauthored by the economist Franco Modigliani.[5] His theory has had a wide influence on economists' thinking about the timing of retirement as well as the determination of saving. For that reason it is useful to describe the theory in some detail.

### Theory

Modigliani's basic idea was that farsighted workers will rationally plan their consumption over a full lifetime. In devising their lifetime consumption plans, they will take account of the likely path of their labor earnings as they age and will prudently accumulate savings in anticipation of their retirement. The goal of a good consumption plan is to maximize the worker's lifetime well-being, subject to the constraint that lifetime consumption cannot exceed the worker's lifetime wealth. Lifetime wealth consists of the worker's initial assets and the present discounted value of antic-

5. Modigliani and Brumberg (1954); and Ando and Modigliani (1963).

ipated labor earnings and other kinds of income such as public assistance and inheritances that are not derived from initial assets or labor earnings. Rational and farsighted workers will plan to avoid situations in which all their lifetime wealth has been consumed long before they expect to die. In the absence of transfers from relatives, public aid, or private charity, the consequences of this kind of planning error might be unappealing.

It is possible to sketch out the implications of this theory for the path of consumption and wealth accumulation using a few simple assumptions. The top panel in figure 1-5 shows the path of a worker's expected earnings over a lifetime. When he first enters the labor force at age 20 his earnings are just $10,000 a year, but they will climb rapidly as he gains work experience. His earnings reach a peak around age 50 and then gradually decline. He withdraws from the work force on his sixty-fifty birthday, at which point his earnings cease. By assumption, he is completely certain about the path of his future earnings, his age at death (85), and the interest rate throughout his life (5 percent). The worker is able to borrow freely at this interest rate, and if he accumulates savings he will receive the same interest rate on his investments. It is also assumed that the worker has stable preferences throughout his life.

A worker who successfully solves the consumption planning problem under these assumptions will plot out a desired path of consumption for each future year of life and will then stick with the plan. The best plan will depend on the relationship between the worker's subjective rate of time preference and the interest rate he can obtain on his savings. The rate of time preference is a measure of the worker's impatience in consumption. People who insist on consuming nine-tenths of a box of chocolate truffles today, leaving only one-tenth of it for consumption tomorrow, are said to have a high rate of time preference; they are very impatient in their consumption.

If the worker's rate of time preference is equal to the market interest rate, the consumption path will be level throughout the worker's life, as I have drawn it in the figure. If instead the rate of time preference is higher than the interest rate, he will attempt to shift his consumption toward the early part of his life, and his consumption will fall as he grows older. People with a very low rate of time preference, those who are very patient in their consumption, will shift consumption to later stages of their life and will plan to increase consumption as they age. Workers may wish to leave bequests to survivors, in which case they will consume all their lifetime wealth except the amount needed to leave to their heirs. I assume in figure 1-5 that the worker plans to make no bequests and will thus consume all his lifetime wealth by the time he dies.

Figure 1-5. *Hypothetical Life-Cycle Consumption and Wealth Accumulation*

Dollars

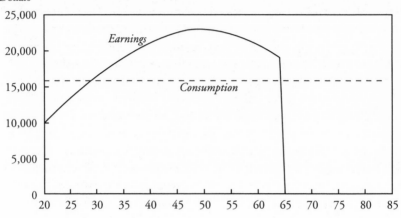

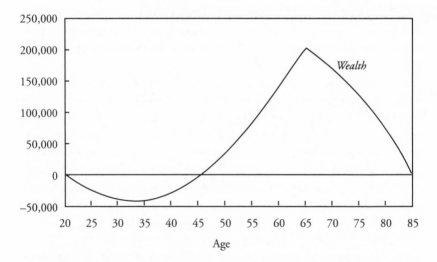

Age

The resulting consumption path is shown as the horizontal line in the top panel. Because the worker's consumption is initially higher than his earnings, he must borrow money when he is young to finance consumption.[6] In the benign world assumed here, he can borrow as much money as he wants as long as he can repay the loan out of his lifetime wealth. The lower panel in figure 1-5 shows the lifetime path of the worker's asset holdings. He accumulates increasing amounts of debt to finance his con-

---

6. He must borrow more than the difference between his earnings and his consumption because he also needs to borrow enough money to make interest payments on his outstanding debt.

sumption until he reaches age 33, when rising earnings allow him to begin paying off liabilities. By age 45 he is free of debt and begins to accumulate assets. The peak of his asset accumulation occurs on his sixty-fifth birthday, the day he retires. His assets are then used up over the last twenty years of his life, when he has no labor income to help pay for consumption.

The characteristic pattern of increasing and then declining asset holdings over the life cycle is one of the central empirical predictions of Modigliani's consumption theory. The asset buildup would not be needed if workers did not expect to retire. In the absence of retirement, saving would be needed mainly to finance bequests and smooth out consumption in comparison with earnings. Readers may notice that some of the assumptions I have mentioned are highly stylized and are unlikely to be true in life. For example, workers cannot borrow money at the same interest rate they obtain on their investments: usually they must pay a much higher rate than the one they can safely earn. More important, few workers can borrow large sums of money to finance current consumption. These are comparatively minor matters for many workers, however, and addressing them does not fundamentally alter many of the implications of the theory.[7]

A more serious problem arises when a realistic picture of the worker's uncertainty about the future is introduced. In formulating an ideal consumption plan, it obviously helps if the worker is completely confident about his future earnings, his age at retirement and at death, and the future interest rate. But no one can predict these with much confidence. In formulating the consumption plan, one must take account of the possibility that the future may turn out to be more or less congenial than anticipated.

In one respect, the life-cycle consumption theory and the closely related permanent-income model represented a major advance in economists' understanding of how consumers handle unexpected events.[8] The two models make a clear and plausible distinction between (unanticipated) changes in flows of income that can be expected to last and changes that are only temporary. According to both theories, an unexpected income

---

7. Even if borrowing constraints prevented workers from borrowing money early in their careers, as they are implicitly able to do in figure 1-5, the life-cycle model still predicts that workers who expect to retire will accumulate substantial wealth holdings toward the end of their active careers. Thus retirement decisively affects the lifetime pattern of asset accumulation and deaccumulation.

8. The permanent-income model was introduced by Milton Friedman (1957) around the same time that Modigliani and his collaborators proposed the life-cycle consumption model. The empirical predictions of the two theories are virtually identical, leading many students of consumption to refer to a common life-cycle–permanent-income model. I have emphasized the life-cycle variant here because early versions of it treated the issue of retirement planning as the central motivation for consumer saving.

improvement that is permanent, such as an earnings gain that accompanies a promotion, will have a much larger impact on a worker's consumption than an improvement that is only temporary, such as a one-time bonus for outstanding job performance. By the logic of the life-cycle model, a person who wins a lottery that pays $10,000 a year for thirty years will plan to make a much bigger change in short-term consumption habits than the person who wins a one-time prize of $10,000. By the same reasoning, the lottery winner who obtains a prize paying a modest annual amount (say $700 a year) that has a present discounted value of $10,000 will alter consumption by the same amount as the winner of a one-time prize equal to $10,000.

Consumers still face the problem of deciding whether an income change will be long-lasting or only temporary. And if it is long-lasting, when will it cease? These considerations are crucial in determining how much workers should adjust their flow of consumption once they have obtained new information about future income flows. In theory, alert consumers will formulate a new lifetime consumption plan every time they receive new information about the future. If an employer's quarterly earnings statement shows an unexpected drop in profits, employees in the company should scale back their consumption in anticipation of layoffs or slower future wage growth. If interest rates rise, workers may postpone consumption until later in life to take greater advantage of improved earnings on their investments. If a worker suffers an unexpected heart attack, he may boost his saving in anticipation of an earlier retirement and lower lifetime earnings.

New information about the future state of the world is seldom clear cut. Does a heart attack mean that retirement will last longer because the victim may be forced to leave the work force earlier? Or will it shorten retirement because the worker can expect an earlier death? The two outcomes, if fully anticipated, would have opposite effects on the rate of consumption over the remainder of life, but a farsighted worker will take account of both possibilities in formulating a consumption plan. Will an interest rate hike be temporary or permanent? Even financial market specialists do not have enough information to answer this question confidently.

## Evidence

To say that solving the consumption planning problem under uncertainty is difficult does not mean it is impossible. Workers who devote enough intelligence and attention to the problem will usually make more prudent and satisfying decisions about consumption than those who approach the issue casually or ignore it altogether. The life-cycle–permanent-income theory has produced important insights into consumption planning. Among economists it remains by far the most influential model of consumption. Whether it provides an accurate explanation for observed consumption behavior remains an open question.

Some evidence supports the theory. Most empirical research suggests that the model is correct in emphasizing that households discount short-run fluctuations in their income when determining current consumption and that retirement is one important motive for saving. There is competing evidence, however, that consumption is more volatile and closely related to current income changes than would be the case if there were complete smoothing of consumption over full lifetime resources.[9] As the theory predicts, economists observe a tendency among many workers to steadily but gradually build up their wealth, increasing their rates of saving in peak earning years and as they approach retirement. The life-cycle theory's implication that consumers have a target wealth-income ratio that increases with age up to retirement also seems to be valid for many households.

Nonetheless, some economists are doubtful of the theory because simple versions of it are not very successful in accounting for important aspects of personal saving. For example, many American workers enter retirement without any assets. A large percentage of others who do have assets apparently continue to add to them after retirement. Neither fact is easy to reconcile with simple versions of the life-cycle model. Theorists are thus forced to adopt modifications in the basic theory to account for obvious empirical contradictions.[10] Different theorists have proposed different modifications to rescue the basic model. Whatever their criticisms of the model, however, few have strayed far from it in trying to explain retirement behavior.

## Economic Models of Retirement

Economic theories of retirement naturally focus on financial aspects of workers' decisions. This section describes some of the financial considera-

---

9. See, for example, Skinner (1988); Zeldes (1989); and, in particular, Carroll and Summers (1991).

10. For example, Hubbard, Skinner, and Zeldes (1994) rescue the model by theorizing that income uncertainty and asset-tested transfer programs erode the incentive to save for a sizable minority of households.

tions affecting workers' choice of retirement age. It then considers the theories economists have advanced to explain retirement choice and the evidence they have used to test them. Although economic studies on choice of retirement age did not begin in earnest until the mid-1970s, their number has grown explosively since then.[11] Rather than provide another survey of them, I will focus on a handful to highlight the growing complexity of economists' models of worker decisionmaking.

## Financial Aspects of Retirement

Modigliani's life-cycle consumption model emphasizes the single most important financial aspect of retirement—the sharp reduction or complete cessation of labor earnings. Most worker households rely heavily on labor earnings to pay for consumption. When earnings cease at retirement, workers must find another way to pay for it. Modigliani stressed personal saving as an alternative source of support in old age. Even though other income sources are now more important (and still others may have been more important in the past), it is useful to think about the choice of retirement age in a world in which retired workers rely solely on their own savings to finance consumption.

Consider a worker who can earn exactly $10,000 in each year she is employed. If she begins working at age 20 and has been reliably informed she will expire on her seventieth birthday, she can work for up to 50 years, potentially earning as much as $500,000 over her life. To keep the calculations simple, let us also assume the interest rate and the worker's rate of time preference are the same and are exactly 0 percent. Under that assumption, she will plan to consume her lifetime wealth at a constant rate over her life span. Her lifetime wealth in this case is simply her lifetime earnings, which in turn are equal to $10,000 times the number of years she chooses to work. If she works 40 years, for example, her lifetime wealth will be $400,000, and she will consume this amount at a rate of $8,000 a year ($400,000 / 50 years).

In this highly stylized case, the worker's retirement choice can be described as a simple trade-off between a higher flow of consumption per year and a longer period of time spent in retirement (figure 1-6). If the worker retires at age 20, she will earn no money, accumulate no assets, and consume $0 a year throughout her life (which is likely to be brief). If

11. For good surveys, see Quinn, Burkhauser, and Myers (1990); Leonesio (1993); Quinn and Burkhauser (1994); and Lumsdaine (1996).

Figure 1-6. *Trade-off between Annual Consumption and Age at Retirement*

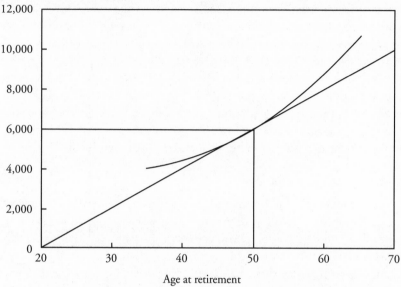

Annual consumption (dollars)

Age at retirement

she works until age 70, she can consume all of her annual wages ($10,000) each year. It seems reasonable to expect that the worker would prefer to consume more each year (holding fixed the amount she works) and would prefer to retire sooner rather than later (holding fixed the amount she consumes). The illustration in figure 1-6 should be familiar to anyone who has studied freshman economics. The worker's problem is to select the best possible combination of consumption and years of retirement in light of her preferences and the trade-off shown in the diagram. In the figure, the most desirable combination occurs if the worker retires at age 50 after working 30 years and consumes her lifetime earnings at a rate of $6,000 a year. Other workers facing the same trade-off might choose to retire at a younger or older age, depending on their preferences for consumption and retirement.

Although the analysis may seem trivial, it can shed light on the retirement trends discussed earlier. Retirement ages have declined in the twentieth century, and the simple economic model suggests three reasons this might have occurred. Workers may now enter their careers with a higher flow of income from inherited assets. This provides a straightforward explanation for earlier retirement because under plausible assumptions about worker preferences greater initial wealth will induce most workers to spend more of their life in retirement.[12] Workers also earn much higher wages in the 1990s than they did in 1910 or 1940. The higher rate of pay provides greater lifetime wealth at any fixed retirement age, which may induce workers to spend more years in retirement.[13] Of course, a higher wage also increases the financial penalty on workers who retire early. If a worker's earnings doubled from $10,000 to $20,000 a year, she would give up $20,000 in lifetime wealth rather than only $10,000 if she chose to retire one year earlier. The larger penalty for early retirement might offset some or all of the effect of higher lifetime wealth. Finally, worker preferences may have changed. Independent of the change in initial wealth or yearly pay, workers today may simply prefer to spend more of their life in retirement.

## Social Security and Pensions

Other changes in the environment have also affected the trade-off between consumption and the age at retirement. Employer-sponsored pensions are now much more prevalent than was the case fifty or a hundred years ago. Workers covered by a pension are provided with a potential source of income in addition to their own savings for financing retirement. Social security, which was introduced in 1935 and greatly liberalized between 1950 and 1975, also offers a reliable source of income in old age.

Social security and pensions affect the lifetime trade-off between consumption and retirement in a complicated way. Here I will focus on social security. Workers who become eligible to receive benefits under social security are entitled to receive a pension starting at age 62 or when they retire, whichever occurs later. Because the system has historically been very generous, all generations retiring up to the present have received larger pensions than their contributions could have paid for if the contributions had been invested in safe assets. In effect, this generosity increased the lifetime wealth of older workers who became vested in the system. If they consumed all of the benefits paid to them, they enjoyed higher lifetime consumption than their labor income alone could have financed.[14] The for-

12. In terms of figure 1-6, higher initial wealth will lift the lifetime budget constraint to a position that is above and parallel to the budget constraint in the figure. Because of inherited wealth, the worker might be able to consume $4,000 a year rather than only $0 if she retired at age 20.

13. Higher wages cause the budget constraint drawn in figure 1-6 to rotate counterclockwise around the origin.

14. This kind of generosity is possible in a pay-as-you-go retirement system because early contributors to the system make much smaller contributions to the program than will be needed when the system is fully mature. Future generations will not receive such a good deal under social security. Young workers today may actually receive lower benefits under the system than their contributions would have earned if they had been invested in safe assets, such as government bonds.

tunate generations that received this windfall may have retired earlier than they would have if social security had not been introduced or if it had offered less generous pensions.

The effect of social security on retirement depends on the social security tax and the benefit formula linking monthly pensions to a worker's past covered earnings. Employers and workers pay into the system a combined tax equal to 12.4 percent of wages. The tax thus reduces workers' wages by about 12 percent in comparison with the wages they would receive if the program were abolished. But, of course, contributions allow a worker to earn credits toward a social security pension. The pension entitlement goes up as the worker's covered lifetime wages increase. Whether the increase in the pension entitlement is large enough to compensate a worker for his extra contributions is an empirical question. Low-wage workers receive favorable treatment under social security, so they usually receive a generous return on their contributions. High-wage workers typically receive lower returns.

Workers who delay their retirement until after age 62 are at least temporarily passing up the opportunity to receive a social security check, which can begin immediately after the worker's sixty-second birthday. If a worker is entitled to a pension of $500 a month, for example, he is sacrificing $500 in retirement income every month he delays retirement past age 62. If his regular monthly pay is $10,000, this represents a small sacrifice. But if his usual pay is $1,000, the sacrifice amounts to half his wage. Between the ages of 62 and 64 the social security formula offers workers a fair compensation for giving up a year's benefits. Monthly benefits are adjusted upward about 8.5 percent for each year's delay in claiming a pension. For workers with average life expectancy and a moderate rate of time preference, this adjustment is just large enough so that the sacrifice of a year's benefits is compensated by eligibility for a higher pension in future years. After age 65, however, the benefit formula is much less generous toward delayed retirement. Postponement of retirement after that age is not fairly compensated by increases in the monthly pension.

The reason that many people must retire in order to collect a social security check is that the program imposes an earnings test in calculating the annual pension. Workers who are between 62 and 64 and who earn more than $8,640 a year lose $1 in annual benefits for every $2 in earnings they receive in excess of $8,640. Workers between 65 and 69 lose $1 in benefits for every $3 in annual earnings in excess of $13,500. (Pensioners age 70 and older do not face an earnings test.) At one time the earnings limitations were much lower and the tax on excess earnings was much higher, dis-

couraging pensioners from work and possibly encouraging them to postpone claiming a pension until they were confident their earnings would
remain low.

Social security has, then, boosted the lifetime wealth of older people
who have received benefits under the program. Its complicated benefit formula provides an incentive for people to become entitled to benefits but
may discourage extra work by high-wage workers, who do not receive
good returns on their marginal contributions to the program. At age 62,
when pensions can first be claimed, eligible people who continue to work
give up a year's benefits every year they postpone their retirement. For
workers who have a high rate of time preference or who do not expect to
live long, this sacrifice is equivalent to a big cut in annual pay. Between the
ages of 62 and 64, however, the pension formula fairly compensates most
workers for this sacrifice. Starting at age 65 the compensation formula is
much less generous, so workers must sacrifice some lifetime benefits every
year they delay retirement past 65. Social security does not provide a simple annuity. Most workers must substantially cut their earnings to collect
a full pension.

Figure 1-7 summarizes the potential effects of social security on the consumption–retirement age trade-off. The trade-off is similar to the one
shown in figure 1-6, except that the diagram focuses on the retirement
age choice late in life. The lower line represents the consumption–retirement trade-off the worker would face in the absence of social security.
The trade-off is shown to be linear because of my assumption that the
worker can earn exactly $10,000 a year from continued work, an amount
that does not change as the worker grows older. The higher dashed line represents the trade-off for the same worker when social security is introduced.
The trade-off under the system permits the worker to enjoy higher annual
consumption at any fixed retirement age because it increases the worker's
pension income by more than it reduces net earnings. The benefit formula also affects the slope of the trade-off, particularly at ages 62 and 65,
for reasons mentioned earlier. At age 65 the slope certainly declines because
the worker must give up pension benefits for continued work without
receiving a fair compensation for the sacrifice. The change in slope at age
62 is less clear cut. From 62 to 64 workers receive better compensation
for postponing retirement than they do at age 65, but the compensation
may not be regarded as fair by a worker with a high rate of time preference or a short life expectancy. In that case, the change in the slope would
look the same as the change in slope at age 65. Workers with a low rate of
time preference and long life expectancy might regard the compensation as

Figure 1-7. *Trade-off between Consumption and Age at Retirement under Social Security*

Annual consumption (dollars)

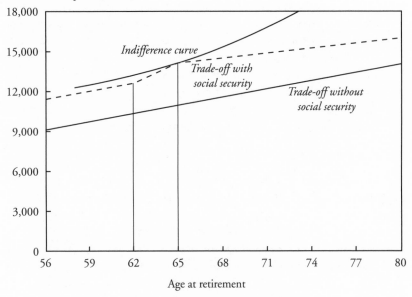

Age at retirement

more than fair. In other words, the compensation they receive is more than enough to make up for the loss in pensions connected with delay in their retirement. The slope in that case would increase at age 62, which is the situation shown in figure 1-7.

Employer-sponsored pensions introduce further complications in the trade-off between consumption and retirement. These are similar to the complications introduced by social security. There is one important distinction between social security and employer-sponsored pensions, however. Social security imposes an earnings test on income received from *all* employment, including self-employment. Employer-sponsored pensions may impose an even more stringent earnings test, but the test applies only to earnings received from the sponsoring employer or perhaps a group of related employers. Workers who wish to claim a pension may be forced to leave the job on which they earned the pension, but they are not forced to leave work altogether. Nevertheless, the effects of employer-sponsored pensions on retirement may be similar to those of social security, because many older workers find it hard to obtain good job offers after they have retired from a career job.

## Health and Job Opportunities

Changes over time in a worker's health and job opportunities also influence the timing of retirement. Many workers experience deteriorating health as they age, which makes it physically more difficult or less pleasant to hold a job and in some cases can make work practically impossible. If deteriorating health is fully anticipated when a person begins to work, it will affect the perceived attractiveness of a consumption plan that postpones retirement until very late in life. This will be reflected in the worker's preferences across various combinations of average consumption and age at retirement. Anticipating that she will be in poor health when she reaches age 70, the worker will avoid lifetime consumption plans that require her to work past that age unless the plans also provide exceptional amounts of lifetime income. Unanticipated changes in health at older ages force workers to reconsider their lifetime consumption plans in light of their new knowledge about their work capacity. In many cases these health changes will force them to retire earlier than they originally planned.

Many workers face worse job prospects when they are old than they did when they were young. This fact is reflected in figure 1-5, which shows declining wages after age 50. It is not reflected in figures 1-6 or 1-7, which are based on the assumption that workers can earn $10,000 a year no matter how long they work. If potential annual earnings decline as workers grow older, the trade-off between consumption and retirement age will look less favorable than it does in figures 1-6 and 1-7. Each added year of work past some critical age (say, age 50) will produce a smaller gain in annual consumption. The decline in potential earnings is an important reason that older workers withdraw from the labor force rather than search for work when they are laid off. At a younger age, when their job opportunities were better, they would have looked for and accepted a job after being laid off.

## Evidence

Before turning to the specific models economists have tried to estimate, it is worth reconsidering the historical evidence in light of this discussion of retirement incentives. Do simple economic models shed any light on the historical trends? Some rough indication of the possible influence of social security on retirement is provided by examining the relationship between social security incentives and the observed distribution of retirement ages.

Social security is now the principal source of cash income of households headed by someone aged 65 or older. Tabulations of the Current Population Survey show that social security benefits account for slightly more than 40 percent of the total cash income of the aged. Among aged households in the bottom 60 percent of the elderly income distribution, social security accounts for more than two-thirds of cash income (figure 1-8). Until 1941 social security provided no income to the aged. Today the program replaces about 42 percent of the final wage earned by a full-career single worker who earns the average wage and claims a pension at age 65. If the worker has a nonworking dependent spouse, the benefit replaces 63 percent of the final wage. Benefits are clearly high enough so they can be economically significant in influencing the choice of retirement age.

The distributions of male retirement ages in 1940, 1970, and 1995–96 are plotted in figure 1-9. The figure shows the percentage of men leaving the labor force at each age from 56 to 70, computed as a fraction of the men in the labor force at age 55.[15] The calculations are based on the data reflected in figure 1-1. Not surprisingly, the retirement distributions for 1970 and especially for 1995–96 show that labor force withdrawal occurred at earlier ages than in 1940. Both the 1970 and 1995–96 distributions also show evidence of clustering in retirement at particular ages. In 1970 the peak rate of retirement occurred at age 65; by 1995–96 the peak occurred at age 62. There are peaks in the distribution of retirements in 1940 at ages 65 and 70, but these are far below the peaks in 1970 and 1995–96.

The discussion of social security suggests an explanation for the clustering of retirements at ages 62 and 65, at least in years after 1940. Workers who continue to work beyond age 65 give up social security benefits for which they are not fairly compensated. We can anticipate that this feature of the benefit formula will encourage retirement at age 65. The clustering of retirements at age 62 is not much more difficult to explain. Starting in 1961 age 62 became the earliest age at which men could claim a social security pension. Before 1961 there was no evidence of retirements clustering at age 62, but by 1970 retirement was more common at 62 than at any other age except 65. By the mid-1990s, age 62 was by a wide margin

---

15. If the labor force participation rate at age 63 is designated $LFPR_{63}$, the retirement rate at age 63 is calculated as $(LFPR_{63} - LFPR_{62}) / LFPR_{55}$. This calculation ignores the complications involved in computing true cohort distributions and the effects of mortality rates, immigration, and temporary withdrawal from the labor force. It offers a picture of the timing of labor market withdrawal based on the participation choices of men aged 55 through 70 in a particular year.

Figure 1-8. *Social Security as a Share of Total Cash Income of Elderly Households, by Quintile, 1996*

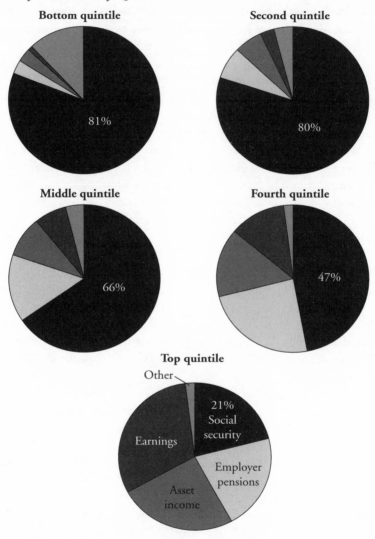

Source: Social Security Administration (1998, pp. 15–16).

the most popular age of retirement. In principle, the social security formula fairly compensates workers if they delay claiming a pension past age 62. But a worker with a high rate of time preference or short life expectancy might not regard the compensation as fair. In those instances one should expect many workers to prefer retiring at age 62 rather than later.

Figure 1-9. *Male Retirement Rate, by Age, 1940, 1970, 1995–96* [a]

Percent

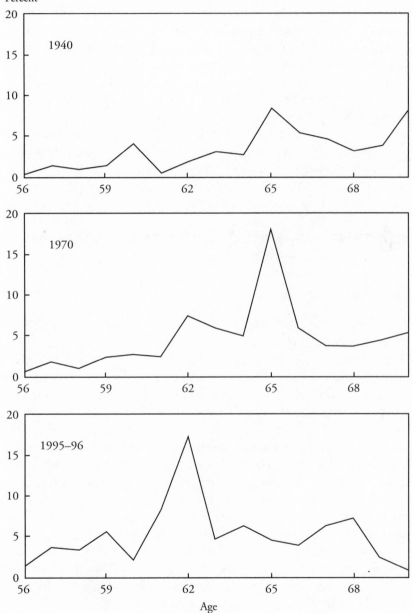

Age

Source: Munnell (1977, p. 70) and author's tabulations of Current Population Survey, March files.

a. Percent reflects the constructed number of men who retire at the designated age, measured as a percentage of men who are labor force participants at age 55.

Of course, the clustering of retirements at ages 62 and 65 may be due to factors other than the availability of social security benefits. It is hard to believe, however, that health or work opportunities decline abruptly at a particular age. Another explanation is that some workers are affected by mandatory retirement rules. This explanation may have been valid in 1940 and 1970, when employers were permitted to dismiss older workers under mandatory retirement rules, but it is not convincing today. Amendments to the Age Discrimination in Employment Act passed in 1986 prohibit employers from dismissing workers solely on account of their age. The simplest alternative explanation for the clustering is that workers are affected by employer-sponsored pension plans. For many older workers private pensions are unlikely to be an important determinant of retirement age, however, because they are not covered by an employer plan. Figure 1-8 shows that employer-sponsored pensions do not provide a large percentage of income to older Americans, except in more affluent households. Among workers who are covered by a private pension plan, some features of the plan may encourage workers to retire at a particular age.

*Early Economic Models*

Two of the earliest economic studies of retirement were based on very straightforward models of the retirement decision. Both focused on the choice between work and retirement faced by workers in a particular year. Michael Boskin analyzed the choices made by a small number of older men who were interviewed in the Panel Study of Income Dynamics, and Joseph Quinn examined the 1969 retirement choices of a much larger sample of older men interviewed in the Retirement History Survey.[16] In essence, both researchers treated the retirement decision as if it were made independently in each year of a worker's later life based on the financial and health circumstances facing the worker in that year. Under this view, workers eligible for a large social security check or employer pension in a particular year might be tempted to leave the work force in that year. Workers capable of earning a high wage might be induced to remain at work.

This model may actually reflect how workers decide when to retire, but it is based on the assumption that workers are not very forward looking. For example, neither Boskin nor Quinn included variables in his model to reflect the future pensions workers could obtain if they delayed their retirement. A 62-year-old worker who delays retirement one year can increase his

16. Boskin (1977); and Quinn (1977).

monthly social security check by as much as 10 percent. Boskin and Quinn disregarded this aspect of the pension formula under the assumption that workers are motivated by the pension they can collect in the current period rather than the increase in their lifetime wealth (including higher future pensions) that they can obtain by delaying retirement.

Most research on older workers suggests that for a majority retirement is a once-in-a-lifetime event. Recognizing this, well-informed workers may not make an independent decision about whether to be retired each year, but may instead treat retirement as a choice they are likely to make only once. They may want to select the most advantageous retirement age possible in light of the pension for which they qualify at each potential retirement age. Researchers do not know, however, whether workers are actually this farsighted. Under the assumption that they are not very farsighted, both Boskin and Quinn found that social security had a very large impact on their behavior.

### Life-Cycle Models

Beginning with a series of articles by Richard Burkhauser, economists started to adopt the life-cycle perspective in their analyses of retirement-age choice.[17] In some cases they examined workers' retirement behavior under specific company pension plans, but most research focused on retirement choice under social security. The information requirements to perform a plausible study are formidable. To analyze the retirement choices of a single cohort of workers requires detailed information about the workers' health, wages, family situation, employment status, and assets over a period that might stretch eight or ten years. To accurately calculate a worker's pension entitlement and determine how the entitlement changes with added work experience, analysts also need extensive information about their past wages and pension service credits. (The social security pension is based on earnings over a forty-year period, for example.)

As economists assembled detailed financial data and put them in a framework that realistically represented the evolution of workers' lifetime pension assets and wealth, their analytical models became increasingly complicated. Part of the complexity reflects the genuine complexity of human behavior. Although many people work in a career job for many years and then leave the job to withdraw permanently from work, others move into transitional jobs with lower pay, less responsibility, and shorter

---

17. See, for example, Burkhauser (1979).

hours. To reflect the wide range of observed or potential paths into full retirement, analysts sometimes specified in great detail the alternative possibilities from which workers could choose.[18] A wider range of choice usually means that the worker's retirement decision problem becomes more difficult to solve, both for the worker and for the researcher who is attempting to analyze it.

The richest source of information about Americans' retirement behavior is provided by the Retirement History Survey, a ten-year panel survey covering about 11,000 families headed by people who were between 58 and 63 years old when the survey began in 1969. Retirement behavior in these 11,000 families has been analyzed by a number of researchers who applied the life-cycle framework in their studies. In many respects the pattern of retirement and postretirement work effort reflected in the survey offered strong confirmation that social security financial incentives matter in determining labor supply late in life.

Figure 1-10 displays a pair of labor supply distributions based on behavior recorded in the survey.[19] The top panel shows the distribution of retirement ages among nondisabled men who were observed to retire by the end of the survey in 1979, when respondents were between 68 and 73 years old. To determine the retirement age, the analysts examined the lifetime pattern of respondents' work effort and selected the point in each worker's life when he made a discontinuous and apparently permanent reduction in labor supply. This definition excludes spells of unemployment or nonemployment that end with the worker's return to a full-time job. However, the definition would include movements from steady full-time into part-time employment. The picture misses the retirements of some men who did not retire before their last completed interviews, and this omission will lead to some underrepresentation of retirements that occur after age 67. Taking account of the different populations included in the tabulations and the differing definitions of retirement, the pattern of retirement in figure 1-10 is broadly similar to that shown for 1970 in figure 1-2.

The lower panel displays the pattern of earnings among retired but working men who are 62 years old or older in the first interview after they retire. Approximately one-fifth of retiring men were still working within the first two years after their retirements, and on average they worked a little more than sixteeen hours a week. The panel shows the distribution of their earnings in relation to the earnings-exempt amount in the social

18. Gustman and Steinmeier (1986).
19. The calculations are described and presented in Burtless and Moffitt (1985).

Figure 1-10.  *Retirement Age and Postretirement Earnings Distributions in the 1969–79 Retirement History Survey*

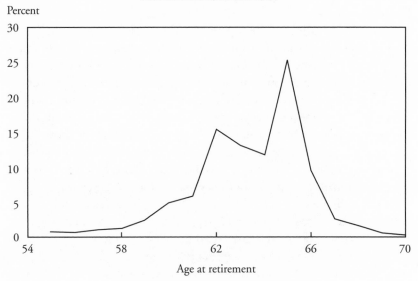

**Retirement age distribution among healthy men born between 1906 and 1912**

Percent

Age at retirement

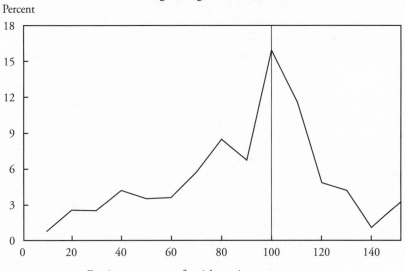

**Distribution of postretirement earnings among men aged 62 and older**

Percent

Earnings as percent of social security exempt amount

Source: Burtless and Moffitt (1985, p. 225).

security benefit formula. Earnings below the exempt amount had no effect on a worker's pension; earnings above the exempt amount caused benefits to be reduced by 50 percent of the amount of excess wages over the exempt amount. (The tax rate on excess earnings has subsequently been reduced for older retirees.)

Casual observation of the top and bottom panels suggests that social security had a powerful effect on both retirement ages and postretirement work effort. The age distribution of retirements has two peaks, a lower one at age 62, when benefits can first be claimed, and a much higher one at age 65, when the social security formula stops making generous adjustments for further delays in claiming a pension. The distribution of postretirement work effort shows an even larger effect of social security. Workers appear acutely sensitive to the high implicit tax on their earnings when annual wages exceed the exempt amount. More than a quarter of working retirees earn within 10 percent of the exempt amount, and more than half earn within 30 percent of it. Although retirees may underreport their true earnings to social security to avoid paying the high implicit tax, the earnings estimates in figure 1-10 are based on workers' responses to a census interviewer, not their earnings reports to the Social Security Administration. Thus, the distribution is likely to reflect a genuine effect of social security on postretirement hours of work.

In view of the apparently dramatic effect of social security on the exact timing of retirement and on postretirement hours worked, readers may be surprised to learn that most of the life-cycle studies in the 1980s found that even big changes in social security produced only modest effects on lifetime work effort. The diagrams may be a bit deceptive, however. Because fewer than a fifth of retirees choose to work after claiming a social security check and only about two-thirds of these earn enough wages to be remotely affected by the earnings test, the potential effect of a change in the earnings test is limited. Even if the postretirement hours of affected workers rose one-third, the average work effort of all retired men would only climb by about one hour a week (from 3.25 hours to 4.25). The effect is even smaller than this because workers do not remain in their postretirement jobs very long. Gustman and Steinmeier reported that the average duration of partial retirement is only about three years.[20] By implication, the apparently dramatic effect of the social security earnings test has only a tiny effect on workers' lifetime labor supply.

---

20. Gustman and Steinmeier (1986).

Even the effect on the timing of retirement may not be particularly large. It is true that many more men retire at ages 62 and 65 than at other ages, exactly as predicted by economists' life-cycle model. It does not follow, however, that sharp reductions in social security would cause workers retiring at ages 62 or 65 to retire very much later or that big increases in pensions would cause them to retire much earlier. After a reduction in benefits, for example, the distribution of retirement ages might show less clustering of retirement at particular ages, but the overall effect of the reduction on the average retirement age might be small. This was the conclusion reached in the great majority of the life-cycle studies conducted in the 1980s and early 1990s. Most analysts reached this conclusion by comparing the cross-sectional distribution of retirements within a group of men born around the same years. The behavior of workers with a large amount of social security or pension wealth was compared with that of workers with less wealth. Differences in the rates at which workers could accumulate social security or pension wealth and earn additional wages were also taken into account. Most studies found that even big changes in social security benefits would cause only small changes in the average retirement age. Gary Burtless and Robert Moffitt predicted, for example, that raising the normal retirement age in social security from 65 to 68 would add only a little more than four months to the full-time working careers of nondisabled men.[21]

Another way to analyze the impact of social security incentives is to examine the behavioral differences among people who face different incentives because the program has been altered in an unanticipated way. In 1969 and again in 1972 social security benefits were increased much faster relative to wages than at any time in the recent past. By 1973 benefits were 20 percent higher in inflation-adjusted terms than would have been the case if pensions had grown with wages as they did during the 1950s and 1960s. In 1977 Congress passed amendments to the Social Security Act that sharply reduced benefits to workers born in 1917 and later years (the "notch" babies) in comparison with benefits payable to workers born before 1917. I examined the first episode, and Alan Krueger and Jörn-Steffan Pishke examined the second using the life-cycle framework.[22] In the period I analyzed, workers born in earlier years planned their retirements when social security was comparatively less generous; workers born in later

21. Burtless and Moffitt (1985, p. 230). For a discussion of other economists' predictions, see Quinn, Burkhauser, and Myers (1990, pp. 108–11).
22. Burtless (1986); and Krueger and Pischke (1991).

years planned their retirement when social security was significantly more liberal. Krueger and Pischke analyzed a period in which younger workers received significantly less generous pensions than those available to older workers. Both studies reached an identical conclusion: major changes in social security generosity produced small effects on the retirement behavior and labor force participation of older men. Burtless estimated, for example, that the 20 percent benefit hike between 1969 and 1993 caused only a two-month reduction in the work career of men who were fully covered by the more generous formula. This was equivalent to a reduction in the labor force participation rates of 62-year-old and 65-year-old men of less than 2 percentage points. The effects of the 1977 amendments found by Krueger and Pischke were even smaller. Even if their largest estimated effects are accepted at face value, less than one-sixth of the drop in labor force participation during the 1970s could be explained by changes in social security.[23]

John Rust has proposed by far the most ambitious framework for understanding retirement decisions and their relationship to workers' choices about consumption, wealth accumulation, and full- or part-time work over an entire career.[24] Many students of life-cycle consumption behavior take the retirement age as fixed and try to model the implications for wealth accumulation during the career (see figure 1-5). Labor economists typically take asset holdings at a particular age (say, 54) as fixed and try to model retirement behavior. In contrast, Rust proposes a model that explains the rate of saving and consumption, the path of annual work hours, and the timing of retirement within a single comprehensive framework. In his setup, workers must use dynamic programming techniques to solve their decision problem. At each point during their lives, they seek out the optimal path for future work, consumption, and wealth accumulation, taking account of their preferences as well as their best current information about future wages, interest rates, rules regarding pension benefits, and expected health. Their behavior in a particular period is guided by the solution they have reached to the decision problem. However, their choice in a future period may turn out to be different from the choice they anticipate in the current period because new information can affect the optimal path of work and retirement.

Noneconomists may find this framework unappealing or unrealistic, but some empirical evidence suggests that the choice of retirement age is often

23. Burtless (1986, p. 800); and Krueger and Pischke (1991, p. 24).
24. Rust (1989, 1990).

guided by the application of a sophisticated decisionmaking rule. Robin Lumsdaine, James Stock, and David A. Wise examined the retirement choices of workers under company pension plans using three decision-making rules, one of which was based on application of a simple rule while the other two were based on more sophisticated decisionmaking approaches.[25] (One used an "option value" technique for evaluating the value of pension offers, and the other used a dynamic reprogramming rule.) They estimated their models using information from one period and then tried to predict retirement patterns in a later period under the three models. Perhaps surprisingly, they found that the models based on more complex decisionmaking rules were much more successful in predicting future retirement patterns. This evidence suggests that at least some workers use information in a sophisticated way to decide when to retire. Of course, within a well-established company plan that covers many workers in the same workplace, information helpful in choosing an optimal retirement age discovered by one worker can easily be shared with co-workers. Where information sharing is more difficult, workers might rely on simpler decisionmaking rules, and some workers may end up retiring at an age that is less than optimal. Also, the evidence collected by the authors does not show that workers use dynamic programming methods that are as complicated as those assumed by John Rust. Lumsdaine and colleagues analyzed the retirement decision in isolation. They did not assume workers were making farsighted and fully consistent plans for both work and consumption over a time horizon of many years. Even the most sophisticated decision rule they consider is much simpler than the planning methods assumed by Rust.

## What Have We Learned?

Research by economists and others has shed light on retirement in the United States. It has shown that the average retirement age of men has declined throughout the twentieth century. Economists have assembled powerful evidence that the exact distribution of male retirement ages is influenced by the financial incentives in social security and private pension plans. However, they have not offered convincing evidence that changes in these incentives can explain a major share of the trend in male labor force

25. Lumsdaine, Stock, and Wise (1992).

participation. Figures 1-1 and 1-3 suggest that the trend toward earlier retirement was already under way during the first decades of the century.

More fundamentally, economists cannot claim to have offered a persuasive explanation for the trend toward earlier retirement within the terms of their basic model. In a trivial sense, of course, the economic model can "explain" earlier retirement. Some combination of changes in wage rates, inherited wealth, pension plan incentives, the population distribution of health, physical and mental requirements for standard occupations, and individual preferences almost certainly accounts for lower participation rates of older men. However, this is a little like explaining the operation of a television set by saying that some combination of metal, plastic, electricity, and electromagnetic signal produces a moving picture on a piece of glass.

In terms of the basic life-cycle model, it would be useful to know what share of the trend can be explained by each of the factors: higher wages, greater initial wealth, private pension and social security incentives, changing health, evolving physical and mental requirements of typical jobs, and changing preferences for consumption and retirement leisure.

It is particularly important to understand the influence of public and private pensions. The cost of the public retirement programs is mounting rapidly, and many observers believe it will be necessary to make them less generous to keep them affordable and politically acceptable. For two reasons it is important to know whether scaling back benefits will cause retirement patterns to change. Policymakers have a practical reason for wanting to know whether retirement rates are likely to change and, if so, by how much. If they cut benefit levels or raise the early retirement age, they need to know how much overall benefit payments are likely to fall. This will be determined, in part, by the work responses of people affected by the cut. If the response is large, the budgetary impact and wider economic consequences will also be large. Both policymakers and the general public also need to understand how much income and consumption levels among the elderly will fall if benefits are scaled back. Social security accounts for more than three-quarters of the cash incomes of elderly families with incomes in the bottom 60 percent of the income distribution. If benefits were scaled back and the average retirement age remained unchanged, low-income retired workers would face large reductions in their old-age income and consumption.

Of the explanations advanced for earlier retirement, two of the least persuasive are declining health and the changing physical requirements of work. While nearly all good retirement studies find that health plays an important role in the timing of retirement, I can find no convincing evidence that the health of 62-year-olds or 65-year-olds has been declining over the period in which their labor force participation rates have fallen. Their declining mortality rates as well as recent evidence about the trend in their physical disabilities suggest instead that male health is improving, at least in early old age. Moreover, analyses of the growth of different kinds of occupations and their physical requirements imply that the physical demands of work are now easier to meet than they were in the past. A much smaller proportion of jobs require strenuous physical effort; a larger percentage require only moderate or light physical exertion.[26]

Evidence about the relative influence of the other factors on retirement is less conclusive. Although most studies since the early 1980s suggest that most of the decline in the retirement age after 1970 was due to factors other than social security, we do not have an accounting of the contributions of the other factors. The most important of these may be a change in workers' preferences. Workers may now prefer to spend a larger part of their lives in retirement. If offered the same trade-off between retirement and lifetime consumption that was available to earlier generations, today's elderly might choose to spend less of their life at work and more of it in retirement. In making that choice, workers would willingly accept lower lifetime consumption of the goods and services their wages can buy. Unfortunately, there is as yet no reliable evidence to tell us whether this conjecture is true.

Even if the hypothesis were true, neither economists nor noneconomists have proposed a convincing explanation of why preferences should have changed. In principle, the introduction and liberalization of social security and private pensions may themselves have contributed to the change in preferences. By providing workers with a secure source of income apart from their wages and savings, pensions may have spurred a handful of alert, farsighted workers to consider the possibility of retirement. Once these pioneers decided to retire, less alert workers were offered a pattern of behavior to emulate. The economically "rational" behavior of a handful of workers may have provoked a slow-motion revolution in the preferences of the wider population. Retirement became an acceptable and even prized part of the typical worker's life. This impact of social security and pensions, if it exists, cannot be measured in the type of statistical study described in the previous section. Those studies attempt to find a correlation between workers' choice of retirement age and the financial incentives that might

26. See Manton and Stollard (1994); and Baily (1987).

motivate them to retire at one age rather than another. If the workers' preferences for retirement versus consumption have gradually changed as a result of a social-security-induced shift, this change would be missed in the statistical study.

Some evidence suggests that behavior is slow to change in the face of changing financial incentives. It took a number of years after the introduction of early social security pensions before retirement at age 62 became common. The financial incentives that eventually induced men to retire at age 62 were presumably present from the first day early pensions became available in 1961. It was only in the late 1960s, however, that a sharp fall-off in labor force participation at age 62 became noticeable. By the late 1970s, the fall-off in participation was greater at age 62 than at age 65. This evidence may suggest either that workers are slow to recognize the financial implications of a complicated innovation or that their preferences are formed, in part, by important changes in the financial incentives facing them.

Without a full accounting of the effect of changing worker preferences or a convincing explanation for the shift in preferences, economists' understanding of the retirement process will remain incomplete. If they wish to propose far-reaching policy reforms, their understanding remains dangerously incomplete.

# References

Ando, Albert, and Franco Modigliani. 1963. "The 'Life Cycle' Hypothesis of Saving: Aggregate Implications and Tests." *American Economic Review* 53 (March): 55–84.

Baily, Martin N. 1987. "Aging and the Ability to Work: Policy Issues and Recent Trends." In *Work, Health, and Income among the Elderly*, edited by Gary Burtless, 59–96. Brookings.

Boskin, Michael J. 1977. "Social Security and Retirement Decisions." *Economic Inquiry* 15 (January): 1–25.

Bureau of the Census. 1975. *Historical Statistics of the United States: Colonial Times to 1970*. Department of Commerce.

Burkhauser, Richard V. 1979. "The Pension Acceptance Decision of Older Workers." *Journal of Human Resources* 14 (Winter): 63–75.

Burtless, Gary. 1986. "Social Security, Unanticipated Benefit Increases, and the Timing of Retirement." *Review of Economic Studies* 53 (October): 781–805.

Burtless, Gary, and Robert A. Moffitt. 1985. "The Joint Choice of Retirement Age and Postretirement Hours of Work." *Journal of Labor Economics* 3 (April): 209–36.

Caroll, Christopher R., and Lawrence H. Summers. 1991. "Consumption and Growth: Some New Evidence." In *National Saving and Economic Performance*, edited by Douglas B. Bernheim and John B. Shoven, 305–43. University of Chicago Press.

Friedman, Milton. 1957. *A Theory of the Consumption Function.* Princeton University Press.

Gustman, Alan A., and Thomas L. Steinmeier. 1986. "A Structural Retirement Model." *Econometrica* 54 (May): 555–84.

Hubbard, R. Glenn, Jonathan Skinner, and Stephen P. Zeldes. 1994. "Expanding the Life-Cycle Model: Precautionary Saving and Public Policy." *American Economic Review, Papers and Proceedings* 84 (2): 174–79.

Krueger, Alan B., and Jörn-Steffen Pischke. 1991. "The Effect of Social Security on Labor Supply: A Cohort Analysis of the Notch Generation." Working Paper 3699. Cambridge, Mass.: National Bureau of Economic Research.

Leonesio, Michael V. 1993. "Social Security and Older Workers." In *As the Workforce Ages,* edited by Olivia Mitchell, 183–204. Ithaca, N.Y.: ILR Press.

Lumsdaine, Robin L. 1996. "Factors Affecting Labor Supply Decisions and Retirement Income." In *Assessing Knowledge of Retirement Behavior,* edited by Eric A. Hanushek and Nancy L. Maritato, 61–122. Washington: National Academy Press.

Lumsdaine, Robin L., James Stock, and David A. Wise. 1992. "Three Models of Retirement: Computational Complexity versus Predictive Validity." In *Topics in the Economics of Aging,* edited by David A. Wise, 19–57. University of Chicago Press.

Manton, Kenneth G., and Eric Stollard. 1994. "Medical Demography: Interaction of Disability Dynamics and Mortality." In *Demography of Aging,* edited by Linda G. Martin and Samuel H. Preston, 217–79. Washington: National Academy Press.

Modigliani, Franco, and Richard Brumberg. 1954. "Utility Analysis and the Consumption Function: An Interpretation of Cross-Section Data." In *Post Keynesian Economics,* edited by Kenneth K. Kurihara, 388–436. Rutgers University Press.

Munnell, Alicia H. 1977. *The Future of Social Security.* Brookings.

Quinn, Joseph F. 1977. "Microeconomic Determinants of Early Retirement: A Cross-sectional View of White Married Men." *Journal of Human Resources* 12 (Summer): 329–47.

———. 1991. "The Nature of Retirement: Survey and Econometric Evidence." In *Retirement and Public Policy,* edited by Alicia H. Munnell, 115–38. Dubuque, Iowa: Kendall-Hunt.

Quinn, Joseph F., and Richard V. Burkhauser. 1994. "Retirement and Labor Force Behavior of the Elderly." In *Demography of Aging,* edited by Linda G. Martin and Samuel H. Preston. Washington: National Academy Press.

Quinn, Joseph F., Richard V. Burkhauser, and Daniel A. Myers. 1990. *Passing the Torch: The Influence of Economic Incentives on Work and Retirement.* Kalamazoo: Upjohn.

Ransom, Roger L., Richard Sutch, and Samuel H. Williamson. 1991. "Retirement: Past and Present." In *Retirement and Public Policy,* edited by Alicia H. Munnell, 23–50. Dubuque, Iowa: Kendall-Hunt.

Rust, John. 1989. "A Dynamic Programming Model of Retirement Behavior." In *The Economics of Aging,* edited by David A. Wise, 359–98. University of Chicago Press.

———. 1990. "Behavior of Male Workers at the End of the Life Cycle: An Empirical Analysis of States and Controls." In *Issues in the Economics of Aging,* edited by David A. Wise, 317–79. University of Chicago Press.

Skinner, Jonathan. 1988. "Risky Income, Life Cycle Consumption, and Precautionary
    Savings." *Journal of Monetary Economics* 22 (2): 237–55
Social Security Administration. 1998. *Income of the Aged Chartbook, 1996.*
Zeldes, Stephen P. 1989. "Consumption and Liquidity Constraints: An Empirical
    Investigation." *Journal of Policical Economy* 97 (2): 305–46.

HENRY J. AARON

# 2 | *Retirement, Retirement Research, and Retirement Policy*

L IFE EXPECTANCIES have increased throughout the twentieth century and are expected to continue rising. Retirement ages have fallen, and few observers expect them to rise much. Labor force participation by men has decreased, while that of women has increased. Together, these facts imply that the portion of life men spend outside the paid labor force has increased and will continue to do so. Trends for women are murkier because their labor force participation rates have increased. Should public policy encourage people to retire later than they do now?

For many observers, the answer to this question is clear. They find it unthinkable—or at least undesirable—that people would spend a steadily expanding share of their lives in retirement. To forestall such trends, they embrace the principle that the ages at which people first become entitled to social security and medicare should be raised. Other public policies might encourage employers to create job opportunities that would appeal to older workers.

I wish to thank George Akerlof, Gary Burtless, William Gale, and Charles Schultze for helpful comments.

43

For other observers the desirability of promoting later retirement is not so obvious. People are free to decide when to retire, they argue, and know better than legislators how much of their lives they want to spend at paid work and how much in leisure or non-labor-force activities. They hold that the goal of public policy should be neutrality and that, if this condition is met, the timing of retirement, like people's choices between spending their incomes on automobiles or vacations, should be matter of indifference to policymakers.

Whether one lines up with the stop-the-trend-to-early-retirement camp or the whatever-people-decide-is-OK-as-long-as-public-policy-is-neutral camp depends on whether one believes that current public policy is neutral toward the retirement decision and whether one thinks that throughout their lives people plan for retirement with foresight and make well-informed decisions based on accurate expectations about when to retire. This chapter is addressed to these two questions. The tentative answer to the first is that public and private policies are almost certainly *not* neutral with respect to the timing of retirement and that they very likely encourage earlier retirement than would occur if policies were neutral. The answer to the second question is more complex. People are poorly equipped to make sound decisions on matters as complex as how much to save and how best to prepare in other respects for retirement. For that reason, they are likely, if responding freely to neutral incentives, to find themselves on the eve of retirement poorly prepared economically and in other respects. Furthermore, there is evidence that many people suffer from distorted expectations about retirement. Nonetheless, the evidence that people willingly accept a sharp drop in consumption at retirement suggests that the decision to leave work is not a close one. There is good reason to think, however, that this decision is shaped by social interactions as much as it is by individualistic preferences.

Because my answer to the second question contradicts many of the assumptions of standard economic analysis, I begin by outlining the reasoning economists normally apply to individual decisions on retirement and then discuss why this reasoning needs to be supplemented. The chapter concludes with a brief and speculative summary.

## How Economists Think about Retirement

Standard economic analysis rests on the following reasoning. People have certain talents and abilities that define their income earning capacity. They can use this capacity to earn money with which they can buy various goods and services, but only by sacrificing leisure to work. The more a person works, the more onerous each added hour of work becomes. People choose to work up to the point at which the value of the additional consumption made possible by more work is just offset by the loss suffered from giving up more leisure.[1] Workers decide how much to consume each period based not only on current earnings but also on unbiased expectations regarding total lifetime earnings and inheritances.

Workers also understand that they will have to decide how much to work each period throughout their lives. Accordingly, decisions about working are influenced not only by current circumstances but also by expected future conditions that will also influence later decisions on how much to work. Among the relevant future conditions are broad economic variables, such as wages, asset prices, consumer goods prices, and interest rates. These depend on such economywide conditions as the rate of growth of productivity, the frequency and severity of recessions, and the general rate of inflation. But they also depend on conditions specific to particular workers, including their personal and family health, the business success of their employers, and the demand for services of people with their particular skills. Public policies such as tax rules, minimum wage laws, pension regulations, monetary policy, and a wide range of actions influencing international trade and capital movements also shape the environment for each worker.

In addition to such objective considerations, workers' work and retirement decisions depend on their current preferences and their beliefs about how those preferences will evolve in the future. For example, 30-year-olds will need to save more and work harder if they are sprinting to retire at age 50 than if they plan never to retire. People who are impatient to consume—that is, those who have a high discount rate—find it harder to accumulate sufficient wealth to support themselves during retirement than do workers who are willing to defer gratification. Those who cannot bear risk are more likely than those who tolerate risk easily to defer retirement until they are sure that they have enough saved to guarantee that they will not outlive their savings.

---

1. Contrary to some naive criticisms, the standard economic model allows for the possibility that work provides deep personal and social satisfactions. All that the model requires is that at some point workers suffer a loss of well-being from *more* work that is sufficient to cause them to decide not to work an additional hour. The total effect of the sacrifice of leisure (which is the mirror image of work) can be to increase welfare, even apart from the consumption goods that earnings from work make possible.

Economists usually assume that people have stable preferences—over leisure and other consumption goods—or that they correctly anticipate how those preferences will change. They do not assume that people correctly anticipate every future event but that they use all available information efficiently and do not make systematic forecast errors.

Personal circumstances, the standard reasoning continues, are expected to vary over the life cycle. The young typically save little and may even go into debt in the expectation that they can pay off their debts later on. Incomes typically increase in middle age, as do saving and wealth. As old age approaches, infirmities or declining productivity eventually make work so burdensome or unremunerative that workers typically retire. To do so voluntarily, they must have sufficient wealth in the form of individual saving, private pensions or public annuities such as social security, or entitlement to in-kind benefits such as health care. In short, people retire when two conditions are satisfied: current labor compensation is no longer sufficient to compensate them for the burden of continuing to work *and* wealth is sufficient to sustain planned consumption during retirement.

*If these conditions are satisfied, individuals will maximize their own welfare, subject to the resource constraints imposed by their skills and other endowments, including inheritances.* If a majority regards endowments as unfair, government may impose taxes or provide transfers to redistribute wealth or income. As long as certain additional conditions are satisfied, the decisions collectively will be socially efficient, in the narrow sense that no person's welfare can be improved without lowering someone else's.

The remainder of this chapter will examine three issues. I first describe certain additional conditions that must be satisfied if behavior is to be optimal in this narrow sense. I next examine important incentives that influence retirement behavior, which can be analyzed within the traditional economic model. Finally, I explain why the traditional economic model is at best an incomplete and imperfect description of human behavior.

## Certain Additional Conditions

Some of the conditions for social optimality are strong. First, prices must reflect all costs of production and consumption, including the costs one consumer or producer may impose on others. If this condition is violated, people may make decisions that are right for themselves but that reduce the welfare of others.

Second, important markets must not "fail." If private markets for important goods do not exist or if they operate inefficiently, people may be precluded from pursuing options they desire. For example, private markets for annuities operate inefficiently. If the price of annuity contracts is based on average life expectancy, people with long life expectancies are more likely to buy annuities than are people with short life expectancies. As a result, the population of purchasers will have higher than average life expectancies, and this will push up the price insurers must charge. As the price rises, even people with average or slightly longer life expectancies will find annuities too expensive. Prices must therefore increase, further limiting the appeal of annuities. In principle, the market could collapse completely. In practice, few people voluntarily purchase annuities because the prices are 10 to 20 percent higher than they would be if they were priced for the average person. Unemployment insurance provides an even starker problem since the private market is entirely unable to provide adequate insurance because no actuarial calculation is possible, and no private agent can provide reliable protection. Government is the only credible purveyor of unemployment insurance.

Third, the political system may reflect popular revulsion against the distribution of income: excessive poverty and the hardships it causes or excessive wealth and the concentration of power it generates. In such cases, measures to redistribute income may be justified, but the taxes and transfers necessary to reduce inequality all impose economic costs because they distort the wage rate or other prices and generate economic inefficiency.[2]

When these qualifications are important, government action *may* improve public welfare by providing commodities that would otherwise be produced in inadequate quantities. Or government may cause markets to operate more effectively—by improving information, as in the case of financial markets; or by taxing, subsidizing, or otherwise regulating private transactions, as in the case of pollution control; or by improving the distribution of income.

Of course, government intervention may make things worse for any number of reasons, including simple error or greed or selfishness by officials. Whether government intervention will make things better or worse

---

2. Okun (1975). In some cases redistribution may actually improve efficiency despite the distortions of taxes. The cases include health or nutritional interventions that boost labor productivity of those who are too poor to afford adequate diets or health care based on their unsubsidized market earnings.

depends on whether the flaws and distortions of public intervention are more or less serious than those of private markets.

Still, one has to start somewhere. Most economists for many years have started with a default position—in legal terminology a "rebuttable presumption"—that decisions are best left to individual households and businesses and that the burden of proof rests with those who would use government authority to overturn these decisions. The strength of this presumption has grown in recent years for some economists; it is virtually unrebuttable for libertarians, to whom it is axiomatic that private decisions, if not optimal, will not be improved by outside interference.

Few people other than economists fully embrace this model of behavior, and doubts are sprouting up even among economists. Nonetheless, these principles provide an organizing framework—a sort of economist's home base—from which deviations or exceptions may be specified. The assumptions underlying this framework sometimes support strong inferences about how people will respond *qualitatively* to policy changes, although the size of responses is always a matter for empirical research and even qualitative responses may be in doubt.[3]

This model of household decisionmaking normally pays little explicit attention to the constraining effects of institutional rules or peer group pressures or influences. To the extent that these factors are important in shaping retirement decisions, their influence will be observed through their effects on the estimated sensitivity of retirement to wealth, income, or other measured variables. Institutional rules are expected to evolve gradually to reflect the preferences of employers and employees. Thus, *retirement is largely an individual decision*, based on such measured, individually differentiated quantities as income, wealth, health status, and—a relatively recent innovation—the labor force status of one's spouse.

## Are Retirement Incentives Neutral?

Neutrality requires that prices—including wages, the price of labor— reflect resource costs and that all relevant markets exist. Neither condition is satisfied. In the past, departures from neutrality in the United States probably accelerated retirement, but the situation is now less clear. Massive

---

3. Some implications of theory involve constraints on responses. For example, economic theory gives no clear signal on whether an increase in wage rates will cause people to delay or accelerate retirement. But if it accelerates retirement, it will increase desired saving.

shifts in retirement norms in foreign countries followed changes in public policies that accelerated availability of retirement pensions.[4]

Wage rates are often more or less than current productivity for many reasons, including taxes and transfer payments that rise or fall with earnings. In principle, taxes can influence labor supply in various ways: the age at which people enter the labor force, hours worked per week, weeks worked per year (that is, the length of vacations), investments in skill-enhancing education and training, and age of retirement. In practice, empirical estimates of the effect of taxes focus almost exclusively on hours worked per year. The theoretical effect of most taxes on labor supply is indeterminate. The empirical estimates suggest that increases in taxes reduce labor supply modestly for adult males and single women and more substantially for married women.[5] Analyses of how ordinary taxes affect the retirement age are rare. For older workers, private and public pensions and health benefits probably influence labor supply more than taxes do. But whether the sum of these nonneutralities favors retirement in the United States is unclear.

## Why Have Pensions?

Why do pensions exist if people make selfishly optimal decisions voluntarily? First, tax laws promote private pension plans by deferring taxation of pension fund income until it is paid out.[6] Voluntary individual behavior can neutralize the effects of pension funds on household saving. People who want to save enjoy the tax advantages. People who do not want to save

4. Gruber and Wise (1998).

5. Typical labor supply elasticities for men run about 0.2, meaning that an increase in a proportional tax from 10 percent to 12 percent—a 20 percent increase in the tax—would reduce labor supply about 11 minutes a week. This calculation assumes that there are no other taxes. Because taxes interact and some taxes are progressive, marginal rates usually exceed average rates. These facts tend to increase the effect of taxes on labor supply, possibly by a large amount.

6. Wage controls during World War II, which encompassed money wages but not fringe benefits, also encouraged the spread of pensions, a form of compensation that employers could legally provide to avoid limits on cash compensation. Until recently, savings vehicles, other than private pensions, that enjoyed tax-favored status included the inside buildup of whole life insurance, owner-occupied housing, social security, and capital gains on any asset. However, life insurance is encumbered by sizable administrative costs. The tax advantages of owner-occupied housing are capitalized into land values and confer no major investment advantage. And similar capitalization occurs with assets that are expected to yield capital gains rather than taxable interest and dividends. Thus, it was profitable to carry out as large a proportion of intended saving through private pensions as possible. In recent years, tax advantages have been extended to savings vehicles that closely resemble personal savings accounts with withdrawal restrictions. This legislation has been associated with a decline of traditional defined-benefit pensions.

can offset pension fund saving by saving less in other forms or by borrowing more heavily than they would otherwise.[7] In addition, employers can
use pensions to encourage older workers to quit. Police and fire depart-
ments and the military provide generous pensions after as little as twenty
years of service and often before age forty.

## Social Security

Social security was initially designed to encourage older workers to retire
and almost certainly encourages retirement.[8] First, social security benefits
are reduced if earnings exceed an exempt earnings threshold—the "earnings test." By way of compensation for this loss, workers whose benefits are
reduced receive increases in future benefits—the "delayed retirement
credit."[9] This credit is currently actuarially equivalent to the benefit reduction for workers between ages 62 and 65 and will be equivalent for all
workers in about a decade.[10]

Despite actuarial equivalence (or near equivalence), empirical research
suggests that the earnings test slightly discourages labor supply.[11] Presumably, workers undervalue the higher future benefits relative to the current
loss of benefits, although the standard economic models indicate that the
effect should be tiny. The finding that the earnings test reduces labor supply may be read in three ways: as evidence against the underlying assumption that workers make rational plans for the future, as evidence the workers have higher discount rates than the Social Security Administration
uses in calculating the delayed retirement credit, or as evidence that workers do not understand how the delayed retirement credit works.

## Private Pensions

Many employers use defined-benefit private pensions to bind workers
when they are young and to get them to quit when they are old. Pensions
create these incentives by substantially raising or lowering the worker's net

---

7. These offsets are likely to be incomplete, however, because pensions and other forms of saving
are imperfect substitutes; pensions cannot normally be withdrawn before the pension is activated and
cannot be used as collateral to secure low-interest loans. Furthermore, interest on personal borrowing
other than home mortgage interest is not normally deductible.

8. Aaron and Reischauer (1998).

9. Social Security Administration (1997).

10. Diamond and Gruber (1997). After age 70 the earnings test no longer applies.

11. See chapter 1. For reasons explained by Burtless, this finding may not be a reliable indicator
of its long-term effect on labor supply.

wage. While pension entitlements are building up, but before workers are eligible for a pension, their total compensation includes current earnings plus the increase in the present value of their future pension entitlement.[12] Once workers can actually claim a pension, and particularly if the growth of pension entitlements slows, they have an incentive to leave their employer because their net wage falls dramatically to the excess of current wages over the pension they could claim if they quit.[13] Faced with this situation, many workers retire rather than accept the adjustment costs and pay cut usually associated with a new job. Such pensions figuratively, if not literally, force retirement.

## Earnings Distortions: Health Benefits

Most, but not all, private workers are covered by employer-financed health insurance. People with low incomes, particularly children in poor families, may be covered by publicly financed health insurance under the medicaid program. Most of the elderly and disabled are covered by medicare. Some employers provide health insurance benefits to retirees as well, although most benefits terminate or decline materially when the worker retires.[14]

These separate sources of health insurance create a host of incentives: to participate or not to participate in the labor force, to retire or not to retire.[15] Among the incentives the following have been the subject of scholarly study and are thought to be significant. First, group insurance is cheaper than individual insurance. Employer-financed health insurance enjoys tax advantages over individually purchased health insurance. Accordingly, the availability of health insurance as a work-related fringe benefit encourages those who value health insurance to enter and remain in the labor force. Second, because some employers do not offer health insurance as a fringe benefit and individually purchased insurance is more costly than group insurance, many workers have an incentive to remain with their

---

12. Under "cliff vesting," for example, employees have no pension entitlement until they have worked a fixed period, which can be up to five years, after which they become entitled to a future pension based on all service up to that date. The real earnings of workers under such plans jump sharply at the cliff. As tenure approaches the cliff, workers have increasingly powerful incentives not to quit.

13. Window plans that provide particularly generous pensions for a short period after workers reach certain ages create even more powerful incentives. Confronted with such offers, most workers leave their current jobs.

14. Because of federal legislation, workers have the right to buy coverage for a period under the plan where they last worked at a premium 3 percent above the average cost to their employer.

15. Gruber (1998) surveys the effects of health insurance on labor supply.

current job and not to leave the labor force or become self-employed. This incentive is particularly powerful for older workers who are not yet old enough to claim medicare because they are at relatively high risk of large medical outlays; and the incentive is strongest if their employers do not provide health benefits for retirees. Third, potential workers who are eligible for medicaid may have an incentive not to take a job with an employer who does not offer health insurance because work usually results in the loss of medicaid coverage. Fourth, the fact that the cost of health care increases with workers' age means that companies that self-insure—pay health costs of their employees directly—have an incentive not to hire older workers or those with a history of illness.

The net effect of health insurance on labor force participation is hard to sort out. Employer-financed benefits for retirees, particularly the more generous plans, represent a large nest egg of deferred compensation. The present value of these benefits at first increases with years of service and then declines as the worker ages.[16] For reasons of custom or formal contract, wages and other fringe benefits probably do not vary with age to fully offset variations in the cost of fringe benefits. At some point, therefore, the existence of retiree health benefits creates a strong incentive for workers to retire. The reason is analogous to the incentives under private pension plans that do not increase actuarially with age—the worker has to "use it or lose it." The effect on employers is more complicated. If workers do not use and do lose retiree health benefits, total employer obligations fall. Thus, the waning in value of retiree health care, which makes retaining older workers attractive, is a factor that should be balanced with other considerations in determining personnel policy.[17]

## Saving and Wealth Distortions

Public policy is pervasively not neutral with respect to retirement saving. But *how* public policy affects this accumulation depends sensitively on

16. The present value rises for two reasons. The period of retiree health insurance coverage usually grows with duration of service. And the nearer the date of using the benefits comes, the less that they are discounted for delay. The value eventually declines, also for two reasons. First, most plans provide more generous benefits before age 65 than afterwards in recognition of medicare eligibility, which starts at 65. As workers approach 65, they lose generous benefit years. Second, as people age, mortality risk increases.

17. If workers and employers quickly and correctly recognized the value of retiree health benefits, and wages and other fringe benefits reflected them on an individual worker basis, retiree health benefits would have no effects. But this assumption seems fanciful. I know of no one who makes it. Even if economic markets worked this way for most workers, the minimum wage laws might short-circuit the process for the small proportion of low-wage workers who have retiree coverage.

what one takes as the baseline situation and how people respond to deviations from it. Relevant wealth includes private savings, private pensions, social security, retiree health benefits, and medicare.[18]

Compared to a situation with reduced spending on government activities other than social security and medicare and with commensurately lower taxes, public policy discourages retirement. By lowering the rate of return on saving, taxes probably discourage retirement. But government regulation, on balance, improves the reliability of information regarding rates of return and risk characteristics of various saving vehicles. Such encouragement to save may well dominate the direct effects of taxes and transfers.

The idea that public policy lowers voluntary *private* saving is hardly controversial, although empirical research suggests that the effects of taxes are small and that taxes may even boost saving.[19] Tax policy does, however, promote private pensions and other forms of compulsory saving. These plans may overcome impulsive behavior and thereby boost saving. Furthermore, tax-sheltered saving cannot generally be used as collateral for loans. And people cannot gain access to these funds before a certain age without paying a penalty. As a result, tax-sheltered saving is an imperfect substitute for other saving, at least for younger people, and more tax-sheltered saving than ordinary saving is necessary to achieve a given level of protection against various risks. Myopia might intensify these effects. Because withdrawal penalties do not apply to the elderly, they may be left with more assets than would otherwise have been the case, relaxing one of the constraints limiting voluntary retirement.

Standard theory suggests that social security will reduce private saving needed if people retire at some given age, but may boost saving if it induces earlier retirement. After a careful review of research on the effects of social security on saving, William Gale and Eric Engen concluded: "The literature has reached inconclusive results on the impact of social security on

18. I omit income- and means-tested benefits, such as supplemental security income, aid to families with dependent children, medicaid, food stamps, and housing assistance, although a significant number of older people subsist on these programs after leaving low-paying jobs. Without such support these people would probably have to remain in the labor force in low-paid employment.

19. Empirical estimates vary. The most commonly cited estimate is that the elasticity of saving with respect to the rate of return is about 0.4, meaning that an increase in the rate of return of 10 percent will boost saving 4 percent. If one assumes that the saving rate is 5 percent, the before-tax rate of return is 10 percent, and the tax rate is 20 percent, cutting the tax rate in half—to 10 percent—would boost the net rate of return from 8 percent to 9 percent, an increase of 11.1 to 12.5 percent, depending on the initial comparison point. This change would increase saving by a bit under 5 percent [0.4 × (0.125 + 0.111)/2 = 0.0472], or from 5 percent to about 5.24 percent.

national saving, although almost all studies show some displacement of private saving."[20] Furthermore, they pointed out, whether reforms raise or lower saving depends sensitively on the details of the proposed change.

On balance, whether public policy as a whole "distorts" private saving plans and results in more or less saving is simply too large a question to be well defined. What seems clear, however, is that the capital stock is too small, judging by the fact that new investment earns returns higher than rates at which most people are willing to save. For this reason, increases in saving would raise national economic welfare.

## Does Current Policy Bias Retirement Decisions?

The simple answer is yes. But how much and in what ways is impossible to say. The social security earnings test probably decreases labor supply, although it would not have such effects for workers age 62 to 65 if they responded to the actuarial incentives. Many private pensions first create incentives for workers to remain with their employer and, at some point, leave their jobs but not necessarily to retire. As Gary Burtless shows in chapter 1, most workers claim benefits at age sixty-two, the age of eligibility for social security, or soon after. Health benefits, private and public, create a crazy quilt of labor force incentives, encouraging some workers to enter the labor force and others to remain outside. These incentives cause some workers not to retire and some to retire. Although the net effect is unclear, the pervasiveness of nonneutralities is indisputable.

# Qualifications to the Standard Model

The most important justifications for incentives to promote saving through private and public pensions or tax rules rest on two sorts of principles: denial of one or more elements of the standard model and the capacity of social insurance to protect people against risks that they cannot handle themselves because the private market offers no insurance.

## Myopia

The basis for social insurance is a conviction that many people are myopic, at least when it comes to retirement saving. Assertions that myopia is wide-

20. Engen and Gale (1997).

spread encounter spirited opposition from adherents of the standard model, who are apt to point out that many people make rational lifetime plans based on fully informed estimates of future earnings, rates of return, and other relevant considerations.[21] If people fail to save as much when young as full lifetime planning indicates would be optimal, building up sufficient assets in later working years implies saving rates of 30 to 40 percent, which few people actually sustain. By forcing people to curtail current consumption when young and providing for pensions at a later age, social insurance ameliorates the adverse consequences of myopia.

Myopia does double duty. The same forces that lead people to save too little when young cause them to undervalue the pension promise, which therefore causes little or no offsetting increase in current consumption. The combination of social insurance and suboptimal private saving (because of myopic disregard of the distant future) could fortuitously lead to the accumulation of wealth approximating that under fully rational lifetime planning.

Economists have tried in recent years to provide systematic explanations for myopia. An important advance is the finding that discount rates applied to choices in the near future are much higher than discount rates applied to the distant future. An example illustrates this finding. Offered $100 in a year, people will accept a much smaller increment for waiting until the thirteenth month to receive payment than the amount they will demand for turning down immediate payment of $100 and waiting one month. Repeated studies have demonstrated that discount rates decline with time for both people and animals.[22] Though amply confirmed, this pattern of decisionmaking is inconsistent with the principles of standard economic theory, according to which people demand the same compensation for waiting a given period, whether the wait occurs now or in the future.

Myopia justifies the compulsion inherent in social insurance. It also explains some specific features of the U.S. social security system—for example, the payment of benefits only as annuities, prohibition of single-

21. Some economists believe that people make not only rational *lifetime* plans, but rational *dynastic* plans, taking into account the effects of their actions and of external events not only on themselves but also on heirs. Controversy over this line of reasoning has led to a large literature. As indicated later, I believe that lifetime decisionmaking clearly exceeds human cognitive capability. Dynastic planning is even more difficult. I shall ignore this literature.

22. For studies of discount rates that decline with time—so-called hyperbolic discounting—see Ainslie (1992) and Laibson, Repetto, and Tobacman (1998). The same patterns apply to choices in the present or in the future when the sums are identical but the probability of receiving them varies. See Loewenstein and Prelec (1992).

life annuities for married workers, and full inflation indexing. Myopia generates two symmetric problems that justify the automatic annuitization of benefits as opposed to payment in a lump sum. Some people might prodigally exhaust their resources before they die because they seriously underestimate future wants. Others, who are morbidly fearful that they will outlive their assets, will not spend enough. If people could buy "real" (that is, inflation-adjusted) annuities from private insurers, advocates of the standard economic assumptions could hold that they were simply expressing their consumption preferences. But no private financial organization offers such annuities. And people who wish to buy the annuities that private insurers offer find that the insurance companies impose large loading charges. As a result, few people buy them.[23]

### Aggregate Economic Events

Risks associated with aggregate economic performance are not explicitly considered in the standard model of personal decisionmaking and constitute an additional motive for social insurance. No private market can effectively insure against extended unemployment, lower-than-anticipated rates of return on savings, or high inflation. Social insurance cannot eliminate these risks. But it can spread them more widely among workers of a given generation or even across several generations, reducing the risk that individual workers would have to face alone if they had to rely solely on private pensions and saving.

Several aspects of social insurance spread what would otherwise be private risks. Payment of benefits that increase less than proportionately with earnings and computation of average earnings, which are used to compute benefits, over less than a full working life reduce the effect of unemployment on ultimate benefits.[24] The defined-benefit character of social insurance subjects workers to an average, economywide rate of return, rather than to a return on the particular portfolio the individual selects. This average return is related to economywide interest rates, but only approximately and with long delays. The unavailability of indexed dollar

23. In the early 1980s only 2 percent of people over age 65 had private annuities. Some proportion, perhaps most, of these annuities were involuntary, having been established by gift or bequest. Poterba and Warshawsky (1999).

24. Under current law, U.S. social security benefits are based on the worker's highest thirty-five years of indexed earnings, where earnings are indexed by a wage index. A worker with earnings spanning forty years can be unemployed or out of the labor force for any reason (child bearing or rearing, education or training, or other reasons) for up to five years with no effect on retirement benefits.

bonds has meant that only government-guaranteed benefits could be reliably insulated on a large scale from the effects of inflation.[25]

## Externalities

If prices inaccurately measure the social costs of individual behavior, some form of collective action—taxes, subsidies, regulations, prohibitions, or mandates—may improve social welfare. Common examples refer to peak-load pricing by utilities or congestion taxes on travelers.[26] But externalities can arise from either private or governmental action.

Private and public health and pension policies and methods of labor compensation cause individual decisions about when to retire to generate external costs and benefits. Under social security, people over age 62 who earn enough to cause their benefits to be deferred generate external benefits even if the benefit reduction is actuarial. They do so because they pay taxes on the earnings at the same rate as other workers do, but such work is unlikely to cause a proportionate increase in the benefits to which they are entitled. If annual earnings after age 62 are not among the highest thirty-five years of a person's working life, they are disregarded in benefit computation. The revenue generated by taxes on such work reduces the taxes that have to be collected from younger workers. Older workers therefore generate a financial external benefit by continuing to work. The same is true of lesser-earning spouses (still typically women) whose earnings records support benefits equal to less than half of that based on their spouses' earnings. Their work creates a right to disability benefits and to an old-age pension before the principal earner retires, but these benefits are worth less than the tax revenue that the work generates. And the actuarial adjustments to benefits under the earnings test take no account of adverse selection (those with short life expectancies probably claim reduced benefits proportionately more often than do workers with high life expectan-

25. Despite the issuance of indexed Treasury bonds, insurance companies and private pension funds have yet to offer inflation-indexed annuities, perhaps because the duration of commitments exceeds the maximum maturity of indexed Treasury securities. It is also possible the companies have concluded that there is little demand for indexed annuities.

26. If utilities charged the same price of use of electricity at all hours, peak-load users would not bear the full costs of their consumption. Such users force the electricity supplier to carry extra peak-load capacity or use high-cost reserve capacity. These costs are in addition to those associated with normal usage. The marginal user thereby inflicts "external costs"—"externalities" for short—on others. Such externalities justify taxes or extra private charges for electricity used during peak-load periods. These charges discourage peak-load demand that is worth less than the peak-load price to the user but at least as much as the normal price. The charges thereby avoid costs that otherwise would be distributed among all users, including those whose demands are more urgent.

cies), age of spouse (the younger the spouse, the longer the spouse's benefits will be payable on average), or number of other dependents.

Each of these externalities and many others mean that society as a whole
has an interest in when workers retire. Although it is possible to come up
with cases in which continued work generates external social costs, I believe
that most *financial* externalities are benefits generated by older workers that
accrue to the nonaged and aged retirees.

If retirement ages should increase, younger workers will bear some possibly important costs, especially during the *transition* to later retirement.
During this transition, opportunities for some younger workers waiting to
succeed to senior positions would diminish or vanish, particularly if promotion is based on age and tenure. But this effect will also occur if promotion is based entirely on merit whenever older workers are more capable
than younger workers, perhaps because of experience. Once the transition
to a longer working life is complete, opportunities for promotion would
improve, but would be slowed permanently on the assumption that the
shape of the job hierarchy is unaffected by the extension of working life. If
the transition occurs slowly, however, the effect may be almost subliminal.

## Are Retirement Decisions *Really* Optimal?

Within the standard model, individual retirement decisions are optimal
in a particular sense: given the choices and opportunities available, each
person retires at the time that is personally optimal. People may make
mistakes, but, the theory holds, systematic improvements are not possible. This conclusion ceases to follow if even the relatively minor qualifications I have listed are admitted. If people are predictably myopic, they
make *systematic*, rather than random, mistakes. Their decisions may be
inferior because market prices send incorrect signals about the resource
costs of individual actions. In addition, "agency" problems may arise. People who are responsible for the economic support of spouses, children, or
others sometimes fail adequately to consider the interests of these dependents. In such cases, externally imposed constraints can *in principle*
improve welfare of the dependents through mandated intrafamily redistribution. And collective action can *in principle* fill in for nonexistent markets—to insure against inflation, for example. Whether restrictions on
individual choice will improve outcomes *in practice* hinges on the importance of distortions in political processes.

However, even if these qualifications to the standard economic model
are ignored, a great many studies from psychology and philosophy raise

questions about whether individual decisions on issues as complex as those concerning retirement are or can be optimal in the sense used by economists—that decisions cannot be systematically improved based on available information or information that can be collected at a cost not greater than the information is worth. This definition corresponds to what J. St. B. Evans calls *rationality₂*, substantive rationality.[27] It contrasts with what he calls *rationality₁*—procedural rationality, which refers to the use of the procedures that balance considerations of accuracy, cognitive and energy demands, and time. My conclusion will not be that the claim of optimality in the standard model is wrong, but that there is little reason to believe that it is correct at the individual level. The line of argument consists of several elements.

## Complexity, Heuristics, and Norms

Decisions about retirement, like decisions concerning other complex events, can be modeled using decision trees. A decision tree is a schematic portrayal of the options a person faces, the probability of each option, and the value of each outcome. Typically, a decision tree consists of many branches and nodes. Mathematicians have shown that once the number of branches and nodes exceeds a relatively modest number, even the fastest digital computer may take millennia to find the optimal outcome. Even if the optimal branch is discoverable in reasonable time, the solution typically will be so difficult to find that no human has the mental capacity to discover it unaided. Many experiments have demonstrated the rather puny capacity of most people to solve problems depicted in decision trees or to infer cause and effect in even small problems.

As a result of these cognitive limitations, people rely on a variety of mental short cuts or heuristics. These heuristics have arisen in various cultures from the efforts of individuals over long periods trying to solve various problems. They work satisfactorily in many situations. People use them, presumably, because they produce satisfactory answers and save time and mental energy. But they lead to systematic errors when applied to problems materially different from those in which the heuristics evolved. The quality of decisions therefore becomes extremely sensitive to a lengthy list of situational factors examined in fascinating detail in the vast literature of social psychology.[28]

27. Evans (1993).
28. See Rabin (1998); Ross and Nisbett (1991); and Nisbett and Ross (1980).

These experiments document, among other things, that individual decisions fail standard tests of rational choice. Decisions are not invariant to irrelevant alternatives. They violate the "sure-thing" principle (that people should prefer a lottery with a given chance of option A or option B if the outcome is guaranteed to be better than option C). They constantly violate theorems of how to make optimal decisions when confronted with decision trees (Bayesian problems). This situation can be viewed in several ways.

One possibility is that habits of thought arose in one setting because they were "good enough," if not optimal. Another possibility is that these habits of thought were ideal practical solutions to problems in the settings in which they arose but are inferior in a new setting. Responses, such as quickness to anger, that promoted survival in violent environments may cease to serve well in circumstances where patience and cooperation are superior strategies.[29] Thus once functional rules may have become inferior or even dangerous in a new setting but can be improved through education and training. The final possibility is that these habits of thought, while easy and "natural," are genuinely inferior and cannot be corrected but are not sufficiently damaging to be eliminated through Darwinian processes.[30]

The existence of systematic errors in individual decisionmaking is not the end of the story, however. Individuals interact, work out problems together, and come up with solutions no single person might have found if working in isolation. This process occurs at various levels, ranging from interactions among small groups grappling with an unfamiliar problem to the exchange of ideas among all members of a given profession. In each instance ideas emerge that no single person would have conceived alone. Education and training consist not only of developing individual analytic skills and learning facts about the world, but also of learning how to cooperate with others, sift good ideas from bad, advance one's own thoughts in ways that are appealing and persuasive, and understand and apply methods that people have developed in the past to solve problems. Thus for some problems, less than fully rational individuals who cooperate may produce

---

29. Nisbett and Cohen (1996) report that American men raised in the South tend to take offense and resort to violence more quickly than men raised elsewhere.

30. Even if one accepts a Darwinian argument for why rational decisions must eventually win out, Eldar Shafir (1993, p. 279) argues that the case is always provisional. Humans have been around for not more than 2.5 million years, he points out. Dinosaurs were dominant for 100 million. "Biological assumptions of optimality notwithstanding, most biologists would not find it incredible if horses were to systematically make some maladaptive decisions; yet, the horse family has been around for more than 60 million years."

more nearly rational solutions than individuals who are superior rational thinkers acting alone.

The social nature of certain decisions is expressed in norms or patterns of behavior that have evolved over time. If norms have force, it is precisely because they reflect accumulated experience and lead people to behave differently from the ways they might otherwise behave. *Norms may serve as group heuristics.* As with individual heuristics, they work well most of the time and probably have survival value, but norms or heuristics that have ceased to have survival value in a changed environment may linger for extended periods, and their loss of value may not be apparent to those who persist in applying them.[31]

Furthermore, it is quite possible that norms lead to clearly suboptimal equilibria, as the following highly artificial, prisoners'-dilemma-like game inspired by the retirement decision illustrates. I assume initially that everyone has identical tastes, which are well defined and well understood. People derive income and social standing from work. Past a certain age, however, they become jealous of others who are enjoying the leisure of retirement. Their welfare is therefore reduced if a sufficient number of others retire while they continue to work—the jealousy factor. Symmetrically, people enjoy retirement a bit more if others are working than if everyone else is retired—the gloat factor. People are happiest if substantially everyone, including themselves, works. The satisfactions from work exceed the gloat factor, but jealousy extinguishes them. If a sizable number of others retire, each person prefers retirement to work. This situation can be depicted as a multiperson game, as in the following matrix. The payoffs reflect what might be called the white-collar professional payoff matrix. The number on the left in each pair is the welfare index for oneself and the number on the right is the welfare index for others.

|  |  | Others | |
| --- | --- | --- | --- |
|  |  | *Retired*† | *Working* |
| *Oneself* | *Retired* | 15/15 | 16/14 |
|  | *Working* | 14/16 | 20/20 |

† at least a "sufficient" fraction retires

31. Identifying dysfunctional norms is extremely difficult. Norms that seem inefficient (for example, the Hindu practice of treating cows as sacred, kosher food practices of Orthodox Jews in modern society, enforced chastity among the Catholic nuns and priests) may reinforce other values that are highly functional and have important survival value. Or, such practices may be genuinely costly, but not costly enough to threaten overall survival.

If everyone works, welfare is 20. If everyone retires welfare is 15. If more than a critical number of others retire while one works, one's own welfare drops to 14 because of the jealousy factor. If one is retired when everyone else is working, one's welfare is 16 because of the gloat factor. The welfare maximizing outcome is for everyone to work. This equilibrium persists as long as substantially everyone works. But if some event causes a sufficient, possibly small, number of others to retire, then welfare for oneself is maximized by retiring. That is true for everyone. So a new equilibrium is established with everyone retired. This new situation is stable but inferior to the previous equilibrium.

The stability of the welfare-maximizing outcome depends on the tipping point, the critical number of people whose retirement makes one feel like a chump for continuing to work. If different people have different tipping points and different payoff matrices—in particular, if continued work becomes suboptimal for even a few, even when everyone else works—the nearly-everybody-works equilibrium may be fragile or may cease to be an equilibrium even if welfare with continued work by all averaged over the group would be higher than it is with all retired.

This example is artificial in every respect. Not least of the artificialities is the white-collar professional nature of the payoff matrix in which work is a positive experience. The payoff matrices for backbreaking labor and dull demeaning jobs would look different. Although artificial, this example illustrates a simple point. Social interaction may produce benign norms and useful information. It may also lead to outcomes that are suboptimal, stable, and resistant to change.

One may also think of the behavior of others as a norm. As long as the norm is work, everyone works and welfare is maximized. If the norm is destroyed by deviation of a sufficient minority, retirement becomes a new norm that is stable but inferior.

## Information: Too Much or Too Little

People clearly lack even rudimentary data about some matters of central importance to retirement decisions and harbor important illusions. For example, surveys have documented the widespread belief that medicare provides extensive insurance against the costs of long-term care, although it offered almost none until recently and now provides considerable home-health coverage but almost no protection against the costs of long-term institutional care. As a second example, understanding the effects of such social security rules as the earnings test and the delayed retirement credit is exceedingly difficult yet critical to understanding the net wage from additional work. Few people have a good idea of how much social security they can expect to receive.

More fundamentally, retirement belongs to an important class of large decisions such as marriage, selection of a college, or choice of occupation that one makes once or only a few times during one's life. One can purchase expert advice or receive it gratis from friends, but I suspect that such advice works about as well as expert advice on how to play tennis or poker. It helps. But it is no substitute for extensive practice. Practice is possible with tennis and poker, but not with retirement.

### Preferences: Conflicts and Definition

The idea that people have well-defined, consistent, and stable preferences is, I believe, insupportable as a description of human behavior.[32] At least three types of evidence are relevant.

SITUATION. The results of laboratory experiments by psychologists and behavioral economists indicate that people's responses vary on the basis of seemingly minor and irrelevant situational factors. Decisions violate transitivity and other necessary conditions for consistent preferences.[33] This evidence does not suggest that people always display poorly defined, inconsistent, or unstable preferences. It is therefore an exceedingly minor accomplishment to find countless instances in which behavior is consistent with the hypothesis that people act on well-defined, consistent, and stable preferences. But such findings are weak evidence, just as sighting several white swans goes little way to disproving that some swans are black. Or as Arthur Okun often quipped, even a stopped clock is right twice a day.

SELF-CONTROL. The second sort of evidence concerns the problems of self-control. As Thomas Schelling has observed, people everywhere struggle not to overeat, drink too much, stay up too late, let the homework pile up, do another crossword puzzle, be unfaithful to their spouses, run red lights, drive too fast, or shout at their children.[34] And people every-

---

32. Kahneman, Ritov, and Schkade (1998). Whether it is useful for research purposes to *assume* that people have well-defined preferences is another matter to which I return later.

33. The psychological literature on this subject is huge, as documented by Rabin. A study of people's responses to torts illustrates the problem. When asked which is the more serious tort—selling improperly fire-proofed children's pajamas that result in serious injuries or marketing fraudulent financial assets, most people judge the former action as more serious. Yet, when asked how much financial compensation they would provide in the two cases, most people would impose larger fines on the marketing of fraudulent stock. Kahneman, Ritov, and Schkade (1998).

34. Schelling (1995).

where lapse, swear to do better, and relapse repeatedly. George Loewenstein has shown that visceral factors strongly influence behavior and that people are very poor at either predicting future responses to such visceral factors or recalling how they responded in the past.[35]

Through mental gymnastics, one can reconcile such behaviors with stable preferences, but only by pushing the stable preferences underground. One might argue, for example, that visceral factors—lack of food, lack of sleep, sexual arousal, or, more generally, "hormones" and neurotransmitters—cause behaviors that seem inconsistent. Deep down inside, one might argue, preferences are stable if such visceral factors held constant. Or one might argue that if one takes into account seemingly irrelevant external situational factors that actually are relevant, preferences are really well defined, stable, and consistent.

This type of explanation is of little practical value. Even if visceral and situational factors are critically important—and there seems little doubt that they are—the existence of underlying preferences with the proper attributes is no more than an article of dogma, until and unless one explicitly measures and models such visceral and situational factors, something that no one has done and that may be impossible.[36] It also entails a view of the "mind," the supposed seat of these immutable preferences, that is divorced from the rest of the body, a position that I believe recent research has rendered untenable.[37] This line of defense can achieve formal success, but at the price of emptying the assertion of well-defined, stable, and consistent preferences of any practical meaning because observable behavior remains inconsistent and only the invocation of something else that cannot be readily observed, a sort of phlogiston of the mind, preserves the supposed stability and consistency of preferences.

MEMORY. Contemporary research on memory and cognition reports that people are able to maintain in short-term memory only a few bits of information. Cognition consists of recalling from long-term memory bits of information, which the brain then uses to construct recollections of events, people, scenes, sounds, and so forth, rather as a paleontologist reconstructs animals from bone fragments.[38]

The capacity of long-term memory is vast but far short of what would be necessary to record all information that becomes available to each person. Each seventy-four-minute compact audio disk contains approximately

35. Loewenstein (1996).
36. Damasio (1994); LeDoux (1996); Loewenstein (1996); and Ross and Nisbett (1991).
37. Damasio (1994).
38. Schacter (1996).

800 megabytes of information. Each video disk contains far more. Every moment of every waking hour humans are bombarded by information in quantities vastly greater than they can record. Various mental processes screen that information and focus attention on those aspects of experience that are important to a person. As I write this sentence, I can make an effort to recognize a part of the stimuli to my various senses. I see out of the corner of my eye a richly variegated landscape. I listen to harp music through earphones. I also hear auto traffic, a jet passing overhead, and other background noise. I feel the clothing on my body, a slight itch in the corner of my eye, a breeze ruffling my shirt. I register the rather appalling effluvia that I have allowed to accumulate in my office. In the normal course of events, I take conscious note of only some of this information, process only a tiny fraction of it, and store in memory even less.

Because people have diverse needs, different people literally experience diverse realities and retain different experiences of all phenomena.[39] What people recall depends not only on what was stored, but also on the nature of the eliciting stimulus and the significance of the stimulus to the individual. Among these recollections are tastes and preferences. It is natural therefore that tastes and preferences will vary depending on the nature of the eliciting stimulus. Memory limitations compel people to construct preferences in each situation rather than "look them up." Such limitations may explain why "framing" influences decisions and expressed preferences, including, for example, why people presented with a list of adjectives describing a person or object evaluate those people or objects differently depending on the order in which the adjectives are listed. Furthermore, for individuals to *act* rationally, in the sense of *rationality*$_2$, on the basis of such preferences demonstrably exhausts memory capacity for problems of even moderate complexity. As Mike Oaksford and Nick Chater point out, "Diagnoses involving just two symptoms, together with some reasonable assumptions concerning the numbers of diseases and symptoms a physician may know about, require upwards of $10^9$ numbers to be stored in memory. Since typical diagnoses may work on upwards of

39. This line of reasoning leads some people to retort—either as an attack on the existence of objective truths or in an attempt to discredit the view through *reductio ad absurdum*—"well, then everything is relative and there is no objective truth." I believe this retort, whatever its motivation, is misconceived. The existence of physical phenomena or of logical truths is not called into question by the fact that each person may recognize or remember only fragments of the information arising from these phenomena. But the assumption that everyone is "reading from the same page" is not tenable. The task of science, and of persuasion more generally, is to seek agreement among people on which bits of information are relevant and important.

thirty symptoms, even if every connection in the human brain were encoding a digit, its capacity would nonetheless be exceeded. Such complexity considerations render it highly unlikely that human decisionmakers are generally employing Bayesian decision theory in their risky decisionmaking."[40] It is possible that other patterns of thought—the use of reference points to evaluate utilities rather than a complete evaluation of every state independently, and the emphasis on procedure in determining whether outcomes are fair—owe their origins to efforts to economize on cognitive effort. Such patterns of thought help explain why repealing a privilege once granted provokes a stronger reaction than does not granting the privilege in the first place.

## So What?

The foregoing line of argument regarding how people make decisions is well supported by research in psychology and philosophy but has troubling implications for the analysis of retirement policy, in particular, and the normative content of economics, in general—and possibly for democratic political theory. I think it has more limited bearing on economics as a *positive* social science.[41]

As far as retirement research and policy are concerned, what should one make of this evidence? Clearly, personal behavior carries *political* weight. Rule changes that force people to revise plans are certainly politically difficult. But apart from such considerations, how much normative weight should be given to individual decisions? Clearly not much if people are receiving incorrect signals from the market or if important markets fail in important ways. In these instances the policy prescription is simple: correct the signals, if feasible.

But what if the market signals are correct? That is, what if prices accurately reflect full resource costs, all externalities are corrected, and the markets for people to trade relevant goods all exist and function well? The answer still seems to be that the *normative* weight *individual* decisions deserve is slight. Retirement is an act that takes on meaning for each person against the background not only of his or her own circumstances (eco-

---

40. Oaksford and Chater (1993, p. 37).

41. The validity of economics as a predictive tool depends, of course, on its capacity to predict. Milton Friedman (1953) held that prediction is the only function of economics or other sciences. But this view is surely false, at least as a description of how economists use their craft. Economists use their tools heavily in support of normative conclusions. And every research field uses its findings for epistemological purposes, as a framework to tie together what would otherwise be unrelated facts.

nomic, physical, family), but also of the behavior of friends, peers, and the community. Retirement may be represented as a decision tree of considerable complexity. People have neither the data nor the analytical capacity to analyze it fully, so they resort to all sorts of decision heuristics and social norms to guide their decisions. These heuristics and norms are not subject to optimality tests.[42] Almost everyone retires only once, so that individual learning and experimenting are not possible. People can secure expert guidance, but the guidance will often fail to produce optimal outcomes because individual circumstances not recognized by expert systems will be important to individuals, because people are not fully aware of their own preferences in states of the world they have never experienced, and because learning through repetition is not generally possible.

Group learning is possible, and the results of interactions among large numbers of people may well be superior to the decisions that individuals would make alone. For reasons analogous to those captured in the game outlined earlier, however, group behavior need not converge to a global optimum. Potential changes in business practices, for example, might cause people to change their behavior in ways they would come to judge an improvement. Nevertheless, business practices may remain unchanged, either because behavior is sticky or because information about how people would respond to the changes is unavailable. For example, part-time work might become widespread if employers made the necessary arrangements and part-time work became sufficiently frequent to become a new norm. But creating a sufficient number of such part-time jobs raises formidable problems of coordination, including transportation arrangements, identifying interested workers, and providing special facilities. Making such arrangements for only a few workers may be prohibitively costly, but the necessary scale may be beyond the capacity of any single employer to engineer, perhaps because a process like that in the game sketched earlier is at work. Thus, no single employer may find it profitable to make the change.[43] Consequently, patterns of individual behavior, *taking behavior*

---

42. For reasons suggested by the quotation from Shafir (note 30), even asserting survival value is risky because the environment within which the norms and heuristics were optimal may have changed in "relevant" ways. An exhaustive definitive determination of what is "relevant" in finite time is impossible because the question involves all possible information and all possible theories among them. Deciding what information is relevant is the essence of the framing problem in artificial intelligence: how should a decisionmaking entity confronted with a concrete problem decide which information among the infinity of data is relevant to the problem at hand. This problem is unsolved.

43. This argument is similar to that advanced by Spence (1974) and Stiglitz (1973) for why patterns of discrimination in labor markets might remain unchanged but respond readily to legislated prohibitions on discrimination.

*of others as given*, are likely to persist unless they produce demonstrably bad results *for the individual.*

Furthermore, many experimental studies by both economists and psychologists indicate that people value outcomes they have actually selected more than they value the identical states of the world when obtained in other ways. Holders of lottery tickets, for example, demand a higher price to sell their tickets if they selected the number than they do if the number was selected for them. If this process is also at work in evaluation of the results of such major personal decisions as when to retire, the result is utility maximization of a sort, but not the kind normally envisaged in economic theory. A situation that arises because of individual choice becomes right *ex post* because the individual has selected it, not because it could be judged superior *ex ante*. In this case, possibly sizable variations around current behavior are unlikely to produce much difference in people's evaluations of their own subjective well-being, provided the behaviors represent voluntary responses to incentives regarded as fair.[44] Nor is there any basis for judging whether subjective well-being would rise or fall if general patterns of behavior were somehow transported to a new norm.

None of this denies that people have a more richly textured understanding of their own circumstances (even if they lack good information about some important technical matters) than others do. Nor does it deny that people may genuinely believe that the course they have chosen is better than any other they could have selected under the circumstances they faced. Indeed, there is evidence that they think the course they have adopted is optimal precisely because they have adopted it. And this fact, ultimately, may be the strongest *normative* argument for treating the decisions of individuals as presumptively optimal.

The implications of this line of argument are that people will do as well as they can given their reading of the incentives they face, the preferences that are elicited by their personal circumstances, and the social norms they have internalized. But there may be no important detectable difference in the well-being people experience under a wide variety of condi-

---

44. A striking finding of psychological research is the insensitivity of measures of subjective well-being to even major differences in objective circumstances. This result may reflect poor instruments for measuring subjective well-being or inadequate theoretical specification of the underlying process so that statistical tests fail to reveal structure. But this result may also reflect a deep truth: that subjective well-being, if that is what we economists mean by *utility*, is determined not entirely, and perhaps not principally, by external conditions, but by the processes through which states are achieved and by a kind of psychological homeostasis.

tions. Other outcomes would also have been judged similarly. Research gives little evidence that subjective well-being is related systematically to any major extent with most measures of personal circumstances. Among these weak relationships, one of the stronger is a positive observed relation between satisfying work and subjective well-being, but I do not think that the causal processes have been "unpacked."[45]

The conclusion is not that any retirement policy will do and that none matters. Rather, the claims to optimality of any particular pattern of behavior, including the current timing of retirement, are weak. If one cannot attach normative weight to observed behavior, one of the most important contributions of economic analysis—support for the belief that one knows the effects of various interventions on welfare—is lost. In that event one must turn to other criteria to determine policy. But which ones? Such criteria could include appeals to evaluations of the consequences of alternative policies. For example, one might support changes in policy that encourage later retirement because sustaining a policy that supports a relatively young retirement age creates serious political problems: the necessity for either large tax increases or large cuts in other activities of government. Alternatively, one might oppose such a policy on the ground that, as indicated earlier, a move to a later retirement age would invalidate expectations for promotion of younger workers. One might base policy on external judgments of fairness, but judgments of fairness are slippery. Just for starters, does one have in mind something analogous to what economists call "horizontal equity"—equal treatment of equals (if so, from what reference point?)—or "vertical equity"—some degree of income redistribution from rich to poor? What one cannot do is point to actual behavior as evidence of optimality or welfare maximization.

## Research Issues

One effect of these qualifications to the standard model is to shift the goal line. Neutral public policy does not necessarily maximize welfare because the concept of welfare maximization loses precise meaning. But public policy still affects behavior, and everyone can remain interested in the positive question of what those effects are, even if they cannot agree on the normative evaluation of whether such changes increase or decrease welfare. The qualifications to the standard model listed here also open up the pos-

45. Diener and Suh (forthcoming).

sibility that policies judged equivalent within the standard model—that is, policies with equal present values when discounted at some market interest rate—may not have equivalent effects on behavior.

## The Retirement Test and Delayed Retirement Credit

When legislative changes enacted in 1983 become fully effective, the social security benefit formula will provide the "average" beneficiary a pension whose amount varies with the age at which benefits are initially received. Workers who are eligible for benefits but earn more than stipulated ceilings will lose part or all of their current benefits because of the earnings test. When earnings fall or after age 70, benefits are paid regardless of earnings. At that point, the pension will be boosted enough—through the delayed retirement credit—to provide equivalent lifetime benefits.[46] Several alternative policies would generate the same long-term costs but might elicit a different labor supply.

First, the earnings test could be repealed so that benefits are paid from the initial age of eligibility, regardless of earnings. This change would accelerate payments but would not change the present expected value of total payments over the average worker's lifetime. President Clinton proposed such a change in his 1999 State of the Union address.

Second, the earnings test could be relaxed gradually, so that a growing portion of the benefit is paid without regard for the earnings test. For example, at age 62 workers might be permitted to receive 20 percent of their pensions regardless of earnings. At age 63, the earner would receive 40 percent of the pension regardless of earnings. And so on, until the full benefit was payable regardless of earnings after the worker reached age 66. The process could begin later—perhaps at age 65 (the so-called normal retirement age)—and phase in differently. In each case a smaller increment in pension benefits would be provided later when earnings fell.

Third, workers who lose benefits because of the earnings test could be awarded a lump-sum payment at some later age equal in present discounted value to the increased pension provided under current law. For example, current law provides that a 65-year-old worker with a benefit of $15,000 who earns enough to zero out that benefit for one year, will receive $15,937.50 starting at age 66.[47] Under the alternative arrangement, the

---

46. The retirement test and delayed retirement credit, rather complicated provisions, are described in detail in the appendix to this chapter.

47. These examples all ignore inflation adjustments.

worker's pension would remain $15,000 starting at age 66, but he or she would also receive (assuming a 2 percent real discount rate) a lump-sum payment of $16,560 at age 70 or a payment to designated heirs, which would average approximately $20,000 (assuming average survival to age 80). If the worker earned enough through age 70 to zero out benefits, the lump-sum benefit at age 70 would be approximately $80,000 or the payment to an heir would run about $100,000.

Would such modifications of the earnings test increase or decrease the labor supply?

The evidence, as reported by Gary Burtless in chapter 1, suggests that simply repealing the retirement test would have little effect on labor supply, where "labor supply" is defined to include both the age at which people substantially withdraw from full-time work *and* the modest amount they work if they partially retire. If "labor supply" refers solely to the amount worked by social security pensioners—ignoring the age when people actually claim pensions—eliminating the earnings test has been found to have a large percentage effect on labor supply. But Burtless presents reasons why these estimates may be too low. In chapter 6 David Fetherstonhaugh and Lee Ross describe survey evidence on the effects of replacing an annuity with a lump-sum payment as compensation for benefits lost from the earnings test. Questionnaire responses may be larger or smaller, or even of different sign, from responses to an actual change in policy.

The problems stem from several sources. First, explaining the offers in comprehensible terms will be difficult. What people learn in the real world may differ from what they learn in the laboratory. Second, even if people correctly comprehend the problem, the amount of time they have to think about it in the laboratory is limited. Third, no one in the laboratory setting is "firing real bullets." Little is at stake. On easy problems this difference may not matter much. On complicated problems, it may. It may not be worth the considerable individual mental effort to imagine responses to such a complicated change of policy. However, widely different responses to financially equivalent offers that differ only in form would indicate that considerations other than present expected value are important and should be considered explicitly in research and in the formulation of policy.

## Procedural Innovations

If information about the conditions of retirement is imperfect and people have a hard time identifying their own preferences regarding situations unlike ones they have experienced, behavior may be sensitive to procedures under which offers are made. Strong evidence supporting this hypothesis comes from studies of patients' responses to various courses of medical treatment.[48]

The most dramatic findings concern the responses of men with prostate cancer to the medical options they face. The options are watchful waiting—a medical euphemism for doing nothing—or surgery.[49] Randomized trials indicate that for men below a certain age—about 60 years old—survival rates are somewhat higher with surgery. Above a certain age, survival rates are lower with surgery because prostate cancers are slow growing, other causes of death are likely to intervene, and surgery can be dangerous. Over a considerable intermediate age range, the comparative results are indeterminate. Apart from their effects on life expectancy, the alternative procedures entail different risks. Watchful waiting carries a high likelihood of low-grade symptoms, mostly difficulty with urination. Surgery carries a smaller risk of serious side effects—death or other serious complications from surgery—and somewhat higher risks of lesser side effects—incontinence and impotence. Wennberg and his colleagues randomized patients into different decision settings. Some made their decisions in the standard doctor-patient interaction. Others were shown films on the disease and the various treatments and then participated in group discussion. The course of therapy varied widely depending on the decision setting. A far larger proportion of the film-and-group-discussion group than of the doctor-patient group chose watchful waiting.

The Wennberg experiment varied many elements of the decision: the relative standing of the treating physician, the information available to the patient, and the influence of fellow patients in the decision. I do not know whether the research on responses of patients tried to distinguish the separate effects of these factors.

Experiments such as this, as well as more general research in psychology and sociology, raise the question of whether decisions about the timing of retirement might be sensitive to interventions analogous to those Wennberg and his colleagues used. Some companies offer retirement counseling. TIAA-CREF offers financial counseling to its potential annuitants. Study of the results of such interventions or new experiments with random assignment could shed light on the effects of such framing variations on retirement behavior.

---

48. Flood and others (1996); and Barry and others (1995).
49. Different surgical procedures are also available with different risks.

## Norm Effects

If the retirement decision is subject to influence not only by standard individual variables—wealth, total income, net wage rate, health status, or retirement status of one's spouse—but also to the behavior of friends, coworkers, or society at large, standard cross-section regressions will generate what amounts to short-run effects of any policy intervention (such as changes in the retirement test). One will observe direct effects operating through net wage rates. But feedback effects arising from the influence of other people, whose behavior is also altered by the policy intervention, may take some years to unfold. Robert Axtell and Joshua Epstein (chapter 5) show that one can replicate the sluggish pattern of responses to changes in public policies if only a small fraction of the population responds directly to such policies and the majority simply imitate the behavior of people within their social networks.

## Conclusion

I began this chapter by describing the standard model used in analyzing retirement planning as a "rebuttable presumption." The rest of the chapter has argued that exceptions to the rebuttable presumption are many and important. The exceptions arise in part from long-recognized problems, including the absence or failure of markets that people would need to use if they were to protect themselves against predictable risks. I have stressed other problems arising from the nature and frailties of memory, cognition, and preference formation and from myopia. These problems are particularly important for decisions spanning many years and with many discrete but important components, because these decisions are extremely difficult analytically and demanding psychologically. Retirement planning is quintessentially such a decision. Analytical difficulty and psychological frailty are not unique to retirement planning, however, but characterize, usually in less severe forms, other economic problems.

It is interesting, but not difficult, to identify these problems. The more important and challenging question is what to do with them. It would be foolish to argue that one should abandon the standard model as a research tool, where its value is remarkable and there is simply no alternative. Still, the research I have reviewed undermines some positive predictions of economic analysis. In particular, the prediction that policies with similar expected present values will affect behavior similarly, which rests on expected utility theory, is inconsistent with experimental evidence. Nonetheless, the failure of positive predictions of orthodox theory that flow from expected utility theory, though troubling, can be regarded as no more than a challenge to research.

The more serious and intellectually challenging difficulties arise from the damage caused by the points raised in this chapter to the *normative* inferences drawn from standard economic analysis. By undercutting the presumption that individual decisions are normatively optimal or close to it, recent research on memory, cognition, and preference formation deprives economists of their customary pole star to guide their policy recommendations.

Some analysts seem blind to the problem, as some models that purport to measure the welfare effects of social security illustrate. A widely shared view that myopia and other mental frailties cause people systematically to make decisions regarding saving for retirement or disability that are not in their self-interest explains the institution of social security. Without challenging the need for some form of mandatory retirement saving, some analysts nonetheless employ models to measure welfare losses from social security that explicitly assume full life-cycle or infinite horizon rational expectations and that require solution of staggeringly difficult dynamic programming problems that were unsolved until recently and are solvable now only because of heroic simplifications.

The erosion of the normative inference from standard economic models that individuals' decisions maximize their own welfare leaves one an uncomfortable choice. One may hold that individuals' decisions, despite their flaws, should be sovereign because any alternative would be worse. Alternatively, one may adopt an unabashedly paternalistic view that collective interference with individual decisions should occur freely because individual decisions are flawed. I believe both positions are unwise, the former because it is demonstrably untrue and the latter because it legitimates tyranny.

One is left, I believe, in an intellectually parlous intermediate position: that unfettered individual decisions should normally be accepted but not regarded with undue reverence. One should be prepared, through democratic processes, to modify individual decisions, but only if a good case can be made that the sorts of frailties described in this chapter are important. In making such a decision, one should keep in mind the usual inefficiencies of government. And one needs to keep in mind the findings of psychological research that an individual's act of making a decision legitimates the consequences of that decision. Collective interference with or regulation of private decisions is warranted not only when markets fail in some way, but when human beings fail, as they do in many, many situations. The general and conclusive assumption that if markets function well, outcomes will be optimal is simply insupportable.

# Appendix: The Retirement Test and Delayed Retirement Credit

Social security provides retirement benefits, not an unconditional annuity. That means that payments begin when people who have reached 62, the age of initial eligibility, have "substantially" stopped working. If people work past age 62, their benefits when they eventually stop working are increased for each month that they do not receive full benefits.

## The Formulas

To make this system work requires a formula for deciding what constitutes the cessation of substantial work, another formula for determining how much to curtail benefits if people work more than some allowable minimum, and still another formula for determining how much benefits should be increased if they work past age 62.

Most discussion of social security focuses on the so-called normal retirement age of 65. However, this emphasis is confusing because eligibility actually begins at age 62 and roughly two-thirds of beneficiaries claim benefits before reaching age 65.

Between the ages of 62 and 65 people are considered to be fully retired if they are retired and earn less than $8,640. This provision is called the earnings test. If workers earn more than that amount and have claimed benefits, the payments are reduced by $1 for every $2 of earnings over $8,640.[50] Starting at age 65, benefits are paid automatically. Between the ages of 65 and 70 people are subject to a more liberal earnings test than applies to people ages 62 to 65. In 2000, workers will be considered fully

50. This implicit tax through benefit reduction is distinct from personal income tax on earnings and benefits. Social security benefits are included in income under a complicated formula. If income including social security and tax-exempt bond interest is less than $32,000 for joint filers ($25,000 for single filers), social security is excluded from tax. If the combination exceeds these thresholds, social security benefits equal to half of the excess are added to income subject to tax. An additional 35 percent of benefits is included to the extent that income exceeds $44,000 for joint filers ($34,000 for single filers).

retired if they earn less than $17,000. Their benefits will be reduced by only $1 for every $3 of earnings over this amount. This earnings amount for people 65 to 67 years old rises over time as follows:

| Year | Allowable earnings (dollars) |
|------|------------------------------|
| 1999 | 15,500 |
| 2000 | 17,000 |
| 2001 | 25,000 |
| 2002 | 30,000 |

After age 70, benefits are paid regardless of earnings.

To illustrate the formula, a 62-year-old entitled to a benefit of $10,000 in 2000 faces a benefit reduction rate of 50 percent of earnings over $9,120 up to $29,120. A person aged 65 to 70 entitled to a $10,000 benefit faces a benefit reduction rate of 33⅓ percent on earnings over the range from $17,000 to $47,000. In 2002 and later, this same beneficiary would have benefits reduced over the range from $30,000 to $60,000. Once a person reaches age 70, the $10,000 benefit will be paid no matter how high earnings may be. The proportion of people age 70 and older in the labor force is tiny.

If benefits are reduced or wholly eliminated because of current earnings, future benefits are increased. The formula is linear: loss of half of benefits triggers half of the applicable delayed retirement credit. If earnings are sufficient to zero out benefits for an entire year, the change in future benefits, as a percent of benefits paid at age 62 is as follows:

| If worker turns age 62 in the year indicated | Benefit increase (percent) |
|------|------|
| 1999 | 8.12 |
| 2000 | 8.24 |
| 2001 | 9.00 |
| 2002 | 9.13 |
| 2003 | 9.93 |
| 2004 | 10.07 |
| 2005 | 10.91 |

This peculiar-looking schedule arises from the fact that benefits payable at age 62 are being lowered relative to the "unreduced" benefits payable at progressively older ages at the same time that the delayed retirement credit is being increased.

Clearly, these adjustments are not exactly actuarial. In principle, they should increase smoothly with age, not in steps. Adjustments should differ for workers whose earnings records provide the basis for their spouse's benefits as well as their own, and these adjustments should vary based on the age difference of the couple.

*Administration*

These formulas are neither transparent nor self-administering. It is not clear how well workers understand the magnitude of the adjustments. The combination of complexity and the fact that progressive increases in allowable earnings means that fewer workers now than in the past actually suffer benefit reductions helps explain why President Clinton in 1999 proposed repeal of the earnings test.

The following explanation of the retirement test is based on a recent report prepared by a study panel of the National Academy of Social Insurance:

> The annual earnings test is administered as follows: 1. Beneficiaries who work are sent a form early in each year on which they are asked to report their earnings for the last year and estimate their earnings for the coming year. They are also asked to report promptly to SSA any change in their earnings estimate. 2. Based on the beneficiary's estimate of earnings for the year, SSA determines the annual amount of benefits to be withheld. Those benefits are withheld in full, starting with the January check, until the requisite amount has been withheld. The remaining benefits are paid in full for the rest of the year. There is no partial withholding of monthly benefits throughout the year [except in cases of hardship or special request]. 3. When the beneficiary submits the report of actual earnings for the past year (along with the estimate for the coming year), SSA reconciles the amount of benefits withheld for the past year with the actual earnings reported. 4. When SSA receives the W-2 forms and posts the earnings to individuals' records, the amount on the W-2 is compared to the amount reported to SSA by beneficiaries. This earnings enforcement operation is designed to ensure that benefits were properly paid. If past benefits were overpaid or underpaid, final adjustments are made.

The most striking feature of this procedure, apart from the administrative burdens it places on the Social Security Administration, is the front-loading of benefit reductions. This feature minimizes the likelihood that SSA will have to go back to beneficiaries to reclaim overpayments, a task that is burdensome and unpopular. Whether front-loading of benefit reductions significantly affects the behavior of beneficiaries, relative to some other system—proportional payment reductions, for example—has never been tested.

Furthermore, a former SSA official reports that administering the partial benefit reduction, and the delayed retirement credit that follows from it, is accorded low priority in SSA. The computations are likely to be slow in coming. For this reason, the connection between earnings and benefit payments is actually much looser than is implied by the adjustment formulas and the connection is further obscured by administrative hassle.

## Medicare

The age of eligibility for medicare is 65. For that reason, medicare costs are not much affected by when *before* age 65 workers choose to retire. Because medicare coverage is "secondary" to private health insurance, work *after* age 65 in employment covered by private health insurance reduces medicare costs. Since entitlement to medicare comes automatically and unconditionally when covered workers turn 65, none of the complexities arising from the earnings test apply.

# References

Aaron, Henry J., and Robert D. Reischauer. 1998. *Countdown to Reform: The Great Social Security Debate*. New York: Century Foundation.

Ainslie, George. 1992. *Picoeconomics: The Strategic Interaction of Successive Motivational States within the Person*. Studies in Rationality and Social Change. Cambridge University Press.

Barry, M. J., and others. 1995. "Potential Reactions to a Program Designed to Facilitate Patient Participation in Treatment Decisions for Benign Prostatic Hyperplasia." *Medical Affairs* 33 (August): 771–82.

Damasio, Antonio. 1994. *Descarte's Error*. Putnam.

Diamond, Peter, and Jonathan Gruber. 1997. "Social Security and Retirement in the U.S." Working Paper 6097. Cambridge, Mass.: National Bureau of Economic Research.

Diener, Edward, and Eunkook Suh. Forthcoming. "Measuring Quality of Life: Economic, Social, and Subjective Indicators." In *Well-Being: The Foundations of Hedonic Psychology*, edited by Daniel Kahneman, Edward Diener, and Norbert Schwarz. Russell Sage.

Engen, Eric M., and William G. Gale. 1997. "Effects of Social Security Reform on Private and National Saving." In *Social Security Reform: Links to Saving, Investment, and Growth*, edited by Steven A. Sass and Robert K. Triest, 103–42. Federal Reserve Bank of Boston.

Evans, J. St. B. 1993."Bias and Rationality." In *Rationality: Psychological and Philosophical Perspectives*, edited by Ken I. Manktelow and David E. Over, 6–30. Routledge.

Flood, A. B., and others. 1996. "The Importance of Patient Preference in the Decision to Screen for Prostate Cancer. *Journal of General Internal Medicine* 11 (6): 342–49.

Friedman, Milton. 1953 "The Methodology of Positive Economics." In *Essays in Positive Economics*, 3–43. University of Chicago Press.

Gruber, Jonathan. 1998. "Health Insurance and the Labor Market." Working Paper 6762. Cambridge, Mass.: National Bureau of Economic Research.

Gruber, Jonathan, and David A. Wise. 1998. "Introduction and Summary." In *Social Security Programs and Retirement around the World*, edited by Jonathan Gruber and David A. Wise. Cambridge, Mass.: National Bureau of Economic Research.

Kahneman, Daniel, Ilana Ritov, and David Schkade. 1998. "Economists Have Preferences, Psychologists Have Attitudes: An Analysis of Dollar Responses to Public Issues." Princeton University, Hebrew University, and University of Texas.

Laibson, David, Andrea Repetto, and Jeremy Tobacman. 1998. "Self-Control and Saving for Retirement." *Brookings Papers on Economic Activity,* 1: 91–172

LeDoux, Joseph. 1996. *The Emotional Brain: The Mysterious Underpinnings of Emotional Life.* Simon & Schuster.

Loewenstein, George. 1996. "Out of Control: Visceral Influences on Behavior." *Organizational Behavior and Human Decision Processes* 65 (March): 272–96.

Loewenstein, George, and Drazen Prelec. 1992. "Anomalies in Intertemporal Choice: Evidence and Interpretation." In *Choice Over Time*, edited by George Loewenstein and Jon Elster, 119–45. Russell Sage.

Nisbett, Richard, and Dov Cohen. 1996. *Culture of Honor: The Psychology of Violence in the South.* Boulder, Colo.: Westview Press.

Nisbett, Richard, and Lee Ross. 1980. *Human Inference: Strategies and Shortcomings of Social Judgment.* Prentice-Hall.

Oaksford, Mike, and Nick Chater. 1993. "Reasoning Theories and Bounded Rationality." In *Rationality: Psychological and Philosophical Perspectives*, edited by Ken I. Manktelow and David E. Over, 31–60. Routledge.

Okun, Arthur. 1975. *Equality and Efficiency: The Big Tradeoff.* Brookings.

Poterba, James, and Mark J. Warshawsky. 1999. "The Costs of Annuitizing Retirement Payouts from Individual Accounts." Working paper 6918. Cambridge, Mass.: National Bureau of Economic Research.

Rabin, Matthew. 1998. "Psychology and Economics." *Journal of Economic Literature* 36 (March): 11–46.

Ross, Lee, and Richard Nisbett. 1991. *The Person and The Situation: Perspectives of Social Psychology.* McGraw-Hill.

Schacter, Daniel. 1996. *Searching For Memory: The Brain, The Mind, and The Past.* Basic Books.

Schelling, Thomas. 1995. *Choice and Consequence.* Harvard University Press.

Shafir, Eldar. 1993. "Intuitions about Rationality and Cognition." In *Rationality: Psychological and Philosophical Perspectives*, edited by K. I. Manktelow and D. E. Over, 260–83. Routledge.

Social Security Administration. 1997. *Annual Statistical Supplement, 1997, to the Social Security Bulletin*.

Spence, Andrew Michael. 1974. *Market Signaling*. Harvard University Press.

Stiglitz, Joseph. 1973. "Approaches to the Economics of Discrimination," *American Economic Review* 63 (May): 287–95.

ANNAMARIA LUSARDI

# 3 Information, Expectations, and Savings for Retirement

M ANY STUDIES indicate that people save less than they need to sustain living standards if they retire at customary ages. Economic studies provide no adequate explanation of why people save so little. The life-cycle model has been the main framework for studying saving and wealth accumulation. Many works have cast doubts on its empirical validity, but it is hard to test the model rigorously.[1] Many data sets have insufficient information about how households make their saving decisions and are therefore limited to looking at very narrow aspects of the theory. Several explanations for the low accumulation could be consistent with the life-cycle model or an enlarged version of the intertemporal optimization model. For example, households may have experienced many adverse events that depleted their assets. Or they may plan to continue working well beyond the standard retirement age. Some, especially those in bad health, may expect brief retirement periods. Others may believe that social security and private pensions will provide sufficient support. Some may expect to realize big capital gains on their houses, which is the main asset in most portfolios, or expect support from families and friends.

1. Deaton (1992); and Bernheim (1991).

81

I consider these reasons for low saving but stress another possible explanation—that many people save little because even at an advanced age they simply do not think about retirement. Contrary to the assumption of the life-cycle model that people plan ahead to provide for retirement, I show that as many as one-third of people aged 51–61 have not begun to think about retirement. Plain lack of planning goes far to explain why saving and wealth holdings are so small. This finding underscores the importance of serious study of how people perceive and plan for the future. My conclusions support the findings of analysts who emphasize the importance of information and financial literacy and the value of financial education.[2]

Many models presume that saving decisions emerge from intertemporal optimization in which people make informed guesses about their lifetime income and plan consumption and saving accordingly. These models disregard the fact that planning for retirement is a complex task that many people may perform only imperfectly. To plan adequately requires extensive information, including an understanding of the elaborate rules governing social security and private pensions. In addition, retirement is not a repeated event that provides people the possibility of learning from their mistakes.[3] There is also no correction mechanism that prevents planners from behaving incorrectly. Apart from the case of personal bankruptcy, poor savers or naive planners are not pushed out of the markets or disciplined in any way. Contrary to businesses, which survive only if they are profitable, households will include successful and unsuccessful groups of retirement planners. Only at retirement will they realize whether they have made mistakes.

I examine saving for retirement with a new data set, the Health and Retirement Study (HRS), which provides detailed information on people's preferences and economic circumstances. I begin with a brief review of studies on savings and describe evidence on savings and retirement plans. I then examine the determinants of savings and the consequences of not thinking about retirement.

## Savings and Retirement Plans

For many years, the life-cycle–permanent-income model has been the basis for the studies of savings. The basic intuition of the model is that house-

2. Bernheim (1996); Bernheim and Garrett (1995); and Thaler (1994).
3. Bernheim (1996).

holds base consumption on their lifetime resources and not simply on their current income. Households smooth consumption over the life cycle, saving during their working years to accumulate assets, which they use to sustain consumption after they retire. This was the original intuition of the model, but other theoretical predictions can be added to it, in particular, when accompanied by the assumption of rational expectations.[4]

*Theory versus Fact*

This basic framework has been subject to a number of criticisms. First, the elderly do not seem to use up their wealth as predicted by the model.[5] The fact that they often leave bequests seems to contradict the life-cycle model. It is possible, however, to reconcile bequests with the life-cycle model in various ways. For one thing, some people *want* to leave bequests. Parents, for example, typically care not only about themselves but also about their offspring. In addition, bequests could be accidental because people may die earlier than they expected or become ill and unable to consume as much as they planned, or *strategic*, if the elderly use bequests to control the behavior of relatives.[6] Unfortunately, it is not easy to distinguish among or evaluate the relative importance of alternative explanations for why people leave bequests.[7]

Another finding, that households do not smooth consumption much over the life cycle, is even more damaging to the life-cycle theory. Lawrence Summers and Christopher Carroll found that consumption is not smoothed but basically tracks income.[8] Angus Deaton has replicated this controversial finding for many countries.[9]

The life-cycle model also implies that saving should be high when workers are in their prime earning years, especially their forties and fifties. Assuming this, many observers predicted that U.S. saving would increase

4. See Browning and Lusardi (1996) and Deaton (1992) for an extensive discussion of these implications.

5. See, for example, the earlier work of Mirer (1979); and Menchick and David (1983).

6. On the role of early death, see Davies (1981); and Abel (1985). On the role of deteriorating health, see Börsch-Supan and Stahl (1991). And on strategic behavior, see Bernheim, Schleifer, and Summers (1985).

7. Altonji, Hayashi, and Kotlikoff (1992). Recent evidence by Wilhem (1996) and Laitner and Juster (1996), using new and unexploited data sets, indicates only limited support in favor of altruism. As Laitner and Juster report, "The data yield several surprises, some of which point to a wide range of tastes among respondents, others to inadequacies of simple formulations of both currently popular theories of saving behavior" (p. 895).

8. Summers and Carroll (1991).

9. Deaton (1992, chap. 2).

as the baby boom generation aged. In fact, saving fell sharply from 7.9 percent in 1980 to 4.2 percent in 1990, just as the baby boomers reached their anticipated high-saving years. Many explanations have been offered to explain this decline, but there seems to be more agreement on reasons that could not explain the decrease than on those that could. In particular, changes in the age structure of the population, as emphasized by the life-cycle model, cannot be responsible for the decline because these changes occur only gradually and should have spurred saving.[10]

Another challenge to the life-cycle model has received much less attention. If the model has general validity, all or most households should follow its strictures. In fact, some households accumulate and hold more wealth than the simple model can rationalize, while most arrive at retirement with little or no wealth.[11] Although this finding helps to explain why assets decline little after retirement, it does so by raising doubts on whether the life-cycle–permanent-income model adequately characterizes household saving behavior.

*An Alternative Approach*

A new approach to analyzing household saving emphasizes the difficulties that households have in acquiring necessary information, solving complex maximization problems implied by the life-cycle theory, delaying gratification, and exercising the self-control necessary for saving.[12] I classify this line of work under the heading "behavioral theories of saving" because this theory gets to the heart of how people make decisions. It also focuses on documented weaknesses people display when making long-run decisions.

Attempts to apply behavioral theories have sometimes been based on small samples. In this work I analyze these theories by using data from a large representative sample of U.S. households and examining the saving behavior before and around the time of retirement. If the life-cycle model is valid, wealth holdings should increase with age and reach a maximum at retirement. Rather surprisingly, this fundamental prediction has been subject to little verification. The data I use to investigate this matter are from the Health and Retirement Study, a longitudinal data set that started in 1992.[13]

10. Bosworth, Burtless, and Sabelhaus (1991).

11. Diamond and Hausman (1984a); Venti and Wise (1993); and Lusardi (1998).

12. Thaler and Shefrin (1981); Shefrin and Thaler (1988); Thaler (1994); Laibson (1996); and Bernheim (1991).

13. Juster and Smith (1997) and Smith (1995) describe the Health and Retirement Study, evaluate the quality of the data, and compare it with other data sets.

## Variation in Wealth Holdings

Contrary to the life-cycle theory, households do not consistently accumulate wealth as they approach retirement but instead have very heterogeneous wealth holdings (table 3-1).[14] Both financial and total net worth vary enormously. Considerable differences in net worth are to be expected because incomes vary widely. But the actual variation—from $850 in net worth for households at the tenth percentile to $475,000 in the ninetieth percentile—is far larger than income differences could explain. The paucity of wealth among households nearing retirement is striking. A quarter of the population has less than $30,000 in total wealth and more than half the population has less than $6,000 of financial wealth. Other studies have reached similar findings.[15] Even if one could claim that households with few personal assets have much wealth in social security and qualified pensions, it is hard to borrow against those assets. In any event, households with only $850 in net worth (the holdings at the tenth percentile) have little capacity to deal with adverse surprises in income, health, or family events.

Table 3-1 demonstrates that housing is an important asset and perhaps one of the main vehicles of accumulation. Seventy-four percent of households in this age group report having housing equity, and 30 percent have other real estate. For many households—in particular, for black and Hispanic homeowners—the house accounts for more than half their wealth. Whether the elderly do or should use housing wealth to support their consumption at retirement is in dispute, and whether housing equity should be used in a measure of net worth is also debated.[16] Some studies indicate that housing wealth is not used to finance consumption, at least until a late age.[17] Even though reverse annuity mortgages are now available, there seems to be little use of them.[18] Other, more recent, studies find some

14. Table 3-1 is based on data from the first wave of the HRS, excluding households whose respondent is partially or fully retired and those with respondents younger than age 50 or older than 61. Questions about wealth are only asked of the financial respondent in the household. The HRS oversamples black and Hispanic households as well as households from Florida. I therefore use household weights to obtain statistics representative of the population.

15. Diamond and Hausman (1984a), using data from the 1966 National Longitudinal Survey of Mature Men, reported that the median value of wealth for households close to or at retirement was as little as $1,500 (approximately $6,500 in 1992 dollars). Using data from the Survey of Income and Program Participation, Venti and Wise (1993) and Poterba, Venti, and Wise (1994) also reported that many households arrived at retirement with very little wealth.

16. Bernheim (1991) and Congressional Budget Office (1993) present conflicting views on this issue.

17. Merrill (1984); and Venti and Wise (1990).

18. Venti and Wise (1991).

Table 3-1. *Distribution of Household Wealth*[a]

Constant 1992 dollars

| Percentile | Financial net worth | IRAs or Keoghs | Housing equity | Other assets | Total net worth |
|---|---|---|---|---|---|
| 5 | –6,000 | 0 | 0 | 0 | 0 |
| 10 | –2,000 | 0 | 0 | 200 | 850 |
| 25 | 0 | 0 | 0 | 3,000 | 27,980 |
| 50 | 6,000 | 0 | 42,000 | 11,000 | 96,000 |
| 75 | 36,000 | 15,000 | 85,000 | 46,000 | 222,200 |
| 90 | 110,000 | 45,000 | 150,000 | 197,000 | 475,000 |
| 95 | 199,500 | 75,000 | 200,000 | 420,000 | 785,000 |
| Mean | 46,171 | 16,492 | 61,613 | 103,207 | 227,483 |
| Standard deviation | 178,654 | 49,754 | 100,646 | 400,233 | 521,467 |

Source: Health and Retirement Study and author's calculations.

a. The number of observations is 5,292. All figures are weighted using survey weights. Financial net worth includes checking and saving accounts, bonds, stocks, and other financial assets minus short-term debt. Other assets includes real estate other than housing equity, business equity, and vehicles.

evidence that households reduce home ownership as they age, even though it is estimated that 42 percent will leave behind a house when the last member dies.[19] It is unclear how households, especially those with little financial wealth, will support consumption at retirement.

Asset holdings differ strikingly by education, race, and marital status (table 3-2). (These characteristics refer to the financially knowledgeable person in the household.) Education is correlated with permanent income and, crudely, with financial literacy. Wealth holdings (especially *financial* wealth holdings) are very low for households whose respondent has less than a high school education.[20] But most households headed by a college graduate have much higher holdings of financial assets and total wealth. Even in these instances, however, half of all college graduates have financial assets of less than $28,000, an amount sufficient to purchase an annuity of approximately $2,200 a year or less.

Wealth holdings also vary widely by race and marital status. Blacks and Hispanics have very little in terms of financial assets (the median is zero)

19. Sheiner and Weil (1992).

20. These findings also confirm the results of previous studies. For example, Hubbard, Skinner, and Zeldes (1995) use data from the Panel Study of Income Dynamics and find that households with low educational attainment have very low preretirement wealth, much too low according to the authors to be consistent with the predictions of the life-cycle model.

Table 3-2. *Wealth, by Education, Race, and Marital Status*[a]
Constant 1992 dollars

| Characteristic | Number of observations | Financial net worth | | Total net worth | |
|---|---|---|---|---|---|
| | | Median | Mean | Median | Mean |
| *Education* | | | | | |
| Elementary | 329 | 0 | –707 | 9,000 | 82,215 |
| Less than high school | 1,042 | 100 | 16,429 | 39,000 | 110,324 |
| High school | 1,876 | 5,500 | 29,668 | 90,000 | 183,678 |
| Some college | 1,041 | 10,000 | 47,312 | 122,700 | 243,571 |
| College | 800 | 28,000 | 90,910 | 186,000 | 358,848 |
| Beyond college | 204 | 41,000 | 175,160 | 234,000 | 636,366 |
| *Race* | | | | | |
| White | 3,645 | 10,000 | 55,308 | 118,500 | 264,615 |
| Black | 983 | 0 | 12,070 | 26,575 | 75,044 |
| Hispanic | 542 | 0 | 5,594 | 28,150 | 72,684 |
| Other | 122 | 6,900 | 30,308 | 113,000 | 188,155 |
| *Marital status* | | | | | |
| Married | 3,265 | 10,600 | 55,950 | 133,500 | 289,113 |
| With partner | 120 | 2,000 | 26,498 | 60,000 | 228,928 |
| Separated | 241 | 0 | 21,810 | 19,500 | 95,892 |
| Divorced | 895 | 1,400 | 28,348 | 38,000 | 124,227 |
| Widowed | 473 | 3,000 | 31,553 | 58,000 | 126,295 |
| Never married | 298 | 3,000 | 45,509 | 41,000 | 148,107 |

Source: See table 3-1.
a. All figures are weighted using survey weights.

and total net worth. The same is true for households whose respondent is divorced or separated.

## The Effects of Contractual Savings

Apart from private assets shown in tables 3-1 and 3-2, many households are covered by pensions. In the sample approximately 49 percent of individuals are covered by pensions and the proportion increases when families rather than individuals are considered. However, coverage varies substantially according to education and other demographic characteristics.

According to behavioral theory, the composition of wealth affects how much people save. Illiquid assets such as IRAs and housing are hard for households to access and spend; for this reason, they indirectly foster saving.[21] The same could be said for pensions. Pensions also may encourage their owners to think more about retirement and therefore recognize the need to save.[22] Homeowners surveyed in the HRS households have substantially more financial wealth on the average than do renters: $55,200 versus $16,805 (table 3-3). But it is not clear whether homeowners are more likely to save or savers are more likely to be homeowners. The same is true for retirement savings. Households that have IRAs or Keogh plans also have more in financial assets. Similarly, households with pensions have more financial and total net worth than households without pensions. Once again, it is not clear whether ownership of assets that are difficult to access boosts other forms of saving or households with a proclivity to save have more of all kinds of assets.

*Future Saving*

Surprisingly, the HRS indicates that respondents, most of whom have little wealth, plan not to save much during the five to ten years remaining before their retirement. They were asked how much wealth, other than IRAs, Keogh plans, and pensions, they planned to have accumulated by retirement. Three-quarters expected to have accumulated $100,000 or less, and a sizable share planned to accumulate nothing (table 3-4). Although the question explicitly excluded IRAs, Keoghs, and pensions, most wealth takes other forms. Households that currently have no IRAs or Keoghs said they expected to accumulate very little by retirement. Once again, those without IRAs or Keoghs expected to have fewer assets of other kinds at retirement than did those that had IRAs or Keoghs. The same is true of pensions; households from which a respondent has a pension reported much higher planned accumulation in nonpension assets than did households from which respondents did not have a pension.

In responding to the question about future accumulation, many people seem not to count home equity, as some current homeowners say their expected accumulated wealth is well below their current housing equity (table 3-5). Although homeowners are not as likely to report zero expected accumulation as renters, many report little expected future wealth. This again supports the idea that one has to use caution in defining the amount of resources that can be used to smooth consumption after retirement.

---

21. Thaler (1994).
22 Katona (1965); and Cagan (1965).

Table 3-3. *Financial Net Worth, by Type*[a]

Constant 1992 dollars

| Percentile | Total | Homeowners | | IRAs or Keoghs | | Pensions | |
|---|---|---|---|---|---|---|---|
| | | Yes | No | Yes | No | Yes | No |
| 5 | -6,000 | -5,970 | -6,566 | -2,800 | -8,000 | -5,900 | -6,800 |
| 10 | -2,000 | -1,600 | -3,000 | 200 | -3,500 | -1,800 | -2,400 |
| 25 | 0 | 700 | 0 | 6,000 | 0 | 1,000 | 0 |
| 50 | 6,000 | 10,177 | 0 | 25,000 | 1,000 | 10,200 | 2,500 |
| 75 | 36,000 | 48,000 | 6,900 | 88,000 | 11,500 | 43,600 | 27,000 |
| 90 | 110,000 | 129,000 | 36,000 | 182,000 | 45,000 | 113,000 | 110,000 |
| 95 | 199,500 | 220,000 | 83,400 | 320,000 | 87,800 | 205,500 | 185,000 |
| Mean | 46,171 | 55,200 | 16,805 | 85,911 | 18,179 | 53,752 | 38,815 |
| Standard deviation | 178,654 | 196,046 | 98,022 | 252,651 | 86,925 | 217,020 | 130,723 |
| Number of observations | 5,292 | 3,965 | 1,327 | 1,948 | 3,344 | 2,504 | 2,788 |

Source: See table 3-1.
a. All figures are weighted using survey weights.

Table 3-4. *Expected Accumulation of Net Wealth at Retirement*[a]

Constant 1992 dollars

| Percentile | Total | Homeowners | | IRAs or Keoghs | | Pensions | |
|---|---|---|---|---|---|---|---|
| | | Yes | No | Yes | No | Yes | No |
| 5 | 0 | 0 | 0 | 0 | 0 | 0 | 0 |
| 10 | 0 | 0 | 0 | 5,000 | 0 | 1,000 | 0 |
| 25 | 5,000 | 10,000 | 0 | 20,000 | 0 | 10,000 | 0 |
| 50 | 30,000 | 40,000 | 10,000 | 60,000 | 10,000 | 40,000 | 20,000 |
| 75 | 100,000 | 100,000 | 50,000 | 200,000 | 50,000 | 100,000 | 100,000 |
| 90 | 250,000 | 300,000 | 100,000 | 375,000 | 100,000 | 250,000 | 250,000 |
| 95 | 405,000 | 500,000 | 200,000 | 500,000 | 250,000 | 400,000 | 500,000 |
| Mean | 107,514 | 122,916 | 56,860 | 164,858 | 65,579 | 121,714 | 91,736 |
| Standard deviation | 360,779 | 381,501 | 276,248 | 411,287 | 312,312 | 445,098 | 232,896 |

a. The number of observations is 4,536. All figures are weighted using survey weights.

Table 3-5. *Financial Net Worth*[a]

Constant 1992 dollars

| Financial net worth | Home ownership | Home equity | | Net worth | | Expected accumulation | |
|---|---|---|---|---|---|---|---|
| | | *Median* | *Mean* | *Median* | *Mean* | *Median* | *Mean* |
| Net worth ≤ 0 | 0.57 | 6,500 | 27,503 | 14,950 | 53,591 | 3,000 | 36,311 |
| | | | (45,262) | | (189,414) | | (125,370) |
| 0 < net worth ≤ 6,000 | 0.75 | 30,000 | 44,300 | 50,100 | 98,711 | 10,000 | 56,120 |
| | | | (62,417) | | (245,834) | | (273,565) |
| 6,000 < net worth ≤ 35,000 | 0.86 | 55,000 | 67,345 | 106,700 | 163,303 | 45,000 | 81,619 |
| | | | (67,267) | | (295,376) | | (132,690) |
| Net worth > 35,000 | 0.90 | 82,000 | 109,070 | 275,000 | 530,758 | 100,000 | 257,820 |
| | | | (161,924) | | (834,151) | | (621,848) |

Source: See table 3-1.

a. Standard deviations are in parentheses. Net worth excludes IRAs and Keoghs. All figures are weighted using survey weights.

A comparison of current accumulation and expected accumulation suggests that low saving will persist. Nearly half of households that report negative or zero current financial wealth also report zero future planned accumulation. Almost one-third with zero to $6,000 of current financial assets report planned accumulation of less than $10,000; only 17 percent of these households plan to have accumulated more than $50,000 by the time they retire.

## Why Are Savings So Low?

People may discount the future, but they are forward looking and plan ahead, according to a fundamental assumption of the life-cycle model. The data shown in table 3-6 cast doubt on the general validity of this assumption. Although respondents in this sample are only five to ten years from retirement, one-third have "hardly thought" about retirement; less than one-third have thought about it "a lot." These findings have profound implications for wealth accumulation. A great many of those who have thought little about retirement expect to have no assets at retirement, and overall planned accumulation is low.

The respondents who have not thought about retirement are more often the younger ones, but there is still a significant percentage who do not think about retirement even at an advanced age. These respondents are also more likely to have little education and low earnings and not to be married. They are also less likely to have private pensions. Respondents who do not think about retirement appear to be generally uninformed about the retirement process. They are less likely to have attended retirement seminars and to have asked the Social Security Administration to calculate their retirement benefits. They are also less likely to have older siblings, who could be already retired (table 3-7).

People without a plan for retirement are unlikely to accumulate just the right amount of savings. Instead, they may well be surprised as they approach retirement at how little they have accumulated and suddenly realize that they must accept a sharp drop in living standards or work longer than they planned. In fact, consumption appears to fall sharply at retirement, much more than traditional models of saving or estimates of reductions in work-related expenses can rationalize. Studies report that consumption by white married couples aged 62–69 exceeds by 14 percent what their financial assets, pensions, and social security wealth can sup-

Table 3-6. *Thinking about Retirement and Expected Accumulation*[a]

Constant 1992 dollars

| Expected accumulation percentile | How much have you thought about retirement? | | | |
|---|---|---|---|---|
| | *A lot* | *Some* | *A little* | *Hardly at all* |
| 5 | 0 | 0 | 0 | 0 |
| 10 | 0 | 0 | 0 | 0 |
| 25 | 10,000 | 10,000 | 7,000 | 0 |
| 50 | 30,000 | 50,000 | 25,000 | 15,000 |
| 75 | 100,000 | 100,000 | 100,000 | 50,000 |
| 90 | 200,000 | 300,000 | 300,000 | 200,000 |
| 95 | 400,000 | 500,000 | 500,000 | 375,000 |
| Mean | 106,395 | 123,489 | 131,978 | 82,505 |
| Standard deviaton | 362,143 | 303,526 | 438,348 | 361,798 |
| Percent zeros | 15 | 11 | 15 | 30 |
| Number of observations | 1,331 | 1,039 | 681 | 1,438 |

Source: See table 3-1.

a. Figures are weighted using survey weights.

port.[23] As a result, households are forced to reduce their consumption when they retire and still more as they age.[24] Not surprisingly, the drop in consumption is smaller among households that have had high rates of saving.[25]

## Factors Influencing Household Savings

Available versions of the life-cycle model provide an inadequate explanation of saving behavior. The heterogeneity of behavior suggests that good alternative theories will require a lot of information. For example, one

23. Hamermesh (1984).

24. Mariger (1987) reported similar results. Hausman and Paquette (1987) also reported a decline in consumption at retirement, which they linked to unexpected and involuntary job loss resulting mainly from health problems.

25. Bernheim, Skinner, and Weinberg (1997). These authors also look into the composition of consumption and find little evidence that relative tastes for leisure or home production or differences in work-related expenses can explain the lack of consumption smoothing. They conclude that their results "appear to suggest that on average individuals who arrive at retirement with few resources experience a 'surprise'—they take stock of their finances only to discover that their resources are insufficient to maintain their accustomed standards of living (for example, because pension income is less than expected, or because they recognize that savings will go less far than they had hoped)" (pp. 4–5).

Table 3-7. *Thinking about Retirement, by Personal Characteristic*[a]

Percent

| Characteristic | How much have you thought about retirement? | | | | Total sample |
|---|---|---|---|---|---|
| | A lot | Some | Little | Hardly at all | |
| Age 50–53 | 0.32 | 0.38 | 0.40 | 0.39 | 0.37 |
| Age 54–57 | 0.36 | 0.36 | 0.33 | 0.37 | 0.36 |
| Age 58–61 | 0.32 | 0.26 | 0.27 | 0.24 | 0.27 |
| Married | 0.64 | 0.68 | 0.61 | 0.53 | 0.61 |
| Less than high school | 0.20 | 0.13 | 0.22 | 0.32 | 0.22 |
| High school | 0.38 | 0.35 | 0.37 | 0.37 | 0.37 |
| More than high school | 0.42 | 0.52 | 0.40 | 0.31 | 0.41 |
| Gross earnings > $25,000 | 0.51 | 0.53 | 0.41 | 0.28 | 0.43 |
| Have pension | 0.63 | 0.64 | 0.53 | 0.34 | 0.53 |
| Attended retirement seminar | 0.26 | 0.20 | 0.11 | 0.07 | 0.16 |
| Retirement seminar offered by employer | 0.18 | 0.14 | 0.07 | 0.05 | 0.10 |
| Social security calculated retirement benefits | 0.31 | 0.26 | 0.19 | 0.12 | 0.22 |
| Number of siblings older than 62 | 0.23 | 0.28 | 0.22 | 0.19 | 0.23 |
| Number of observations | 1,331 | 1,039 | 681 | 1,438 | 4,489 |

Source: See table 3-1.

a. The total number of observations is 4,489.

would need to know about people's preferences as well as their resources, about past and current economic circumstances, and what households expect for the future. Unlike other sources of data, the HRS provides information on each of these subjects.

## Expectations

People's expectations influence their saving decisions. To some extent these explanations are correlated with ordinary variables, such as earnings and health status, on which many surveys provide information. But people differ in their reactions to the same objective circumstances.

The HRS asks a number of questions about people's expectations that are relevant to their saving behavior.[26] These variables are analytically important because they convey information on how people perceive the future, which affects saving. Many authors have examined subjective data and found that responses to these questions are sensible. Few, however, have examined how expectations influence behavior, which is the focus of my work. These variables are important determinants of accumulation, and they may explain the low wealth holdings of many households.

SURVIVAL. Respondents were asked to evaluate the probability of surviving to age 75 and age 85. More than half of the respondents report a probability greater than 0.5 of surviving to age 75. Responses to this question vary with known risk factors in an intuitively sensible way. Women, for example, expect to live longer than men, and smokers and heavy drinkers report much lower probabilities of survival. Respondents whose parents lived to old ages report relatively high probabilities of surviving to an older age.[27]

RETIREMENT. Workers were asked about whether they would be working full time after age 62.[28] A sizable fraction said they planned to work full time through age 62, but most expected to be retired by age 65.[29] There are

26. A few studies have looked at subjective data and examined whether it conforms with realizations. See, for example, Bernheim (1988); Hurd and McGarry (1995a,b); and Honing (1995).

27. Hurd and McGarry (1995b) also analyze successive waves of the HRS and find that expressed survival probabilities change in a systematic and sensible way with the arrival of new information and predict accurately mortality outcomes across waves.

28. There is also a question on the probability of working full time after age 65, but the bulk of the empirical analysis so far has concentrated on the probability of working after age 62.

29. Hurd and McGarry (1994) show that these subjective probabilities are rather close to a population probability, and they vary with known risk factors for retirement, such as the eligibility for defined benefit pensions. Honing (1997) shows that married women's subjective expectations of

some, however, who say they will never retire completely; a large share of these are self-employed. One might expect that those who say they will retire early have saved more than those who say they will retire late. In fact, this expectation is not confirmed. Poorly educated workers, those in bad health, and those who worked less than thirty weeks in the previous year, for example, are likely both to expect to retire relatively young and to have little wealth.

ECONOMIC CONDITIONS. The HRS asks respondents to judge the likelihood that Congress will cut social security benefits and that housing prices in their neighborhood will outpace general inflation over the next ten years. Both housing and social security are important components of total household resources, and it is relevant to take account of expectations about them. The HRS also asks some general questions about the probability of double-digit inflation and that the economy will experience a major depression in the next ten years. I do not consider them in the empirical analysis reported here because even experts find these two variables difficult to forecast and their effects on saving behavior are unclear.

EARNINGS AND UNEMPLOYMENT. Respondents were also asked whether they expected their real earnings to rise, fall, or remain the same in the next several years. Theory predicts that households expecting earnings increases will save less than those that expect wages to fall or remain unchanged because consumption should be more stable than income. Respondents were also asked about the chance that they will lose their job in the next year. Although the chance of job loss is usually small for members of this age group, losses from unemployment can be large. Defined benefit pensions depend heavily on earnings in the last years of work. In addition, job loss often leads to retirement.[30]

OTHER FACTORS. People may save less than theory would predict for various other reasons. For example, family members or charities may ensure basic income. The presence of these floors (and related tax incentives) may make it rational for consumers to hold little or no wealth.[31] Although it is difficult to test the influence of such protections on saving, the HRS asks respondents whether they have relatives or friends who

---

working after age 62 are strongly influenced by their expected wage and nonwage compensation and expected social security entitlements. Hurd (1996) and Honing (1995) examine these expectations across the first two waves and show that they vary with age, gender, and race in the expected way, and have predictive power for actual retirement.

30. Diamond and Hausman (1994b); and Hausman and Paquette (1987).

31. Hubbard, Skinner, and Zeldes (1995).

would be both willing and able to help out over a long period if the respondents ran into severe financial problems. The presence of such relatives seems to have little effect on saving, however.

## Past Economic Circumstances

Bad fortune is a major reason why many households have little wealth. Many respondents report that there have been large unexpected expenses or events—extended unemployment or bad health or divorce or separation—that have made it difficult to meet financial goals. Good fortune, such as large inheritances, would have the opposite effect. Not many households receive inheritances or money from relatives or insurance companies, but those that do often receive large amounts. In short, simple luck—good or bad—goes a long way in explaining the differences among wealth holdings of people of similar age and income.

## Individual Preferences

The HRS is an unusual economic survey because it reports information on respondents' characteristics from which it is possible to derive measures of individual preferences. Among the most important questions are those that provide information on respondents' attitudes toward risk.[32] Respondents' choices about risky behaviors, such as the decision to smoke and drink, to buy insurance, to immigrate, to be self-employed, and to hold stocks are related to their answers to these questions.[33]

How far people look ahead is clearly relevant to financial decisions. People may not look far ahead because they are impatient which prevents them from acting on long-term saving plans.[34] In addition, people save for

32. The wording of the question is: "Suppose that you are the only income earner in the family, and you have a good job guaranteed to give you your current (family) income every year for life. You are given the opportunity to take a new and equally good job, with a 50-50 chance it will double your (family) income and a 50-50 chance that it will cut your (family) income by a third. Would you take the new job?" If the answer to this question is yes, then the interviewer continues: "Suppose the chances were 50-50 that it would double your (family) income, and 50-50 that it would cut it in half. Would you still take the new job?" If the answer to the first question is no, then the interviewer continues: "Suppose the chances were 50-50 that it would double your (family) income and 50-50 that it would cut it by 20 percent. Would you then take the new job?"

33. Barsky and others (1997). The authors already recognize there can be problems with the wording of the question, which may at the end not characterize well the category of risk aversion. This variable can still serve as a crude proxy.

34. In past work (Alessie, Lusardi, and Kapteyn, 1995) I have found that the length of the horizon is strongly related to wealth. This study confirms that finding.

motives other than to provide for retirement: to leave bequests or to protect themselves against such contingencies as unemployment or illness.
Many authors have studied the importance of the bequest motive. The
HRS asked respondents whether they expected to leave a sizable inheritance to their heirs. The desire to leave large bequests could help explain
particularly great wealth. In addition, if people have a precautionary saving
motive, an increase in risk will reduce consumption and increase wealth
accumulation.[35] In this case, they care, for example, about the variability of
earnings, and it is possible to use responses in the HRS to calculate how
much respondents expect earnings to vary.

## Explaining Household Savings: Empirical Analysis

All the previously mentioned variables are *individually* correlated with
wealth holdings, positively or negatively. But it is important to evaluate
their contribution in regressions that take account of their influence simultaneously. In the empirical work reported later, I present the results of
regressing wealth on an extensive set of variables. These results test how
well one can explain household wealth by using the information about
households contained in the Health and Retirement Study.[36] In addition,
and most important, these regressions permit me to determine whether
lack of planning plays any important role in explaining why savings are so
low.

I use three different definitions of wealth: financial net worth (measured
by the sum of checking and saving accounts, bonds, stocks, IRAs or
Keoghs, and other financial assets, minus short term debt), total net worth
(financial net worth plus housing equity, other real estate, business equity,
and vehicles, minus other debt), and expected accumulation at the time
of retirement. I consider both financial and total net worth because it is
unclear what the correct definition of resources for retirement is and
whether housing should be included. "Financial net worth" includes both
IRAs and Keoghs because they are important components in the portfolios
of many households and to differentiate from the third measure of wealth,
which excludes those types of assets. I divided each measure of wealth by
permanent income to take account of the tendency for wealthy households

---

35. A precautionary motive for saving is a property of utility functions that exhibit nonincreasing
absolute risk aversion. Kimball (1990); and Browning and Lusardi (1996).

36. Each equation can also be regarded as a reduced-form version of a life-cycle model.

to have larger wealth holdings.[37] To construct the final sample, I deleted records of respondents who did not report information on the variables of interest, and, in particular, on the expectations variables. Because the distribution of the ratio of wealth to permanent income is very wide, I excluded the top and bottom 1 percent. The appendix provides descriptive statistics of the variables used in the empirical estimation. Appendix tables 3A-1, 3A-2, and 3A-3 report the results of a regression of wealth on a large set of explanatory variables.

Apart from these variables, there may be another reason why households accumulate little wealth: individuals do not plan ahead and do not think about retirement. Many people in the sample indicated that they did not think about retirement, even at an advanced age. It is important to verify whether this variable has any predictive power for wealth after controlling for many of the other explanations for the lack of accumulation.

Two crucial findings stand out. First, despite the inclusion of a large number of explanatory variables, more than four-fifths of the variation in wealth holdings and more than nine-tenths of the variation in expected wealth accumulation remains unexplained. This result is common to most studies of individual behavior.

Second—again despite the inclusion of many explanatory variables— saving depends on how much people say they have thought about retirement. Respondents who did not think at all about retirement had much lower wealth than respondents who had thought, a little or a lot, about retirement (see table 3-8).[38]

The economic significance of whether one thinks about retirement is not minor. For the average household in which a respondent has not thought about retirement, financial net worth is 12 to 19 percent less, total net worth 9 to 15 percent less, and expected accumulation 7 to 11 percent less than in households with respondents who say they have thought

37. I construct a measure of permanent income by regressing household income on demographic and company characteristics—age, sex, and marital status—in addition to education and occupation dummies that are interacted with age. I also use dummies for whether the respondent works in a small company (fewer than twenty employees), belongs to a union, and does not work full time. Because all respondents were aged 50 to 61 in the first year of the HRS, I have not accounted for cohort effects in income. The predictions from this regression are used as a proxy of the permanent component of income.

38. It is possible that people who report that they do not think about retirement simply have high rates of time preference. Although it is hard directly to measure time preference, I can control for it by adding to the regression dummies for the planning horizons (column 2 of tables 3A-1, 3A-2, and 3A-3). These variables have a strong effect on wealth, and it is noteworthy to see how wealth monotonically increases with the lengthening of the planning horizon. Even with these controls, however, the dummy for not thinking about retirement remains negative and statistically significant.

Table 3-8. Effects of Thinking about Retirement on Wealth Holdings and Expected Accumulation, Average and Median Households[a]

|  | | Amount of thinking about retirement | | | | | |
|---|---|---|---|---|---|---|---|
|  | Ordinary least squares[b] | | | Median regression[c] | | | |
| Dependent variable | A lot | Some | A little | Not at all | A lot | Some | A little | Not at all |
| Financial net worth | 0.745 | 0.740 | 0.677 | 0.591 | 0.208 | 0.216 | 0.196 | 0.134 |
| Total net worth | 2.578 | 2.550 | 2.428 | 2.151 | 1.417 | 1.437 | 1.497 | 1.139 |
| Expected accumulation | 1.237 | 1.264 | 1.217 | 1.103 | 0.633 | 0.681 | 0.594 | 0.507 |

a. Wealth holdings over permanent income.
b. Ordinary least squares estimates apply to households with average values of the independent variables, as shown in appendix table 3A-4.
c. Median estimates are based on median regressions and apply to households with median values of the independent variables, as shown in table 3A-4.

about retirement. This effect persists even after controlling for planning horizons and education, which are strong predictors for accumulation.

Table 3-9 shows the effect on the two measures of wealth and expected wealth holding of additional selected variables. The effects shown in the previous tables are reconfirmed even after accounting for the many factors that can influence saving. For example, the large differences in wealth holdings across race and education groups persist even after accounting for income, past economic circumstance, and expectations about the future. There are large differences in wealth holdings depending on health status. Shocks in the past, such as having been unemployed or having received inheritances, also lead to large differences in observed wealth holdings.

Some of the variables shown in table 3-9 may be revealing the mental habits that cause people to plan or not to plan for retirement. For example, respondents who have a very short planning horizon accumulate much less wealth than respondents with a long horizon. As far as preferences and expectations about the future are concerned, households that expect their earnings to decrease in the future have greater assets.[39]

One reason for not thinking about retirement might be that people expect adequate income from social security or private pensions. However, people with private pensions actually have greater net worth than do people who do not have them.[40] Additionally, people might not think about retirement because they plan to work until a very old age or expect to die young. If so, the estimates of the effect on wealth of not thinking about retirement would be smaller once such plans or expectations have been controlled. In fact, controlling for these variables reduces the difference in wealth associated with those who have thought about retirement a lot and those who have thought about it hardly at all, but the difference remains statistically significant (tables 3A-1 to 3A-3).

Not thinking about retirement is associated with reduced wealth even when one controls for such saving motives as the desire to provide bequests, the probability of receiving help from friends or relatives, and the

39. Median and robust regressions, not reported but available on request, indicate that households whose respondents are more risk averse accumulate more total net worth. Households who expect house prices to go up in the future also tend to accumulate less.

40. Gustman and Steinmeier (1997) report similar results. They use the pension data from the employer-provided survey, which is a data set that can be matched with the HRS data. In my work, I have used a dummy for whether the respondent has a pension as well as the pension value constructed from the self-reported data in the first wave of the HRS. Results are similar, and for brevity, I only report the estimates using the pension dummy. For a detailed explanation of the construction of the pension data, see Venti and Wise (1997).

Table 3-9. *Effect of Selected Variables on Actual and*
*Anticipated Wealth Accumulation*[a]

| Variable | Financial net worth | Total net worth | Expected accumulation |
|---|---|---|---|
| 1. Male | 0.701 | 2.347 | 1.366 |
|    Female | 0.695 | 2.566 | 1.018 |
| 2. White | 0.802 | 2.715 | 1.273 |
|    Black | 0.390 | 1.595 | 0.969 |
|    Hispanic | 0.516 | 2.120 | 1.119 |
| 3. College education | 0.963 | 2.994 | 1.297 |
|    High school degree | 0.624 | 2.257 | 1.177 |
| 4. Good health | 0.706 | 2.373 | 1.157 |
|    Poor health | 0.625 | 2.147 | 1.125 |
| 5. Has been unemployed | 0.669 | 2.259 | 1.105 |
|    No past unemployment | 0.715 | 2.562 | 1.257 |
| 6. Received inheritances, etc. | 0.904 | 2.958 | 1.338 |
|    No inheritance, etc. | 0.654 | 2.341 | 1.172 |
| 7. High risk aversion | 0.691 | 2.444 | 1.182 |
|    Low risk aversion | 0.761 | 2.440 | 1.279 |
| 8. Expect to leave a bequest | 0.897 | 3.063 | 1.494 |
|    No bequest motive | 0.549 | 1.989 | 0.981 |
| 9. Have pension | 0.688 | 2.503 | 1.189 |
|    Don't have pension | 0.720 | 2.334 | 1.230 |
| 10. Planning horizon: next year | 0.652 | 2.351 | 1.102 |
|     Planning horizon: > 10 years | 0.946 | 2.832 | 1.366 |
| 11. Can rely on help from relatives and friends | 0.724 | 2.457 | 1.207 |
|     No help | 0.679 | 2.446 | 1.197 |
| 12. Earnings expected to be stable | 0.677 | 2.430 | 1.061 |
|     Earnings expected to fall | 0.691 | 2.646 | 0.983 |

a. Wealth holdings over permanent income. All values are calculated at the mean for all variables other than the pair shown in each cell.

variance of expected earnings.[41] To the extent that people save for reasons other than retirement, uncertainty about the future as well as the average expectation of future events can influence saving. The precautionary motive for saving can be important and may explain the lack of a long

41. There can be objections to the interpretations of the bequest motive. The question regarding bequests is a rather crude measure of the bequest motive. The exact wording is: "Do you expect to leave

planning horizon and the presence of what can resemble a high discount rate for the future. However, wealth accumulated for such motives accounts for only 2.0 to 4.5 percent of total wealth in the age groups covered by the Health and Retirement Study.[42] It is difficult to claim that households in this age group are facing so much uncertainty that it prevents them from planning for the future.

## Conclusion

A large percentage of U.S. households that are nearing retirement age have little or no wealth. Although many explanations can be found, people have often simply not thought about retirement and they have done little or no planning. A lack of planning is associated with meager wealth accumulation, measured as financial net worth or total net worth or as expected future accumulation. This finding casts doubts on the assumption made in many models of intertemporal optimization that people look ahead and make plans for the future.

## Appendix

Tables 3A-1, 3A-2, and 3A-3 report the complete regressions on which the text tables 3-8 and 3-9 are based. I have also used median and robust estimators, which can take better account of outliers. For brevity, those estimates are not reported, but are available from me upon request.

In the first column of tables 3A-1 through 3A-3, I consider all variables described in the text. This list includes not only age and age squared to capture the hump-shaped profile of wealth holdings, but also some simple demographics, such as the total number of children, and the number of children still living at home, gender, race, marital status, and education, that can account for heterogeneity in tastes. I also include dummies

---

a sizable inheritance to your heirs?" The possible answers are yes, definitely; yes, probably; yes, possibly; probably not; no, definitely. Respondents may have interpreted the question in different ways. It is also not clear whether the probability of receiving help from friends and relatives does or does not result in endogenous (or strategic) behavior on the part of the family. However, these variables serve as proxies for the motives why households do or do not accumulate and to check whether results are robust across different specifications for wealth.

42. Lusardi (1998).

Table 3A-1. *Ordinary Least Squares Regressions, Financial Net Worth*[a]

| Variable | 1 | | 2 | | 3 | | 4 | | 5 | |
|---|---|---|---|---|---|---|---|---|---|---|
| Constant | 2.9783 | (6.773) | 3.6187 | (6.769) | 6.0571 | (6.743) | 6.0934 | (6.745) | 5.4137 | (6.674) |
| Not think of retirement | -.1392 | (.0505) | -.1342 | (.0505) | -.0905 | (.0507) | -.0914 | (.0508) | -.0865 | (.0503) |
| Age | -.1213 | (.2450) | -.1503 | (.2449) | -.2426 | (.2440) | -.2438 | (.2441) | -.2227 | (.2415) |
| Age squared | .0014 | (.0022) | .0016 | (.0022) | .0025 | (.0022) | .0025 | (.0022) | .0023 | (.0021) |
| Number of children | -.0471 | (.0121) | -.0448 | (.0121) | -.0442 | (.0120) | -.0443 | (.0120) | -.0387 | (.0119) |
| Number of children at home | -.0583 | (.0231) | -.0555 | (.0230) | -.0486 | (.0229) | -.0485 | (.0229) | -.0499 | (.0227) |
| Male | .0375 | (.0499) | .0306 | (.0497) | .0438 | (.0495) | .0441 | (.0495) | .0061 | (.0492) |
| White | .2379 | (.0812) | .2163 | (.0812) | .2255 | (.0808) | .2253 | (.0808) | .2858 | (.0803) |
| Black | -.1066 | (.0876) | -.1066 | (.0873) | -.1381 | (.0870) | -.1373 | (.0871) | -.1262 | (.0861) |
| Married | .1435 | (.1283) | .1275 | (.1280) | .1233 | (.1272) | .1199 | (.1278) | .1230 | (.1266) |
| Living with partner | -.0622 | (.1881) | -.0880 | (.1876) | -.0901 | (.1866) | -.0914 | (.1867) | -.0504 | (.1847) |
| Divorced | .0304 | (.1061) | .0234 | (.1059) | .0446 | (.1054) | .0448 | (.1054) | .0205 | (.1043) |
| Widowed | .0352 | (.1245) | .0244 | (.1242) | .0287 | (.1235) | .0279 | (.1235) | .0041 | (.1222) |
| Separated | -.0356 | (.1440) | -.0372 | (.1436) | -.0274 | (.1428) | -.0286 | (.1428) | -.0653 | (.1414) |
| Northeast region | .1067 | (.0645) | .0982 | (.0643) | .0874 | (.0640) | .0868 | (.0640) | .0841 | (.0633) |
| Midwest region | .2352 | (.0540) | .2342 | (.0538) | .2170 | (.0536) | .2178 | (.0537) | .2199 | (.0531) |
| West region | .0906 | (.0666) | .0999 | (.0665) | .0973 | (.0661) | .0971 | (.0661) | .1168 | (.0654) |
| High school | .1326 | (.0671) | .1284 | (.0669) | .1303 | (.0665) | .1298 | (.0666) | .1206 | (.0659) |
| Some college | .2527 | (.0930) | .2430 | (.0927) | .2596 | (.0923) | .2583 | (.0924) | .2510 | (.0914) |
| College | .4508 | (.1299) | .4321 | (.1296) | .4575 | (.1290) | .4545 | (.1294) | .4598 | (.1281) |
| More college | .3757 | (.2004) | .3560 | (.2000) | .4129 | (.1991) | .4073 | (.2001) | .4154 | (.1980) |
| Excellent health | .1322 | (.0765) | .1155 | (.0763) | .1322 | (.0760) | .1322 | (.0760) | .1255 | (.0752) |
| Very good health | .0777 | (.0717) | .0664 | (.0715) | .0874 | (.0712) | .0877 | (.0712) | .0811 | (.0705) |
| Good health | .0470 | (.0697) | .0389 | (.0695) | .0486 | (.0691) | .0492 | (.0691) | .0531 | (.0684) |

| | (.0463) | (.0462) | (.0460) | (.0461) | (.0457) |
|---|---|---|---|---|---|
| Past unemployment | -.0724 (.0463) | -.0710 (.0462) | -.0612 (.0460) | -.0621 (.0461) | -.0464 (.0457) |
| Past shocks | -.3079 (.0459) | -.3027 (.0458) | -.2873 (.0456) | -.2873 (.0456) | -.2738 (.0451) |
| Inheritances | .2950 (.0564) | .2973 (.0563) | .2948 (.0560) | .2952 (.0560) | .2501 (.0557) |
| Money from relatives | .2978 (.0816) | .3065 (.0814) | .3030 (.0809) | .3029 (.0809) | .2547 (.0803) |
| Money from insurance | .5416 (.1025) | .5439 (.1022) | .5339 (.1016) | .5336 (.1017) | .4927 (.1007) |
| High risk aversion | -.0507 (.0675) | -.0518 (.0673) | -.0722 (.0670) | -.0702 (.0674) | -.0699 (.0667) |
| Medium risk aversion | -.0389 (.0861) | -.0424 (.0859) | -.0572 (.0855) | -.0560 (.0856) | -.0623 (.0847) |
| Moderate risk aversion | -.0958 (.0891) | -.0952 (.0888) | -.1072 (.0884) | -.1054 (.0886) | -.0850 (.0877) |
| Permanent income/1,000 | -.0044 (.0029) | -.0046 (.0029) | -.0048 (.0029) | -.0047 (.0030) | -.0056 (.0029) |
| Income expected to fall | .0684 (.0818) | .0679 (.0816) | .0320 (.0814) | .0322 (.0814) | .0140 (.0806) |
| Income expected to rise | .0230 (.0459) | .0253 (.0458) | .0547 (.0458) | .0550 (.0458) | .0351 (.0454) |
| Probability live to 75 | .0582 (.0795) | .0374 (.0795) | .0630 (.0792) | .0635 (.0792) | .0354 (.0785) |
| Probability SS less generous | -.0004 (.0710) | -.0138 (.0709) | .0042 (.0705) | .0050 (.0706) | .0241 (.0699) |
| Probability house prices up | -.1203 (.0733) | -.1251 (.0731) | -.1020 (.0728) | -.1030 (.0729) | -.1281 (.0722) |
| Probability job loss | .0117 (.0832) | .0301 (.0831) | .0278 (.0826) | .0272 (.0827) | .0152 (.0837) |
| Planning horizon: next year | | .1556 (.0860) | .1405 (.0855) | .1404 (.0855) | .1397 (.0846) |
| Planning horizon: next few years | | .1863 (.0626) | .1775 (.0622) | .1784 (.0623) | .1858 (.0617) |
| Planning horizon: 5–10 years | | .2306 (.0648) | .2310 (.0644) | .2323 (.0646) | .2365 (.0640) |
| Planning horizon: >10 years | | .4279 (.0922) | .4306 (.0917) | .4315 (.0918) | .4335 (.0908) |
| Probability work after 62 | | | -.3359 (.0561) | -.3369 (.0563) | -.3037 (.0558) |
| Pension | | | | -.0138 (.0486) | -.0323 (.0481) |
| Bequest | | | | | .3479 (.0428) |
| Variance of income | | | | | .0043 (.0029) |
| Help from relatives | | | | | .0445 (.0423) |
| Adjusted $R^2$ | 0.113 | 0.118 | 0.128 | 0.128 | 0.147 |

a. The mean of the dependent variable is 0.698. The total number of observations is 3,094. Standard errors are in parentheses.

Table 3A-2. *Ordinary Least Squares Regressions, Total Net Worth*[a]

| | 1 | | 2 | | 3 | | 4 | | 5 | |
|---|---|---|---|---|---|---|---|---|---|---|
| Constant | -4.339 | (14.231) | -3.1142 | (14.236) | 3.3726 | (14.131) | 2.7755 | (14.124) | 1.1474 | (13.800) |
| Not think of retirement | -.3892 | (.1062) | -.3739 | (.1062) | -.2577 | (.1063) | -.2431 | (.1065) | -.2330 | (.1041) |
| Age | .2176 | (.5148) | .1615 | (.5150) | -.0838 | (.5113) | -.0639 | (.5111) | -.0145 | (.4993) |
| Age squared | -.0015 | (.0046) | -.0010 | (.0046) | .0013 | (.0046) | .0011 | (.0046) | .0006 | (.0045) |
| Number of children | -.0817 | (.0255) | -.0777 | (.0255) | -.0759 | (.0252) | -.0742 | (.0252) | -.0564 | (.0247) |
| Number of children at home | -.0635 | (.0486) | -.0579 | (.0485) | -.0398 | (.0481) | -.0415 | (.0481) | -.0456 | (.0470) |
| Male | -.1263 | (.1048) | -.1367 | (.1046) | -.1018 | (.1038) | -.1075 | (.1037) | -.2195 | (.1018) |
| White | .4115 | (.1708) | .3751 | (.1709) | .3997 | (.1694) | .4035 | (.1693) | .5950 | (.1661) |
| Black | -.4633 | (.1841) | -.4610 | (.1837) | -.5446 | (.1824) | -.5574 | (.1823) | -.5247 | (.1781) |
| Married | .8173 | (.2696) | .7940 | (.2692) | .7830 | (.2667) | .8394 | (.2677) | .8320 | (.2617) |
| Living with partner | .4177 | (.3953) | .3796 | (.3947) | .3738 | (.3910) | .3947 | (.3909) | .5040 | (.3820) |
| Divorced | -.1057 | (.2231) | -.1097 | (.2228) | -.0533 | (.2209) | -.0576 | (.2207) | -.1254 | (.2157) |
| Widowed | .2718 | (.2616) | .2613 | (.2612) | .2725 | (.2588) | .2852 | (.2587) | .2144 | (.2527) |
| Separated | -.0849 | (.3026) | -.0813 | (.3020) | -.0553 | (.2992) | -.0362 | (.2991) | -.1428 | (.2924) |
| Northeast region | .3243 | (.1355) | .3089 | (.1353) | .2802 | (.1341) | .2905 | (.1341) | .2853 | (.1310) |
| Midwest region | .3392 | (.1135) | .3356 | (.1133) | .2899 | (.1124) | .2765 | (.1125) | .2774 | (.1099) |
| West region | .5196 | (.1401) | .5374 | (.1398) | .5305 | (.1385) | .5344 | (.1385) | .5887 | (.1353) |
| High school | .2478 | (.1410) | .2375 | (.1408) | .2425 | (.1395) | .2514 | (.1394) | .2294 | (.1363) |
| Some college | .4909 | (.1954) | .4751 | (.1951) | .5195 | (.1934) | .5409 | (.1935) | .5290 | (.1891) |
| College | .8476 | (.2731) | .8187 | (.2727) | .8862 | (.2703) | .9361 | (.2711) | .9667 | (.2649) |
| More college | 1.2335 | (.4211) | 1.1976 | (.4207) | 1.3492 | (.4174) | 1.4414 | (.4191) | 1.4818 | (.4095) |
| Excellent health | .7030 | (.1607) | .6749 | (.1606) | .7194 | (.1592) | .7197 | (.1591) | .7007 | (.1555) |
| Very good health | .2137 | (.1508) | .1937 | (.1505) | .2496 | (.1493) | .2452 | (.1492) | .2257 | (.1458) |
| Good health | .1756 | (.1464) | .1619 | (.1461) | .1879 | (.1448) | .1782 | (.1448) | .1884 | (.1415) |
| Past unemployment | -.3938 | (.0974) | -.3893 | (.0972) | -.3633 | (.0964) | -.3486 | (.0965) | -.3037 | (.0944) |

| | (1) | (2) | (3) | (4) | (5) |
|---|---|---|---|---|---|
| Past shocks | -.5556 (.0965) | -.5433 (.0963) | -.5023 (.0956) | -.5016 (.0955) | -.4653 (.0934) |
| Inheritances | .7561 (.1186) | .7608 (.1185) | .7542 (.1174) | .7485 (.1173) | .6170 (.1153) |
| Money from relatives | .8780 (.1715) | .8903 (.1712) | .8809 (.1696) | .8827 (.1695) | .7437 (.1661) |
| Money from insurance | .9566 (.2153) | .9611 (.2150) | .9345 (.2130) | .9391 (.2129) | .8167 (.2082) |
| High risk aversion | .0931 (.1419) | .0868 (.1416) | .0327 (.1405) | .0007 (.1412) | .0034 (.1379) |
| Medium risk aversion | .1485 (.1810) | .1418 (.1807) | .1017 (.1791) | .0781 (.1793) | .0541 (.1752) |
| Moderate risk aversion | .0144 (.1873) | .0136 (.1869) | -.0181 (.1852) | -.0469 (.1856) | .0145 (.1813) |
| Permanent income/1,000 | -.0293 (.0062) | -.0300 (.0062) | -.0304 (.0062) | -.0331 (.0063) | -.0361 (.0061) |
| Income expected to fall | .3668 (.1719) | .3649 (.1718) | .2693 (.1706) | .2665 (.1705) | .2163 (.1667) |
| Income expected to rise | -.0193 (.0966) | -.0137 (.0964) | .0642 (.0961) | .0593 (.0960) | .0058 (.0940) |
| Probability live to 75 | .2212 (.1672) | .1884 (.1673) | .2565 (.1660) | .2478 (.1659) | .1735 (.1623) |
| Probability SS less generous | -.2126 (.1492) | -.2357 (.1491) | -.1875 (.1479) | -.2012 (.1479) | -.1476 (.1446) |
| Probability house prices up | -.1522 (.1541) | -.1601 (.1538) | -.0987 (.1526) | -.0819 (.1527) | -.1579 (.1492) |
| Probability job loss | -.1329 (.1749) | -.0994 (.1748) | -.1055 (.1732) | -.0954 (.1731) | -.1220 (.1730) |
| Planning horizon: next year | | .3024 (.1808) | .2624 (.1793) | .2647 (.1791) | .2701 (.1750) |
| Planning horizon: next few years | | .4385 (.1316) | .4152 (.1304) | .3999 (.1305) | .4276 (.1276) |
| Planning horizon: 5–10 years | | .4406 (.1362) | .4416 (.1350) | .4203 (.1352) | .4400 (.1323) |
| Planning horizon: >10 years | | .7517 (.1940) | .7590 (.1922) | .7442 (.1922) | .7514 (.1878) |
| Probability work after 62 | | | -.8936 (.1177) | -.8762 (.1178) | -.7737 (.1154) |
| Pension | | | | .2274 (.1018) | .1689 (.0995) |
| Bequest | | | | | 1.0749 (.0885) |
| Variance of income | | | | | .0093 (.0062) |
| Help from relatives | | | | | .0102 (.0875) |
| Adjusted $R^2$ | 0.109 | 0.113 | 0.129 | 0.130 | 0.170 |

a. The mean of the dependent variable is 2.451. The total number of errors is 3,094. Standard errors are in parentheses.

Table 3A-3. Ordinary Least Squares Regressions, Expected Accumulation[a]

| | 1 | | 2 | | 3 | | 4 | | 5 | |
|---|---|---|---|---|---|---|---|---|---|---|
| Constant | 4.6435 | (10.509) | 6.8026 | (10.519) | 8.3899 | (10.526) | 8.4088 | (10.528) | 7.1641 | (10.413) |
| Not think of retirement | -.1380 | (.0759) | -.1304 | (.0761) | -.0932 | (.0774) | -.0951 | (.0779) | -.0869 | (.0771) |
| Age | -.1297 | (.3802) | -.2154 | (.3807) | -.2761 | (.3810) | -.2766 | (.3811) | -.2368 | (.3769) |
| Age squared | .0010 | (.0034) | .0018 | (.0034) | .0024 | (.0034) | .0024 | (.0034) | .0020 | (.0034) |
| Number of children | -.0272 | (.0190) | -.0248 | (.0190) | -.0246 | (.0190) | -.0247 | (.0190) | -.0165 | (.0188) |
| Number of children at home | -.0752 | (.0358) | -.0721 | (.0357) | -.0675 | (.0357) | -.0674 | (.0357) | -.0691 | (.0353) |
| Male | .4066 | (.0769) | .3979 | (.0768) | .4066 | (.0768) | .4069 | (.0768) | .3478 | (.0763) |
| White | .1038 | (.1271) | .0712 | (.1272) | .0768 | (.1271) | .0766 | (.1271) | .1626 | (.1263) |
| Black | -.1405 | (.1362) | -.1418 | (.1359) | -.1597 | (.1360) | -.1589 | (.1360) | -.1417 | (.1345) |
| Married | -.0636 | (.1977) | -.0758 | (.1975) | -.0780 | (.1973) | -.0823 | (.1983) | -.0662 | (.1962) |
| Living with partner | -.1553 | (.2929) | -.1981 | (.2925) | -.1903 | (.2923) | -.1920 | (.2925) | -.1095 | (.2894) |
| Divorced | .1214 | (.1633) | .1018 | (.1632) | .1130 | (.1631) | .1132 | (.1632) | .0921 | (.1614) |
| Widowed | .1111 | (.1929) | .0927 | (.1927) | .0959 | (.1925) | .0945 | (.1926) | .0664 | (.1905) |
| Separated | .0682 | (.2210) | .0600 | (.2207) | .0658 | (.2205) | .0641 | (.2206) | .0315 | (.2182) |
| Northeast region | -.0023 | (.0995) | -.0024 | (.0994) | -.0080 | (.0993) | -.0089 | (.0994) | -.0035 | (.0983) |
| Midwest region | .0576 | (.0838) | .0563 | (.0836) | .0464 | (.0836) | .0471 | (.0837) | .0514 | (.0828) |
| West region | .1108 | (.1036) | .1234 | (.1035) | .1268 | (.1034) | .1262 | (.1035) | .1541 | (.1024) |
| High school | .0838 | (.1038) | .0816 | (.1036) | .0808 | (.1035) | .0803 | (.1036) | .0743 | (.1024) |
| Some college | .1142 | (.1457) | .1167 | (.1455) | .1239 | (.1453) | .1224 | (.1455) | .1181 | (.1440) |
| College | .1718 | (.2027) | .1677 | (.2025) | .1830 | (.2024) | .1795 | (.2030) | .1946 | (.2009) |
| More college | .2447 | (.3122) | .2628 | (.3122) | .2964 | (.3121) | .2899 | (.3137) | .3190 | (.3103) |
| Excellent health | .2404 | (.1196) | .2214 | (.1195) | .2309 | (.1195) | .2309 | (.1195) | .2319 | (.1182) |
| Very good health | .0317 | (.1112) | .0160 | (.1110) | .0302 | (.1111) | .0305 | (.1111) | .0315 | (.1099) |
| Good health | .0104 | (.1081) | .0043 | (.1079) | .0115 | (.1079) | .0122 | (.1079) | .0276 | (.1068) |
| Past unemployment | -.1870 | (.0723) | -.1879 | (.0722) | -.1821 | (.0722) | -.1832 | (.0724) | -.1522 | (.0717) |

| | (1) | (2) | (3) | (4) | (5) |
|---|---|---|---|---|---|
| Past shocks | −.1997 (.0712) | −.1940 (.0711) | −.1840 (.0711) | −.1841 (.0711) | −.1703 (.0704) |
| Inheritances | .2214 (.0874) | .2307 (.0873) | .2307 (.0872) | .2309 (.0873) | .1662 (.0868) |
| Money from relatives | .0711 (.1267) | .0890 (.1266) | .0863 (.1265) | .0861 (.1265) | .0280 (.1253) |
| Money from insurance | .2729 (.1623) | .2696 (.1621) | .2591 (.1619) | .2589 (.1620) | .1946 (.1604) |
| High risk aversion | −.0936 (.1082) | −.0914 (.1080) | −.1024 (.1080) | −.1004 (.1085) | −.0974 (.1073) |
| Medium risk aversion | −.1009 (.1362) | −.1112 (.1360) | −.1178 (.1359) | −.1167 (.1360) | −.1299 (.1345) |
| Moderate risk aversion | −.0154 (.1400) | −.0077 (.1398) | −.0101 (.1396) | −.0083 (.1399) | .0212 (.1384) |
| Permanent income/1,000 | −.0020 (.0046) | −.0030 (.0046) | −.0031 (.0046) | −.0029 (.0047) | −.0045 (.0047) |
| Income expected to fall | −.0423 (.1269) | −.0296 (.1269) | −.0482 (.1270) | −.0478 (.1271) | −.0777 (.1257) |
| Income expected to rise | .2617 (.0711) | .2603 (.0710) | .2812 (.0714) | .2816 (.0714) | .2568 (.0708) |
| Probability live to 75 | .4625 (.1243) | .4520 (.1244) | .4675 (.1244) | .4680 (.1244) | .4190 (.1233) |
| Probability SS less generous | .1719 (.1106) | .1554 (.1105) | .1659 (.1105) | .1667 (.1105) | .1966 (.1094) |
| Probability house prices up | −.0290 (.1133) | −.0346 (.1131) | −.0198 (.1131) | −.0207 (.1132) | −.0577 (.1120) |
| Probability job loss | −.0455 (.1290) | −.0206 (.1290) | −.0242 (.1288) | −.0251 (.1289) | −.0838 (.1304) |
| Planning horizon: next year | | .1180 (.1350) | .1133 (.1349) | .1131 (.1349) | .1115 (.1334) |
| Planning horizon: next few years | | .1615 (.0991) | .1621 (.0990) | .1629 (.0991) | .1733 (.0980) |
| Planning horizon: 5–10 years | | .3478 (.1028) | .3547 (.1027) | .3559 (.1029) | .3533 (.1018) |
| Planning horizon: >10 years | | .3864 (.1472) | .3874 (.1471) | .3882 (.1471) | .3754 (.1455) |
| Probability work after 62 | | | −.2273 (.0884) | −.2280 (.0885) | −.1800 (.0877) |
| Pension | | | | −.0166 (.0777) | −.0407 (.0769) |
| Bequest | | | | | .5122 (.0665) |
| Variance of income | | | | | .0117 (.0045) |
| Help from relatives | | | | | .0101 (.0660) |
| Adjusted $R^2$ | 0.045 | 0.049 | 0.051 | 0.051 | 0.072 |

a. The mean of the dependent variable is 1.204. The total number of observations is 2,784. Standard errors are in parentheses.

Table 3A-4. *Descriptive Statistics*[a]

|  | Mean | Standard deviation |
| --- | --- | --- |
| Financial net worth/permanent income | .6982 | 1.2244 |
| Total net worth/permanent income | 2.4507 | 2.5669 |
| Expected accumulation/permanent income | 1.2040 | 1.7340 |
| Not think of retirement | .2333 | .4230 |
| Age | 55.0526 | 3.1772 |
| Age squared | 3,040.89 | 352.0737 |
| Number of children | 3.0911 | 2.0265 |
| Number of children at home | .8173 | 1.0357 |
| Male | .5281 | .4992 |
| White | .7175 | .4502 |
| Black | .1835 | .3872 |
| Married | .6102 | .4877 |
| Living with partner | .0190 | .1367 |
| Divorced | .1890 | .3916 |
| Widowed | .0901 | .2864 |
| Separated | .0387 | .1931 |
| Northeast region | .1929 | .3946 |
| Midwest region | .2488 | .4324 |
| West region | .1522 | .3593 |
| High school | .3791 | .4852 |
| Some college | .2042 | .4032 |
| College | .1803 | .3845 |
| More college | .0365 | .1876 |
| Excellent health | .2521 | .4342 |
| Very good health | .3164 | .4651 |
| Good health | .2941 | .4557 |

Table 3A-4. *(continued)*

|  | Mean | Standard deviation |
|---|---|---|
| Past unemployment | .3674 | .4821 |
| Past shocks | .3196 | .4664 |
| Inheritances | .1780 | .3826 |
| Money from relatives | .0723 | .2591 |
| Money from insurance | .0542 | .2266 |
| High risk aversion | .6599 | .4737 |
| Medium risk aversion | .1199 | .3249 |
| Moderate risk aversion | .1043 | .3058 |
| Permanent income/1,000 | 49.3218 | 21.8723 |
| Income expected to fall | .0811 | .2730 |
| Income expected to rise | .5730 | .4947 |
| Probability live to 75 | .6597 | .2802 |
| Probability SS less generous | .5945 | .2990 |
| Probability house prices up | .4882 | .2942 |
| Probability job loss | .1781 | .2594 |
| Planning horizon: next year | .0901 | .2864 |
| Planning horizon: next few years | .3493 | .4768 |
| Planning horizon: 5–10 years | .3154 | .4647 |
| Planning horizon: >10 years | .0765 | .2659 |
| Probability work after 62 | .4967 | .3905 |
| Pension | .6890 | .4629 |
| Bequest | .4298 | .4951 |
| Variance of income | 1.8219 | 7.0083 |
| Help from relatives | .4214 | .4938 |

a. For the variables used in the empirical estimation.

for health status.[43] Permanent income is included among the regressors to account for nonhomothetic preferences. I also control for the risk-aversion coefficient. To account for past economic circumstances, I include a dummy for whether the respondents have been unemployed in the past, and for whether they have received inheritances, money from relatives, and money from an insurance settlement. To account for future economic circumstances, I include respondents' expectations concerning future events, such as expected longevity up to age 75, the expectations that social security will become less generous, that house prices will go up, and that they will lose their job. I also include whether respondents expect their income to increase or decrease in the next year.

Table 3A-4 lists values and standard deviations for all variables used in this chapter.

# References

Abel, Andrew. 1985. "Precautionary Saving and Accidental Bequests." *American Economic Review* 75: 777–91.
Alessie, Rob, Annamaria Lusardi, and Arie Kapteyn. 1995. "Saving and Wealth Holdings of the Elderly." *Ricerche Economiche* 49 (September): 293–315.
Altonji, Joseph, Fumio Hayashi, and Laurence Kotlikoff. 1992. "Is the Extended Family Altruistically Linked? New Tests Based on Micro Data." *American Economic Review* 82 (December): 1177–98
Barsky, Robert, and others. 1997. "Preference Parameters and Behavioral Heterogeneity: An Experimental Approach in the Health and Retirement Survey." *Quarterly Journal of Economics* 62 (May): 537–79.
Bernheim, B. Douglas. 1988. "Social Security Benefits: An Empirical Study of Expectations and Realizations." In *Issues in Contemporary Retirement,* edited by E. Lazear and R. Ricardo Campbell. Palo Alto, Calif.: Hoover Institution, 312–45.
———. 1991. *The Vanishing Nest Egg: Reflections on Saving in America.* Priority Press.
———. 1993. *Is the Baby Boom Generation Preparing Adequately for Retirement? Summary Report.* New York: Merrill Lynch.
———. 1996. "Personal Saving, Information, and Economic Literacy: New Directions for Public Policy." In *Tax Policy for Economic Growth in the 1990s,* 53–78. Washington: American Council for Capital Formation.
Bernheim, B. Douglas, and Daniel Garrett. 1995. "The Determinants and Consequences of Financial Education in the Workplace: Evidence from a Survey of Households." Stanford University.

---

43. The reference group is represented by Hispanics or other races (such as moreno, brown, and combination of black and American Indian), the never married, those with less than high school education, and those in poor health.

Bernheim, B. Douglas, Andrei Schleifer, and Laurence Summers. 1985. "The Strategic Bequest Motive." *Journal of Political Economy* 93 (December): 1045–75.

Bernheim, B. Douglas, Jonathan Skinner, and Steven Weinberg. 1997. "What Accounts for the Variation in Retirement Wealth among U.S. Households?" Working Paper 6227. Cambridge, Mass.: National Bureau of Economic Research.

Börsch-Supan, Axel, and Konrad Stahl. 1991. "Life-Cycle Savings and Consumption Constraints." *Journal of Population Economics* 4 (August): 233–55.

Bosworth, Barry, Gary Burtless, and John Sabelhaus. 1991. "The Decline in Saving: Evidence from Household Surveys." *Brooking Papers on Economic Activity*, 1: 183–256.

Browning, Martin, and Annamaria Lusardi. 1996. "Household Saving: Micro Theories and Micro Facts." *Journal of Economic Literature* 34 (December): 1797–1855.

Cagan, Phillip. 1965. "The Effect of Pension Plans on Aggregate Saving: Evidence from a Sample Survey." Occasional Paper 95. Cambridge, Mass.: National Bureau of Economic Research.

Congressional Budget Office. 1993. *Baby Boomers in Retirement: An Early Perspective.*

Davies, James. 1981. "Uncertain Lifetimes, Consumption and Dissaving in Retirement." *Journal of Political Economy* 89: 561–78.

Deaton, Angus. 1992. *Understanding Consumption.* Oxford University Press.

Diamond, Peter, and Jerry Hausman. 1984a. "Individual Retirement and Saving Behavior." *Journal of Public Economics* 23 (February-March): 81–114.

———. 1984b. "The Retirement and Unemployment Behavior of Older Men." In *Retirement and Economic Behavior*, edited by Henry Aaron and Gary Burtless, 97–132. Brookings.

Gustman, Alan, and Thomas Steinmeier. 1997. "Effects of Pensions on Saving: Analysis with Data from the Health and Retirement Study," report to the U.S. Department of Labor, Pension and Welfare Benefits Administration.

Hamermesh, Daniel. 1984. "Consumption During Retirement: The Missing Link in the Life Cycle." *Review of Economics and Statistics* 66 (February): 1–7.

Hausman, Jerry, and Lynn Paquette. 1987. "Involuntary Early Retirement and Consumption." In *Work, Health and Income among the Elderly*, edited by Gary Burtless, 151–81. Brookings.

Honing, Marjorie. 1995. "Retirement Expectations over Time: Differences by Gender, Race and Ethnicity." Hunter College.

———. 1997. "Married Women's Retirement Expectations: Do Pension and Social Security Matter?" Hunter College.

Hubbard, Glenn, Jonathan Skinner, and Stephen Zeldes. 1995. "Precautionary Saving and Social Insurance." *Journal of Political Economy* 103 (April): 360–99.

Hurd, Michael. 1990. "Research on the Elderly: Economic Status, Retirement, and Consumption and Saving." *Journal of Economic Literature* 28 (June): 565–637.

———. 1996. "Labor Market Transitions in the HRS: Effects of the Subjective Probability of Retirement and of Pension Eligibility." RAND.

Hurd, Michael, and Kathleen McGarry. 1994. "Evaluation of the Subjective Probability Distributions in the HRS." Health and Retirement Working Paper 94-004. Institute for Social Research, University of Michigan.

———. 1995a. "Evaluation of the Subjective Probabilities of Survival in the Health and Retirement Study." *Journal of Human Resources* 30 (supplement): S268–S292.

————. 1995b. "The Predictive Validity of the Subjective Probabilities of Survival in the Health and Retirement Study." RAND.

Juster, Thomas, and James Smith. 1994. "Improving the Quality of Economic Data: Lessons from the HRS and AHEAD." *Journal of the American Statistical Association* 92 (December): 1268–78.

Katona, George. 1965. *Private Pensions and Individual Saving*. University of Michigan Press.

Kimball, Miles. 1990. "Precautionary Saving in the Small and in the Large." *Econometrica* 58 (January): 53–73.

Laibson, David. 1996. "Hyperbolic Discount Functions, Undersaving, and Saving Policy." Working Paper 5635. Cambridge, Mass.: National Bureau of Economic Research.

Laitner, John, and Thomas Juster. 1996. "New Evidence on Altruism: A Study of TIAA-CREF Retirees." *American Economic Review* 86 (September): 893–908.

Lusardi, Annamaria. 1998. "On the Importance of the Precautionary Saving Motive." *American Economic Review, Papers and Proceedings* 88 (May): 449–53.

Mariger, Randall. 1987. "A Life-Cycle Consumption Model with Liquidity Constraints: Theory and Empirical Results." *Econometrica* 55 (May): 533–57.

Menchik, Paul, and Martin David. 1983. "Income Distribution, Lifetime Saving and Bequests." *American Economic Review* 73 (September): 672–90.

Merrill, Sally. 1984. "Home Equity and the Elderly." In *Retirement and Economic Behavior*, edited by Henry Aaron and Gary Burtless, 197–225. Brookings.

Mirer, Thad. 1979. "The Wealth-Age Relation among the Aged." *American Economic Review* 69 (June): 435–43.

Poterba, James, Steven Venti, and David Wise. 1994. "Targeted Retirement Saving and the Net Worth of Elderly Americans." *American Economic Review, Papers and Proceedings* 84 (May): 180–85.

Shefrin, Hersh, and Richard Thaler. 1988. "The Behavioural Life Cycle Hypothesis." *Economic Enquiry* 26: 609–43.

Sheiner, Louise, and David Weil. 1992. "The Housing Wealth of the Aged." Working Paper 4115. Cambridge, Mass.: National Bureau of Economic Research.

Smith, James. 1995. "Racial and Ethnic Differences in Wealth in the Health and Retirement Study." *Journal of Human Resources* 30 (supplement): S159–S183.

Summers, Lawrence, and Christopher Carroll. 1991. "Consumption Growth Parallels Income Growth: Some New Evidence." In *National Saving and Economic Performance*, edited by B. Douglas Bernheim and John Shoven, 305–43. University of Chicago Press.

Thaler, Richard. 1994. "Psychology and Savings Policies." *American Economic Review, Papers and Proceedings* 84 (May): 186–92.

Thaler, Richard, and Hersch Shefrin. 1981. "An Economic Theory of Self-Control." *Journal of Political Economy* 89: 392–406.

Venti, Steven, and David Wise. 1989, "Aging, Moving and Housing Wealth." In *The Economics of Aging*, edited by David Wise, 9–48. University of Chicago Press.

————. 1990. "But They Don't Want to Reduce Housing Equity." In *Issues in the Economics of Aging*, edited by David Wise, 13–29. University of Chicago Press.

————. 1991. "Aging and the Income Value of Housing Wealth." *Journal of Public Economics* 44 (April): 371–95.

————. 1993. "The Wealth of Cohorts: Retirement Saving and the Changing Assets of Older Americans." Working Paper 4600. Cambridge, Mass.: National Bureau of Economic Research.

————. 1997. "Choice, Chance, and Wealth Dispersion at Retirement." Dartmouth College.

Wilhelm, Mark. 1996. "Bequest Behavior and the Effect of Heirs' Earnings: Testing the Altruistic Model of Bequests." *American Economic Review* 86: 874–92.

116

COMMENT BY

# William G. Gale

The most fundamental assumption in standard economic models is that individuals are rational decisionmakers who put to good use information available to them. This assumption implies that individuals and households are forward looking; that is, they form expectations (which may turn out to be false) about the future and act on the basis of those expectations. This general framework is quite flexible. It can incorporate a variety of assumptions regarding borrowing constraints, uncertainty, motives for saving, public policies, labor supply, family structure, and other factors. It can even incorporate different views regarding how far people look into the future. In the life-cycle model, for example, people maximize utility over their own lifetime. In the dynastic model, agents maximize the utility of a multigenerational family. In all cases, however, a key building block of the economic approach to the analysis of human behavior is that agents are forward looking and rational.

The behavioral approach is an alternative framework for analyzing human behavior, based on principles and insights from psychology. In the analysis of saving, the behavioral approach, in the author's words, "emphasizes the difficulties that households have in acquiring necessary information, solving complex maximization problems . . . , delaying gratification, and exercising the self-control necessary for saving."

Lusardi's paper has the laudable and ambitious goal of distinguishing between these two approaches.[1] Because both frameworks are broad and flexible and can accommodate, with a few additional assumptions, a wide range of observed behavior, distinguishing between the two approaches can be quite difficult. To cut through this Gordian knot, the paper focuses on the extent to which people are forward looking and the economic impact of being forward looking by examining the impact of self-reported measures of "thinking about retirement." The paper develops two novel findings. First, about one-third of households made up of persons between the ages of 50 and 61 say they have thought about retirement "hardly at all." Second, even after one controls for other variables, a statistically significant correlation exists between how much respondents say they have

---

1. Distinguishing between the two approaches need not be an "either-or" decision. It is plausible that the relative importance of the forward-looking and behavioral models varies over time, across households, and even over time for a particular household.

thought about retirement and how much wealth they have accumulated. Lusardi interprets the two findings as evidence in favor of behavioral models and against the life-cycle model.

My comments can be briefly summarized. First, to its credit, the paper examines an important distinction between the models that assume rational, forward-looking behavior and those that emphasize incomplete rationality and myopia. Many criticisms of the life-cycle model—some of which are featured in the literature review in the author's paper—focus on inessential issues. Second, I believe the empirical findings are open to conflicting interpretations. In particular, the meaning of the key survey question is somewhat ambiguous, and other evidence presented in the paper suggests that the author's interpretation of the question may be inappropriate. In addition, while Lusardi suggests that the measured impact of "thinking about retirement" is economically significant, my reading of the evidence is that the estimated effect is quite small and likely to be biased. Thus, I conclude that Lusardi's interpretations of the results are unduly critical of the life-cycle approach, in particular, and forward-looking models, in general, and are unduly supportive of the behavioral model.

## Testing the Life-Cycle Model

The paper focuses on a truly fundamental issue in the debate over the appropriate model of saving behavior—the extent to which people are forward looking. Unfortunately, Lusardi's paper fails to draw the distinction between the life-cycle approach and other forward-looking models, and so misinterprets some rejections of the simple life-cycle model as rejections of forward-looking behavior. For example, as originally formulated, the life-cycle model ignored bequests, presumably to focus on the dynamics of individual lifetime saving. But forward-looking people can plan bequests, and some "augmented" life-cycle models incorporate a "bequest motive," as do models that assume people plan for their descendants as well as themselves. Thus, the finding that people leave bequests does not rule out such augmented life-cycle models.

Likewise, Lusardi notes that some households "hold more wealth than the simple [life-cycle] model can rationalize." This fact, which requires some explanation, is not a reason to reject forward-looking models—which focus on foresight and planning—in favor of a behavioral approach, which argues that behavior deviates widely from forward-looking, rational saving decisions.

A second empirical finding—that consumption fluctuates nearly as much as income does—could imply that people fail to make forward-looking decisions, but it is also compatible with the assumption that people look ahead but are subject to borrowing constraints.

Lusardi argues that the failure of aggregate saving to rise in recent years is evidence against the life-cycle model. Baby boomers have been reaching their peak earning years, and, according to the life-cycle model, their saving should rise. Indeed, microeconomic data clearly show that saving rates rise with age through the peak earnings years, as predicted by the life-cycle model.[2] Aggregate saving may have fallen for other reasons—for example, because booming stock market prices have emboldened consumers—and standard measures of aggregate saving, which exclude capital gains, mismeasure the concept of saving embodied in the life-cycle model.[3] Thus, the performance of aggregate measured saving in recent years cannot be taken as evidence that people are not forward looking.

Lusardi's most important charge against the life-cycle model is that "most [households] arrive at retirement with little or no wealth." However, the finding that most households on the eve of retirement have little wealth is based on a very narrow measure of wealth. For example, Lusardi's data omit social security and pension wealth. Yet Gustman and Steinmeier, *using the same data set as the author*, but including social security and pension wealth, find very substantial amounts of wealth and conclude that including social security and pension wealth is crucial for understanding wealth accumulation.[4] Lusardi claims that a study by Poterba, Venti, and Wise supports the finding that low wealth accumulation is common.[5] Those authors, however, found that while median financial assets of households aged 60–64 in 1991 was about $14,000, median wealth—including housing, pensions, and social security—was $280,000, or twenty times larger.

Other studies claiming to show that most households are saving too little suffer from a series of flaws highlighted in the work of Engen, Gale, and Uccello.[6] Gale shows that about one-third of all households are saving quite substantial amounts, more than enough to sustain living standards in retirement.[7] About one-third appear to be saving very little, while

2. Attanasio (1994).
3. Gale and Sabelhaus (1999).
4. Gustman and Steinmeier (1998).
5. Poterba, Venti, and Wise (1994).
6. Engen, Gale, and Uccello (1999).
7. Gale (1997).

another third are saving just enough. Thus, the majority of households appear to be saving adequately, with tremendous heterogeneity in wealth accumulation patterns. This finding is perfectly consistent with the life-cycle model. A point that is not generally appreciated is that even if households were following the life-cycle model exactly, one would expect, in a cross section, that some of them would have accumulated too little wealth at a particular point in time to support their current income or living standards in retirement. This would occur, for example, if they experienced a recent shock to income or expenses, or because their expectations turned out to be flawed. Indeed, as Lusardi points out, "simple luck—good or bad—goes a long way in explaining the differences among wealth holdings of people of similar age and income." If so, then evidence of low wealth accumulation is not, by itself, evidence against the life-cycle model or against forward-looking behavior.

A related point is that it is impossible—not difficult, but impossible— simply to examine raw data and conclude households are saving "too little" to be consistent with the life-cycle model. For example, Lusardi notes that households in the 10th percentile of the distribution of financial assets have only $850 in financial assets. It turns out, however, that about 7 percent of householders in their fifties were in poverty in 1992. Thus, households at the 10th percentile were very near poverty. Even in a life-cycle model, one would not expect households in or very near poverty to accumulate much financial wealth for retirement because they will likely receive social security, medicare, and possibly supplemental security income in retirement, and because government means-tested programs, such as medicaid, provide strong incentives not to save before retirement.[8] The life-cycle model does not say that everyone will have a high wealth-income ratio before retirement. Rather, it maintains that households will try to smooth consumption over time. Thus, a family that is poor during working years would be expected to remain poor in retirement.

Finally, Lusardi writes: "Contrary to the life-cycle theory, households do not consistently accumulate wealth as they approach retirement but instead have very heterogeneous wealth holdings." This criticism has several problems. First, because this paper uses the Health and Retirement Study as a cross-sectional data set, it cannot provide any information on whether a household consistently accumulates wealth over time. Second, heterogeneous wealth holdings are not evidence against the life-cycle model or evidence that households do not accumulate wealth consistently.

8. Hubbard, Skinner, and Zeldes (1995).

For all of these reasons, the so-called "evidence" against the life-cycle model presented in the review of the literature in the paper is unpersuasive, and I believe that better evidence could be provided. Fortunately, however, the test involved in the paper does focus on an essential difference between the forward-looking economic models and behavioral models.

## Interpreting the Question on "Thinking about Retirement"

The HRS asks respondents, "How much have you thought about retirement?" While this question may appear straightforward, what it means is not at all clear. Lusardi appears to interpret the question as a direct test of the broad proposition that people's economic behavior is forward looking and of the narrow proposition that people have some sort of financial plan for retirement. But it could mean something more like "have you thought about your everyday existence in retirement" or "have you thought about what activities you will be involved in?" How respondents view the question might depend on the surrounding questions in the HRS. Further analysis of how respondents understood the question would be helpful.

In evaluating what the question means, it is important to note that the HRS and other data sources suggest that people do think about the future. For example, according to Lusardi and the literature she cites (see footnotes 26, 27, and 29), HRS respondents appear to be fairly accurate at predicting their own mortality probabilities at a point in time and the changes in their mortality probabilities over time as circumstances (besides age) change, and they appear to have a good sense of whether they will be working at particular ages in the future. Black households and households with low levels of education, both groups with lower than average income, are less likely to expect that social security will be cut back, which is consistent with the perception that social security provides a safety net. Douglas Bernheim has shown that households in the Retirement History Survey could predict their social security benefits fairly accurately.[9]

There is also evidence that households *act* on the basis of such information. In the regression analysis, the author shows that people in good health accumulate more (perhaps due to a longer life expectancy); people who are more risk averse accumulate more wealth (perhaps as a precautionary measure); people who think they will still be working at age 62

9. Bernheim (1988).

have saved less (perhaps because they expect a shorter retirement period); people who expect their earnings to fall in the future accumulate more wealth (perhaps as a precaution); and people who have higher variance of earnings save more (again, perhaps as a precaution). All of these items represent rational, forward-looking responses to expected future events.

In summary, the author's work and the rest of the literature appear to agree that people can predict their life expectancy, changes in their life expectancy, their social security benefits, and their likelihood of working past age 62 in sensible ways and that people with longer life expectancy, longer retirement period, greater risk aversion, and greater demand for precautionary saving save more. It seems too strong, therefore, to conclude that these very same people are not forward looking because of answers to an ambiguous question concerning how they think about retirement. On the other hand, it is fair to acknowledge that the evidence above can be interpreted in different ways. The fact that people's responses are broadly consistent with what happens could be because most people answer randomly and only a small proportion of people make knowledgeable forecasts. Even if enough people are forward looking to produce a significant regression coefficient with the theoretically expected sign, it may still be true that many or most people are not forward looking. Thus, the main points here are simply that the underlying survey question is ambiguous and that the author may be reading too much into the respondents' answers.

## Interpreting the Coefficient on "Thinking about Retirement"

There are two problems with interpreting the coefficient as showing that thinking about retirement causes people to save more by substantial amounts. First, it is unclear how large the estimated effects really are because the main results are presented in a manner that obscures their economic relevance (see table 3-8). Lusardi claims that the effects are economically important and that "for the average household in which a respondent has not thought about retirement, financial net worth is 12 to 19 percent less, total net worth 9 to 15 percent less, and expected accumulation 7 to 11 percent less than in households who say that they have thought about retirement."

This way of reporting the results, however, overstates the importance of thinking about retirement in three ways. First, it examines the results from ordinary least squares equations, which are affected significantly by outliers, rather than from median regressions, which describe the typical household. Second, it is based on percentage changes rather than dollar magnitudes. Since typical financial asset holdings are small, even a large percentage change may not translate into very large level changes. Third, by omitting social security and pension wealth, the results examine only one part of retirement wealth and therefore overstate the effect of thinking about retirement on retirement consumption.

Other ways of examining the results suggest that the estimated impact of the "thinking about retirement" variable on saving is small. For example, suppose that for the typical household social security and defined-benefit pensions will provide about three-quarters of retirement income and private assets will provide the remaining quarter.[10] If so, then the 12–19 percent decline in financial assets due to not thinking at all about retirement would reduce retirement consumption by only 3–5 percent. If one thought that undersaving for retirement was systematic and large, changing retirement consumption by 3–5 percent would hardly put a dent in the underlying problem. Put differently, if raising retirement consumption by 3–5 percent solved the "adequacy of saving" problem, the problem would not be very big in the first place, and therefore the life-cycle model may not be doing so badly.

A second example notes that the median estimates in table 3-8 suggest that the difference in assets between thinking "a lot" and "not at all" about retirement is about 7.4 percent of permanent income. Appendix table A-4 shows that mean permanent income was about $49,000. This suggests that thinking about retirement "a lot" compared to "not at all" raises financial assets by about $3,600 (= $49,000*0.074). If this amount were annuitized at 10 percent, the resulting increase in retirement consumption would be $1 per day. Evaluating the results at the median permanent income would surely give a smaller impact, but median permanent income is not reported.

Even using the ordinary least squares estimates in table 3-8 suggests an increase in retirement consumption, due to thinking about retirement "a lot," of about $2 per day. If those who have thought "not at all" about retirement have lower than average permanent income—as seems plausible—then the effect would be even smaller than reported above. Thus,

---

10. About one-sixth of elderly households depend on social security alone for all of their income, and about two-thirds depend on social security alone for half or more of their income (Social Security Administration, 1997, p. 20).

the *estimated* economic impact of "thinking about retirement" appears to be small.

This result may be explained in part, however, by the second problem: it may be that wealth accumulation affects thinking about retirement, rather than—or in addition to—the other way around. As wealth increases from relatively low levels, households may think more about retirement. For example, a household that receives an inheritance will have to decide how to allocate the funds. On the other hand, very high levels of wealth may cause a household *not* to think about retirement, since the adequacy of retirement income is assured. As a result, the regression coefficient could be biased in either direction. The coefficient would overstate the impact of "thinking about retirement" on saving if people with relatively low levels of wealth—for whom more wealth might induce more thinking about retirement—are dominating the results, but would understate the impact if people with high wealth—who no longer have to worry about retirement—are dominating the results.

# References

Attanasio, Orazio. 1994. "Personal Saving in the United States." In *International Comparisons of Household Saving*, edited by James M. Poterba, 57–123. University of Chicago Press.

Bernheim, B. Douglas. 1988. "Social Security Benefits: An Empirical Study of Expectations and Realizations." In *Issues in Contemporary Retirement*, edited by E. Lazear and R. Ricardo Campbell, 312–45. Palo Alto, Calif.: Hoover Institution.

Engen, Eric, William G. Gale, and Cori Uccello. 1999. "The Adequacy of Saving." *Brookings Papers on Economic Activity*, 2 (forthcoming).

Gale, William G. 1997. "Will the Baby Boomers Be Ready for Retirement?" *Brookings Review* (Summer): 5–9.

Gale, William G., and John Sabelhaus. 1999. "Perspectives on the Household Saving Rate." *Brookings Papers on Economic Activity*, 1: 181–224.

Gustman, Alan, and Thomas Steinmeier. 1998. "Effects of Pensions on Saving: Analysis with Data from the Health and Retirement Survey." Working paper 6681. Cambridge, Mass.: National Bureau of Economic Research (August).

Hubbard, R. Glenn, Jonathan Skinner, and Stephen P. Zeldes. 1995. "Precautionary Saving and Social Insurance." *Journal of Political Economy* 103 (April): 360–99.

Poterba, James M., Steven Venti, and David Wise. 1994. "Targeted Retirement Saving and the Net Worth of Elderly Americans." *American Economic Review, Papers and Proceedings* 84 (May): 180–85.

Social Security Administration. 1997. *Social Security Bulletin, Annual Statistical Supplement*.

TED O'DONOGHUE
MATTHEW RABIN

# 4 Procrastination in Preparing for Retirement

For many years economists have hypothesized that people may save too little because they lack self-control.[1]
Such studies have examined how people who seek immediate gratification
may sacrifice too much future consumption for the sake of current consumption and end up with too little retirement savings. We explore a second way through which lack of self-control can lead to too little retirement
saving: self-control problems combined with a lack of awareness of those
problems can lead people to procrastinate in finding and initiating profitable investment strategies, even when they recognize the enormous
importance of these decisions.[2] Through a series of "calibration" exercises

The authors thank Peter Diamond and other participants in the Conference on Retirement held
at the National Bureau of Economic Research in Stanford, California, May 1–2, 1998, for useful
comments, and Kitt Carpenter and Erik Eyster for research assistance. For financial support, we
thank the National Science Foundation (award 9709485), and Matthew Rabin thanks the Russell Sage
Foundation, the John D. and Catherine T. MacArthur Foundation, and the Sloan Foundation. This
research was started while Rabin was a fellow at the Center for Advanced Study in the Behavioral Sciences, supported by National Science Foundation grant SBR-960123. He is extremely grateful for
the center's hospitality and the NSF's support.
    1. This research dates to Strotz (1956); for more recent studies, see Laibson (1994, 1995, 1997).
    2. While we believe that people procrastinate in preparing for other aspects of retirement as well,
we shall throughout this chapter maintain this narrow focus on delay in investing wisely.

125

we shall show that for plausible degrees of self-control problems people can hurt themselves severely by procrastinating on personal investment decisions.[3]

Because investing for retirement is among the most important economic tasks people perform—or *should* perform—in their lives, positing procrastination as a major source of inferior retirement planning may seem odd. Given its immense importance, will people *really* harmfully procrastinate in preparing for retirement? We are afraid so. One of us, for example, has kept an average of over $20,000 in his checking account during the last ten years despite earning an average of less than 1 percent interest on this account and having easy access to very liquid alternative investments earning much more. While he (Rabin) may be an unusually bad procrastinator, economically significant procrastination seems prevalent. When explaining our research to colleagues, we have been told numerous anecdotes of people leaving pots of money in low-interest accounts, pots of money they realize they should have reinvested and had always *meant* to get around to reinvesting. These anecdotes come from economists, a group more sophisticated and less likely to procrastinate than average.

There is systematic evidence that people spend little time thinking productively about their retirement.[4] There is also research that identifies major problems in observed investment behavior.[5] Making explicit the mathematical implications of their decisions can cause people to behave more sensibly in hypothetical investment decisions.[6] But these results indicate a lack of attentiveness to retirement investments, because otherwise virtually all people over the age of thirty *should* already be familiar with the mathematical implications of investment decisions.

We are skeptical that procrastination as we have conceptualized it causes all or even most poor investments. But the fact that people do not bother to deal adequately with this immensely important decision invites serious investigation of plausible alternatives to the rational-choice model. Indeed, our final reason for investigating the procrastination hypothesis is that procrastination follows as a natural consequence of "present-biased preferences" in which people discount delays in gratification more severely in the

---

3. O'Donoghue and Rabin (1999b) illustrate how even mild difficulties with self-control can cause severe procrastination, and O'Donoghue and Rabin (1999a) show in an abstract model how procrastination is likely to be especially severe in situations similar to personal investment decisions.

4. See, for example, Benartzi and Thaler (forthcoming); Laibson, Repetto, and Tobacman (1998); Lusardi (1998); and Loewenstein, Prelec, and Weber in chapter 7 of this volume.

5. Benartzi and Thaler (1995).

6. Gneezy and Potters (1997); Thaler and others (1997).

short term than in the long term.[7] Such preferences lead to "time inconsistency," the systematic desire to reverse decisions made at an earlier date. Time inconsistency is among the most robust and extensively documented facts about human nature, confirmed by hundreds of experiments and millennia of folk wisdom. Because theories that incorporate time inconsistency often yield more realistic predictions regarding investment and other decisions than the rational-choice model, it is sensible to investigate such theories.

We shall set forth below a simple, formal model of present-biased preferences. The main characteristic of this model is that in any period people pursue immediate gratification more than they would have preferred if asked in any previous period. That is, people have self-control problems. We also examine an important matter for people with self-control problems: are they *sophisticated* or *naive*? That is, do they foresee or fail to foresee that they will have self-control problems in the future? Mild self-control problems cannot cause severe procrastination if people are fully sophisticated in this sense, and we focus on calibrations that assume people are fully naive. Even so, we show that our procrastination examples really only rely on people being a little naive.[8]

Our first set of calibration exercises explores the following question: does a person who has retirement savings in account A but knows it would be more beneficial to have the money in account B switch accounts? The person *should* transfer money if the resultant increase in retirement savings offsets the immediate cost of making the transfer. For example, suppose the person has $10,000 in an account and is planning to retire in thirty years. Suppose further that this account pays no interest whatsoever—a checking account, for example—and that the person has the opportunity to transfer the principal to an account yielding 5 percent annually. Making this transfer immediately will increase retirement savings by nearly $35,000 relative to never making the transfer. Thus, the person should transfer the money if the additional $35,000 in retirement savings thirty years from now is worth the immediate effort required to make the transfer.

For any plausible discounting and transfer costs, fully rational people would make this transfer immediately. But since the retirement benefits are

---

7. Hyperbolic discounting is one example of such present-biased preferences; see Ainslie (1992), for example.

8. O'Donoghue and Rabin (1999a) show that any degree of naivete can cause severe and costly procrastination. To our knowledge, that paper and this chapter are the only places that provide a formal analysis of partial naivete.

delayed and the transfer costs are immediate, people with self-control problems may want to incur the transfer costs in the future rather than today. Even so, people who are fully sophisticated and therefore correctly predict their own future behavior will not tolerate a significant delay unless their taste for immediate gratification is enormous.

If people are naive about their self-control problems, however, they perceive a very different problem. On any given day, they think they will make the transfer tomorrow if they do not do so today. Because the lost retirement savings from a one-day delay are minimal, even a small taste for immediate gratification can spark a desire to put off until tomorrow exerting the unpleasant effort required to transfer the funds. Each day, however, they make the same decision, and so tomorrow never comes.[9] Our calibrations show that for plausible investment decisions people ought to transfer the funds unless the transfer cost is enormous, and yet naive people might never make the transfer even when the transfer cost is very small. For the previous example of switching $10,000 from a 0 percent account to a 5 percent account, for instance, naive people might never make the transfer even when the immediate effort cost of doing so is as little as $7.

Our second set of calibration exercises introduces the idea that people can find better investments by exerting more effort and must decide how much effort to exert. We show that even when there is a superior alternative that requires no effort or cost to initiate—and therefore would not on its own spark the urge to procrastinate—people may still procrastinate if they ought to exert some effort toward finding a better investment. For example, even if it is *cost free* to transfer $10,000 from a 0 percent account to a 5 percent account, people may procrastinate severely if the optimal course is to exert some effort to find a 6 percent account. In such situations, people believe they are merely deciding when to transfer their funds to the 6 percent account, and therefore view other alternatives as irrelevant.[10]

We also find a paradox: as retirement planning becomes more important, people may become *more* likely to procrastinate. For example, with

9. For previous papers exploring this theme, see Akerlof (1991); O'Donoghue and Rabin (forthcoming a, forthcoming b, 1999a, 1999b). For other papers discussing procrastination as related to present-biased preferences, see Prelec (1989), who discusses delay of unpleasant tasks in a one-shot context (where naivete is irrelevant), and Fischer (1997), who develops a formal model of procrastination on big projects assuming complete sophistication.

10. Of course, this conclusion requires that there be some cost associated with transferring funds first to the 5 percent account and later to the 6 percent account.

$10,000 to invest, people might decide that exerting effort to find anything better than a 6 percent return is not worthwhile and immediately move the funds. But with $20,000 they might decide it is worthwhile to look for something better than the 6 percent account—a 6.5 percent account, for example—and put off until "tomorrow" the effort necessary to find this better investment. By similar reasoning, the more people value their retirement consumption, the more effort they decide to exert toward finding a good investment, but the more they may procrastinate. In contrast to many other types of suboptimal behavior, procrastination may often be *worse* for important decisions than for unimportant ones.[11] So, returning to the question of whether people are really likely to procrastinate on this most important of life decisions, our somewhat provocative answer is that people may procrastinate on investing for retirement exactly *because* it is one of the most important life decisions.

In the concluding section we suggest policies that might help people correct this major error they may make in preparing for retirement. These policies are inherently paternalistic. However, we shall emphasize policy prescriptions that satisfy the idea of "cautious paternalism," meaning that the policies can be extremely valuable if people are making errors, but they have relatively small costs if people are fully rational. Our policy prescriptions revolve around two principles that emerge from our analysis: people tend not to transfer savings out of their "default" investment plans, and people are highly sensitive to short-term incentives. The specific policies include manipulating default options; using 401k plans, IRAs, or other tax incentives for saving; providing workplace seminars on retirement planning; and using deadlines.

## Present-Biased Preferences and Procrastination

The standard economics model assumes that intertemporal preferences are time consistent. That is, a person who prefers future option A over future option B will not systematically reverse those preferences as time passes. But evidence indicates that preferences are *time inconsistent*. People often pursue immediate gratification in a way that their "long-run selves" do not appreciate.[12] To illustrate, suppose a person must choose between doing seven hours of an unpleasant task on April 1 versus eight hours of the

---

11. This theme is laid out in more detail in O'Donoghue and Rabin (1999a).

12. See, for instance, Ainslie (1975, 1991, 1992); Ainslie and Haslam (1992a, 1992b); Loewenstein and Prelec (1992); and Thaler (1991).

same task on April 15. If no new information becomes available, time consistency requires a person make the same choice if asked on February 1 or on April 1. We think, however, that if asked on February 1, most people would prefer the seven hours on April 1 ("to do less work next month"), whereas if asked on April 1 many people would prefer the eight hours on April 15 ("to not work today").

The example above reflects a specific form of time-inconsistent preferences that we call "present-biased" preferences: when considering trade-offs between two future moments, people give stronger *relative* weight to their well-being at the earlier moment as it gets closer. That is, people have a self-control problem in that they seek immediate gratification in ways they earlier would not have approved. We employ the following simple, formal model of present-biased preferences.[13] Let $u_t$ be the instantaneous utility people get in period $t$. Then their intertemporal preferences at time $t$, $U^t$, can be represented by the following utility function:

$$U^t (u_t, u_{t+1}, \dots, u_T) \equiv u_t + \beta \sum_{\tau=t+1}^{T} \delta^{\tau-t} u_\tau.$$

The parameter $\delta \leq 1$ represents time-consistent impatience, whereas the parameter $\beta \leq 1$ represents a bias for the present. For $\beta = 1$, these preferences are simply the discrete version of exponential discounting and are therefore time consistent. We shall refer to the people with time-consistent preferences as TCs. But for $\beta < 1$, these preferences parsimoniously capture the time-inconsistent preference for immediate gratification.

To illustrate, consider a simple formalization of the example above. Assume that the instantaneous disutility from doing work is simply the number of hours of work, so that $u_t(7) = -7$ and $u_t(8) = -8$ for all $t$; and that there is no time-consistent discounting, so $\delta = 1$. Suppose also that $\beta = 0.8$. On February 1 people discount both dates by $\beta$ and therefore choose to work seven hours on April 1 rather than eight hours on April 15. On April 1, however, people can experience a utility of $-7$ by working today, or experience a discounted utility of $0.8(-8) = -6.4$ by delaying the work two weeks, and therefore delay work.

A number of economists have formally modeled intertemporal choice given time-inconsistent preferences.[14] The standard approach is to treat a

13. This model was originally proposed by Phelps and Pollak (1968) to model intergenerational altruism and later adopted by Laibson (1994) to study self-control problems. It has since been used by Laibson (1995, 1997); Laibson, Repetto, and Tobacman (1998); O'Donoghue and Rabin (forthcoming a, forthcoming b, 1999a, 1999b, 1997); Fischer (1997); and others.

14. See, in particular, Strotz (1956); Pollak (1968); Phelps and Pollak (1968); Peleg and Yaari (1973); Goldman (1979, 1980); Laibson (1994); and O'Donoghue and Rabin (1999b).

person at each point in time as a separate "agent" who chooses current behavior based on current preferences and predictions of future behavior. These studies consider two extreme assumptions concerning a person's beliefs about future behavior. *Sophisticated* people are fully aware of their future self-control problems and correctly predict future behavior. That is, sophisticates have rational expectations about their future behavior. *Naive* people are fully *un*aware of their future self-control problems and believe their future selves will behave exactly as they currently would like them to behave. With the simple preferences we have described above, naive people believe that they will behave like TCs in the future.[15]

Severe procrastination does not arise merely from present-biased preferences, but rather from present-biased preferences combined with naivete. Because sophisticated people correctly predict future behavior, they always know exactly how long they will procrastinate if they do not complete some task now. In contrast, naive people can repeatedly incorrectly believe that they will complete some task tomorrow if they do not do so now. The examples of investment behavior in the next two sections will therefore concern naifs, with examination of the behavior of TCs and sophisticates included only to emphasize this point. But we shall also illustrate that our examples do not rely on complete naivete by modeling and analyzing the behavior of less-than-complete sophistication.

## Procrastination in Making a Known Investment

We now explore a simple investment decision in which a person *should* immediately transfer retirement savings from a current account to some alternative that yields higher interest, but may procrastinate because this transfer requires some effort.[16]

---

15. Strotz (1956) and Pollak (1968) carefully lay out the two extreme assumptions. Most research on time-inconsistent preferences has assumed sophistication (for example, Peleg and Yaari, 1973; Goldman, 1979, 1980; Laibson, 1994, 1995, 1997; and Fischer, 1997). O'Donoghue and Rabin (forthcoming a, forthcoming b, 1999a, 1999b, 1997) consider both sophistication and naivete. Akerlof's (1991) model of procrastination is not explicitly framed as a model of time-inconsistent preferences, but is formally equivalent to a model with time-inconsistent preferences combined with naivete (and indeed Akerlof emphasizes the role that mispredicting future behavior plays in procrastination).

16. This example is analogous to examples of procrastination in Akerlof (1991) and O'Donoghue and Rabin (forthcoming b, 1999b), where people procrastinate on an unpleasant task that they should complete immediately. While those papers and this chapter assume that the task at hand can be done instantly, Fischer (1997) considers procrastination when people must put in a fixed number of hours before some deadline.

Suppose a person has retirement savings $\$P$ and will retire in $T$ days (we often consider $T = 10{,}950$, which is 30 years). The person's retirement savings are currently in account A, yielding $r_A$ percent annually, and can be moved to account B, yielding $r_B$ percent annually, where $r_B > r_A$, at a cost of $C > 0$. $C$ incorporates transactions costs and the opportunity cost of the effort required to carry out the transfer. We assume that all costs incorporated in $C$ are immediate: $C$ does not include such costs as the loss of other investment opportunities that yield benefits only in the long term, but $C$ does include such costs as a forgone afternoon nap, a missed rerun of *21 Jump Street*, or any other attractive alternative. We further assume that interest is compounded daily, so that the daily interest rate is the annual rate divided by 365. Given these assumptions, the lost retirement savings from a $\tau$ day delay in moving the funds, $L(\tau)$, is

$$L(\tau) = P[(1 + r_B/365)^T - (1 + r_A/365)^\tau (1 + r_B/365)^{T-\tau}].$$

Table 4-1 shows the cost of a one-day delay and of never making the transfer. The cost of never transferring the funds is very large. In contrast, the cost of a one-day delay is usually very small. These are precisely the conditions that can generate costly procrastination.

We assume that the utility of retirement savings is proportional to assets held at retirement.[17] We also assume that the transfer cost, $C$, is measured in terms of the utility equivalent of dollars of retirement savings, and that this cost is incurred immediately. Finally, we assume that the investor has the present-biased preferences we have described. Thus if the person expects to incur transfer cost $C$ in period $\tau$ and expects to retire in period $T + 1$ with savings S, then period-$t$ intertemporal utility is given by $U^t = -C + \beta\delta^{T+1-t}S$, if $\tau = t$, and by $U^t = -\beta\delta^{\tau-t}C + \beta\delta^{T+1-t}S$, if $\tau > t$.

With this formulation, on day $t$ the person values a dollar invested in plan B at $[\delta(1 + r_B/365)]^{T+1-t}$ from a long-run perspective. If $[\delta(1 + r_B/365)] < 1$, plan B is more attractive the *closer* a person is to retirement. In this case, both TCs and naifs initially delay but eventually will transfer the money when plan B becomes attractive enough. If $[\delta(1 + r_B/365)] > 1$,

---

17. Our model also assumes that people discount retirement savings as if they will consume all the money on the first day of retirement. This assumption is not innocuous. First, because consumption will be continued during retirement, the value of retiring with a fixed amount depends on the discount factor and the interest rate, which are parameters we vary. Second, when people must choose their consumption allocation after retirement, their perceived value of savings entering retirement may depend on their sophistication, making our comparisons below between sophistication and naivete potentially misleading. We nonetheless believe that the basic insights of our model, and even the calibration exercises, would not be much altered by the more realistic and complicated model.

Table 4-1. *Lost Retirement Savings from Delay in Transferring $10,000 by One Day or Thirty Years*

| $r_A$ (percent) | $r_B$ (percent) | Lost retirement savings from one-day delay (dollars) | Lost retirement savings if never transferred (dollars) |
|---|---|---|---|
| 0 | 1 | 0.37 | 3,499 |
|   | 5 | 6.14 | 34,812 |
|   | 10 | 54.99 | 190,773 |
| 5 | 6 | 1.66 | 15,675 |
|   | 10 | 27.50 | 155,961 |
|   | 15 | 246.29 | 854,527 |
| 10 | 11 | 7.42 | 70,219 |
|   | 15 | 123.15 | 698,567 |
|   | 20 | 1,102.87 | 3,826,891 |

meaning that the interest rate, $r_B$, is high relative to the person's discount rate, $1-\delta$, plan B is more attractive the *further* a person is from retirement. In this case, both TCs and naifs will either transfer the funds immediately or never transfer the funds (though naifs may, of course, be planning to make the transfer at some future date). We shall restrict attention to cases where $\delta(1 + r_B/365) > 1$ because we think this assumption is more realistic and because it simplifies our analysis.

We now analyze behavior assuming that the person can make the transfer on any given day. Time-consistent people will choose on day 1 the best day to make the transfer (and stick to this plan). When $[\delta(1 + r_B/365)] > 1$, the best day will either be the first day or never. Because the lost retirement savings from never transferring the funds is $L(T)$ and the transfer cost is $C$, TCs will transfer funds immediately if and only if $C \leq \delta^T L(T)$ and never transfer funds if and only if $C > \delta^T L(T)$. That is, TCs transfer the money if and only if the present discounted value of the extra interest earned over $T$ years—$\delta^T L(T)$—is larger than the immediate cost of transferring the funds, $C$.

Unlike TCs, naifs do not directly compare transferring the funds immediately to never transferring the funds. Rather, if TCs make the transfer immediately, naifs repeatedly *believe* they will make the transfer tomorrow if they do not do so today. As a result, naifs make the transfer immediately if and only if doing so is preferred to a one-day delay; otherwise, they procrastinate forever, persistently planning to make the same transfer tomorrow. Because the lost retirement savings from a one-day delay is

$L(1)$ and the transfer cost is $C$, naifs prefer delaying one day if $C >$ $\beta\delta C + \beta\delta^T L(1)$. Naifs therefore transfer funds immediately if and only if $C \leq [\beta/(1 - \beta\delta)]\delta^T L(1)$ and never transfer funds if and only if $C >$ $[\beta/(1 - \beta\delta)]\delta^T L(1)$.[18]

## Behavioral Results: Naive Procrastinators versus Time-Consistent Planners

Table 4-2 presents our main calibration results for this environment: for various values of $r_A$, $r_B$, $\delta^{365}$, and $\beta$, the table provides the transfer costs above which TCs and naifs would never transfer the funds. The table shows striking differences between the circumstances under which time-consistent planners and naive procratinators transfer the funds. For all parameter values, TCs immediately transfer funds unless the cost of doing so is immense; naifs may never transfer funds, even if transfer costs are small. Table 4-2 illustrates not only the differences between naifs and TCs, but also the scale of the problem for naifs. Using our earlier example, when does a person switch $10,000 from a 0 percent interest account to a 5 percent interest account? Doing so increases retirement savings thirty years from now by $34,812. Naifs with yearly discount factor $\delta^{365} = 0.96$ and $\beta = 0.9$ value the benefits of this transfer at $(0.9)(0.96)^{30} \, \$34,812 = \$9,207$, but never make the transfer if the cost of doing so is merely $16. This seemingly self-destructive behavior is made more comprehensible, but no less harmful, by understanding the mind-set of naifs. They know that it would be insane not to make the transfer and plan to do so, but always *tomorrow*.[19]

Table 4-2 illustrates our basic point: Whether people *ought* to transfer the funds—and whether TCs do transfer them—depends on whether the present discounted value of making the transfer exceeds the immediate cost. But naive people with self-control problems transfer the funds only if the lost interest from a short delay is sufficient to overcome the desire to delay incurring the transfer cost.

18. Technically, this condition merely guarantees that naifs prefer a one-day delay on day 1. This condition is necessary and sufficient, however, for indefinite delay by naifs because a one-day delay becomes less costly in terms of lost retirement savings as the investment horizon becomes shorter.

19. The entries in table 4-2 are homogeneous of degree one in the principal. That is, if we multiplied the principal by 10, all entries would be multiplied by 10. For example, naifs with $\beta = 0.9$ and a yearly discount factor of 0.96 do not transfer $100,000 from a 5 percent to a 6 percent interest account even if it takes merely $40 worth of effort.

We urge readers not to infer too much from the calibration exercises in table 4-2. For instance, the results depend on whether people can transfer funds at any time or only at intervals. In the table people can transfer funds each day. Table 4-3 is identical to table 4-2, except that people can transfer funds only once a week. This change does not affect whether TCs transfer funds, but naifs become more likely to make the transfer. When naifs can transfer funds on any given day, they believe they'll do it tomorrow if they wait now. If they can make the transfer only once a week, they believe they'll do it next week if they wait now. Because a seven-day delay is more costly than a one-day delay, once-a-week transfers cause naifs to become less likely to procrastinate. In general, the less frequently naifs can transfer funds, the less likely they are to procrastinate.[20]

The results also depend on whether transfer opportunities arrive at irregular intervals. For example, people can often make transfers only on weekdays, in which case, each Friday people face a three-day delay if they do not make the transfer then. Such irregularity has no effect on TCs. But naifs now fail to make the transfer only if they prefer a three-day delay to making the transfer immediately. The general principle is that the delay that determines whether naifs procrastinate indefinitely is the longest delay they might face. In addition, transfer costs might vary from day to day— for example, because time has a higher value on some days than on others. In such a situation people never make the transfer only if the *lowest* cost is sufficient to induce procrastination.

These considerations would likely diminish the scale of procrastination from that in our calibrations. But we believe that such factors would have to cut predicted procrastination substantially—perhaps by several orders of magnitude—before it could be dismissed as an important factor in investment behavior.

## Behavioral Results: Sophisticated Procrastinators versus Time-Consistent Planners

The assumption of naivete is also critical in tables 4-2 and 4-3. We have earlier observed that sophisticates, who are fully aware of their self-control problems, are unlikely to severely procrastinate in this environment. Because sophisticates correctly predict future behavior, they fail to make the transfer if and only if on day one they prefer never to make the transfer

---

20. However, a "seven-day $\beta$" is likely to be smaller than a "one-day $\beta$," which would partially counteract the effects of less frequent transfer opportunities.

Table 4-2.  *When Time-Consistent People (TCs) and Naïfs Procrastinate Transferring $10,000 (Daily Transfers, Thirty-Year Horizon)*

| | | | | *Funds are never transferred if C is greater than values shown below (dollars)* | | | | |
| | | | | *Naïfs* | | | | |
| $r_A$ (percent) | $r_B$ (percent) | $\delta^{365}$ | TCs | β = .99 | β = .98 | β = .95 | β = .90 | β = .80 |
|---|---|---|---|---|---|---|---|---|
| 0 | 1 | .99 | 2,588 | 27 | 13 | 5 | 2 | 1 |
| 5 | 6 | .99 | 11,595 | 121 | 60 | 23 | 11 | 5 |
| | | .96 | 4,606 | 48 | 24 | 9 | 4 | 2 |
| 10 | 11 | .99 | 51,941 | 542 | 269 | 104 | 49 | 22 |
| | | .96 | 20,634 | 214 | 106 | 41 | 20 | 9 |
| | | .91 | 4,147 | 42 | 21 | 8 | 4 | 2 |
| 0 | 5 | .99 | 25,751 | 448 | 222 | 86 | 41 | 18 |
| | | .96 | 10,230 | 177 | 88 | 34 | 16 | 7 |
| 5 | 10 | .99 | 115,364 | 2,008 | 995 | 386 | 183 | 81 |
| | | .96 | 45,830 | 791 | 394 | 153 | 73 | 32 |
| | | .91 | 9,210 | 157 | 79 | 31 | 15 | 6 |

| | | | | | | | | |
|---|---|---|---|---|---|---|---|---|
| 10 | 15 | .99 | 516,730 | 8,994 | 4,457 | 1,730 | 820 | 364 |
| | | .96 | 205,279 | 3,543 | 1,764 | 686 | 325 | 145 |
| | | .91 | 41,252 | 702 | 352 | 137 | 65 | 29 |
| 0 | 10 | .99 | 141,115 | 4,016 | 1,990 | 772 | 366 | 163 |
| | | .96 | 56,060 | 1,582 | 788 | 306 | 145 | 65 |
| | | .91 | 11,266 | 313 | 157 | 61 | 29 | 13 |
| 5 | 15 | .99 | 632,094 | 17,987 | 8,915 | 3,460 | 1,639 | 729 |
| | | .96 | 251,109 | 7,087 | 3,527 | 1,372 | 651 | 289 |
| | | .91 | 50,462 | 1,404 | 704 | 275 | 131 | 58 |
| 10 | 20 | .99 | 2,830,753 | 80,544 | 39,920 | 15,492 | 7,340 | 3,263 |
| | | .96 | 1,124,561 | 31,733 | 15,794 | 6,145 | 2,914 | 1,296 |
| | | .91 | 225,989 | 6,287 | 3,151 | 1,231 | 585 | 260 |

Table 4-3. *When Time-Consistent People (TCs) and Naïfs Procrastinate Transferring $10,000 (Weekly Transfers, Thirty-Year Horizon)*

| $r_A$ (percent) | $r_B$ (percent) | $\delta^{365}$ | TCs | Naïfs | | | | |
|---|---|---|---|---|---|---|---|---|
| | | | | *Funds are never transferred if C is greater than values shown below (dollars)* | | | | |
| | | | | $\beta = .99$ | $\beta = .98$ | $\beta = .95$ | $\beta = .90$ | $\beta = .80$ |
| 0 | 1 | .99 | 2,588 | 186 | 93 | 36 | 17 | 8 |
| 5 | 6 | .99 | 11,595 | 833 | 416 | 162 | 77 | 34 |
| | | .96 | 4,606 | 313 | 161 | 64 | 30 | 14 |
| 10 | 11 | .99 | 51,941 | 3,733 | 1,865 | 727 | 345 | 154 |
| | | .96 | 20,634 | 1,403 | 720 | 286 | 136 | 61 |
| | | .91 | 4,147 | 258 | 138 | 56 | 27 | 12 |
| 0 | 5 | .99 | 25,751 | 3,086 | 1,542 | 601 | 285 | 127 |
| | | .96 | 10,230 | 1,160 | 596 | 236 | 113 | 50 |
| 5 | 10 | .99 | 115,364 | 13,825 | 6,908 | 2,694 | 1,279 | 569 |
| | | .96 | 45,830 | 5,195 | 2,668 | 1,058 | 505 | 225 |
| | | .91 | 9,210 | 954 | 511 | 209 | 101 | 45 |

| | | | | | | | | |
|---|---|---|---|---|---|---|---|---|
| 10 | 15 | .99 | 516,730 | 61,919 | 30,939 | 12,066 | 5,726 | 2,548 |
| | | .96 | 205,279 | 23,265 | 11,949 | 4,740 | 2,263 | 1,010 |
| | | .91 | 41,252 | 4,273 | 2,291 | 935 | 451 | 202 |
| 0 | 10 | .99 | 141,115 | 27,639 | 13,810 | 5,386 | 2,556 | 1,137 |
| | | .96 | 56,060 | 10,385 | 5,334 | 2,116 | 1,010 | 451 |
| | | .91 | 11,266 | 11,907 | 1,022 | 417 | 201 | 90 |
| 5 | 15 | .99 | 632,094 | 123,787 | 61,853 | 24,122 | 11,448 | 5,093 |
| | | .96 | 251,109 | 46,511 | 23,888 | 9,477 | 4,524 | 2,019 |
| | | .91 | 50,462 | 8,543 | 4,579 | 1,869 | 901 | 404 |
| 10 | 20 | .99 | 2,830,753 | 554,302 | 276,971 | 108,015 | 51,264 | 22,806 |
| | | .96 | 1,124,561 | 208,271 | 106,968 | 42,437 | 20,258 | 9,039 |
| | | .91 | 225,989 | 38,253 | 20,505 | 8,368 | 4,034 | 1,809 |

to making it immediately, that is, if and only if $C > \beta\delta^T L(T)$. This value differs from that of TCs only in the inclusion of the parameter $\beta$. Because $\beta$ in our examples takes on values ranging from 0.8 to 0.98, the cost thresholds for sophisticated procrastinators are 80–98 percent as high as for TCs. Like TCs, sophisticated procrastinators almost surely make the transfer.

In contrast to naifs and TCs, who under the assumptions we have adopted either make the transfer immediately or never make it, sophisticates might delay making the transfer. Intuitively, if sophisticates (correctly) perceive that they would make the transfer in the near future, given their self-control problem they might prefer not to make the transfer now. But such delays are brief (table 4-4). In short, people with sophisticated self-control problems will not severely procrastinate in executing profitable investments.

## It Only Takes a Little

Unfortunately, even a little naivete may be sufficient for people never to make the transfer. That is, even if people know they have self-control problems, but underestimate them slightly, they may still severely procrastinate.

As $\beta$ captures the magnitude of a person's self-control problem, we let $\hat{\beta}$ capture a person's beliefs concerning future self-control problems. Then sophisticates have $\hat{\beta} = \beta$ and naifs have $\hat{\beta} = 1$. People who are aware that they will have self-control problems in the future but who underestimate their size have $\beta < \hat{\beta} < 1$. We call such people partial naifs. Understanding the behavior of sophisticates helps one to understand the behavior of partial naifs. For any $\beta \leq 1$, there is some maximum delay that people are willing to tolerate, and in any given period they transfer funds if and only if waiting now would lead to an intolerably long delay. Because sophisticates correctly predict their future behavior, their "strategy" involves periodically planning to make transfers. Suppose, for instance, that people with $\beta = 0.9$ are willing to tolerate at most an eleven-day delay. Sophisticates might, for instance, plan to make transfers on day one, anticipating that if they do not make the transfer then they will do so on day thirteen (and if not then, on day twenty-five, and so on.).[21] The important point is that sophisticates complete the task when they do because they perceive future behavior to be *just bad enough* to make delay too costly.

21. Sophisticates might follow any plan that completes the task within twelve days and has twelve-day cycles—in other words, make the transfer on days two, fourteen, twenty-six and so on or on days three, fifteen, twenty-seven, and so on.

Table 4-4. *Maximum Delay for Sophisticated Procrastinators to Transfer $10,000 (Thirty-Year Horizon, 4 Percent Discount Rate)*

| $r_A$ (percent) | $r_B$ (percent) | $C$ | Maximum delay (days) | | | | |
|---|---|---|---|---|---|---|---|
| | | | $\beta = 0.99$ | $\beta = 0.98$ | $\beta = 0.95$ | $\beta = 0.9$ | $\beta = 0.8$ |
| 0 | 5 | 100 | 0 | 1 | 2 | 6 | 13 |
| | | 300 | 1 | 3 | 8 | 18 | 42 |
| | | 500 | 2 | 5 | 15 | 31 | 71 |
| 5 | 10 | 200 | 0 | 0 | 1 | 2 | 6 |
| | | 800 | 1 | 2 | 5 | 11 | 25 |
| | | 1,400 | 1 | 3 | 9 | 19 | 44 |
| 10 | 15 | 1,000 | 0 | 0 | 1 | 3 | 6 |
| | | 3,000 | 0 | 1 | 4 | 9 | 20 |
| | | 5,000 | 1 | 2 | 7 | 15 | 35 |

Now consider partial naifs who have self-control problem $\beta = 0.9$, but who naively think that $\hat{\beta} = 0.95$. Suppose that people with $\beta = 0.95$ would tolerate at most a ten-day delay. On any given day such partial naifs must believe that waiting today will lead to a delay of at most eleven days, because they incorrectly think that beginning tomorrow they would tolerate a delay of at most ten more days. But because our hypothetical example assumes that people with $\beta = 0.9$ are always willing to tolerate an eleven-day delay, people with $\beta = 0.9$ and perceptions $\hat{\beta} = 0.95$ never make the transfer. This example illustrates why even a little naivete can be sufficient to permanently forestall a desirable transfer. All that is required is that people be sufficiently naive to believe their future tolerance for delay will be at least one day smaller than their true tolerance for delay.

Table 4-5 shows the extent of naivete—the difference between $\beta$ and $\hat{\beta}$—required to permanently forestall transfers for various values of $r_A$, $r_B$, and $C$, assuming a $10,000 principal, a thirty-year investment horizon, and a discount factor of $\delta^{365} = 0.96$ (a 4 percent annual discount rate).[22] Table 4-5 illustrates that in general $\hat{\beta}$ need not be much larger than $\beta$ to induce severe procrastination.

To summarize, all that is required for severe procrastination is for people to believe they will be a little better behaved in the future than they

---

22. The conditions in the table are sufficient but not necessary to guarantee severe procrastination. See the appendix to this chapter for a derivation of these conditions.

Table 4-5.  *Degree of Naivete Required for Procrastination*
*(Principal = $10,000, Thirty-Year Horizon, 4 Percent Discount Rate)*

| $r_A$ (percent) | $r_B$ (percent) | C | Values of $\hat{\beta}$ above which funds will never be transferred | | | |
|---|---|---|---|---|---|---|
| | | | $\beta = 0.98$[a] | $\beta = 0.95$ | $\beta = 0.9$ | $\beta = 0.8$ |
| 0 | 5 | 100 | .9975 | .9665 | .9148 | .8116 |
| | | 300 | .9857 | .9554 | .9048 | .8038 |
| | | 500 | .9834 | .9532 | .9028 | .8022 |
| 5 | 10 | 200 | . . . | .9878 | .9339 | .8266 |
| | | 800 | .9897 | .9591 | .9082 | .8064 |
| | | 1,400 | .9855 | .9551 | .9046 | .8036 |
| 10 | 15 | 1,000 | . . . | .9837 | .9302 | .8238 |
| | | 3,000 | .9916 | .9609 | .9098 | .8077 |
| | | 5,000 | .9869 | .9565 | .9058 | .8046 |

a. The two blank cells are cases in which naifs will make the transfer immediately, and hence people with any degree of sophistication do so as well.

would believe if they were sophisticated.[23] This same intuition applies to the calibrations in the next section, although we shall not formally demonstrate it.

## Procrastinating in Choosing among Investments

If one interprets the transfer costs of tables 4-2 and 4-3 to be merely the cost of moving funds, the critical costs for naifs may seem so large that procrastination should not be a problem. However, the transfer cost should be interpreted to include not only the cost of moving funds but also the effort people *plan* to exert to determine where to transfer their money. Our calibrations in this section introduce the idea that a person can find better investments by exerting more effort and must decide how much effort to exert. When people must choose how much effort to put into some task, whether they procrastinate depends on how much effort they *should* exert. Because the optimal effort for important decisions like investing for retirement may be high, severe procrastination is likely to be a problem.

23. In an analysis that parallels that above, O'Donoghue and Rabin (1999a) show formally, in a more abstract environment, that any degree of naivete is sufficient to induce severe and costly procrastination.

The general formulation below is a stylized version of a more realistic situation that we wish to capture. People initially have their money in a low-interest account. There are many options through which they can earn increased returns, but costly investigation is required to identify the best one. There is a good alternative that can be initiated relatively easily—choosing one at random; and there is a better alternative that requires more effort—the probable improvement that comes with additional search effort.

Because even small differences in interest rates have huge effects on retirement savings, in such situations people *ought* to work hard to find the better investment unless the cost of doing so is prohibitive. Time-consistent people do so immediately. People with sophisticated self-control problems do so with at most a short delay. People with naive self-control problems *plan* to do so with at most a short delay, and therefore consider the good investment irrelevant. But if the effort required is large enough, naifs procrastinate just as we showed in the previous section.

Formally, we again suppose people have retirement savings $P and will retire in $T$ days, and that their retirement savings are currently in default plan A that has yearly rate of return $r_A$. Each day, they can keep their money in plan A; can transfer it without cost to an alternative investment, plan B, that yields return $r_B$; or can exert some effort $C$ to put it in a second alternative, plan C, that yields return $r_C$. We make the important additional assumption that people cannot invest in plan B now and later transfer to plan C.[24] Our analysis again assumes that $\delta(1 + r_B/365) > 1$, so that shifting to plan B or to plan C is more attractive the further people are from retirement.

In this environment people clearly should not leave money in plan A forever, because plan B dominates plan A. Time-consistent people will either choose plan B or plan C immediately. Because plan B yields intertemporal utility $\delta^T P(1 + r_B/365)^T - 0$, and plan C yields intertemporal utility $\delta^T P(1 + r_C/365)^T - C$, TCs behave as follows: transfer to plan C at $\tau = 1$ if and only if $\delta^T P[(1 + r_C/365)^T - (1 + r_B/365)^T] \geq C$; transfer to plan B at $\tau = 1$ if and only if $\delta^T P[(1 + r_C/365)^T - (1 + r_B/365)^T] < C$.

Now consider naive people with self-control problems. On any given day they perceive that if they wait they will choose either plan B or plan C tomorrow (in other words, TCs would do something the next day). In

---

24. But we note that we need only assume there is a small transactions fee for such a transfer. For example, if $r_B$ = 10 percent and $P$ = \$10,000, then the first day's interest is \$2.74. If people plan to transfer to plan C tomorrow, they would not choose plan B today for any transaction fee larger than \$2.74.

addition, plan B today is clearly better than plan B tomorrow. Thus on day $\tau$ naifs consider three options: choose plan B today, choose plan C today, and (plan to) choose plan C tomorrow. These options yield the following period-$\tau$ intertemporal utilities: plan B today yields utility $\beta\delta^{T+1-\tau}P(1 + r_A/365)^{\tau-1}(1 + r_B/365)^{T+1-\tau}$; plan C today yields utility $\beta\delta^{T+1-\tau}P(1 + r_A/365)^{\tau-1}(1 + r_C/365)^{T+1-\tau} - C$; and plan C tomorrow yields utility $\beta\delta^{T+1-\tau}P(1 + r_A/365)^{\tau}(1 + r_C/365)^{T-\tau} - \beta\delta C$.

Naifs behave in one of two ways.[25] First, when TCs choose plan B immediately, naifs also choose plan B immediately. Intuitively, when TCs find plan C to require too much effort, so will naifs, and because plan B is costless, when naifs intend to choose plan B they clearly do so immediately.

The more interesting and more relevant case is when TCs choose plan C immediately. When, as is typical, plan C is by far the right thing to do, naifs prefer plan C today to plan B today (unless they have a very serious problem with self-control). As a result, plan B is irrelevant to their decision, and the relevant question becomes whether to do plan C today or tomorrow. In other words, an analysis of whether naifs procrastinate here is essentially the same analysis as in the previous section, where we proceed *as if the best action were the unique action*. Introducing a costless option does not overturn procrastination of a costly option when the costly option is the right thing to do.

There is, however, a difference between this case and those we examined previously. In previous examples, if on day one naifs prefer to complete plan B tomorrow rather than today, they will feel this way on all future days and will never make the transfer. For the case we are now examining, we can similarly conclude that if on day one naifs prefer to complete plan C tomorrow rather than today, they will feel this way on all future days. But here this condition is not sufficient to ensure that the transfer is never made because people will eventually prefer plan B today to plan C tomorrow: as the investment horizon becomes shorter, the advantage of plan C over plan B decreases and eventually will not be worth the extra effort. Thus naifs will eventually make a transfer, albeit to plan B.

## Behavioral Results: The Good May Be Irrelevant

Table 4-6 describes the behavior of TCs and naifs for various values $r_A$, $r_B$, $r_C$, $C$, and $\delta^{365}$. Once again the calibrations assume a principal of \$10,000 and a thirty-year investment horizon. In all cases, TCs immediately move

---

25. For simplicity, we are ignoring the knife-edge case where TCs "barely" prefer plan C to plan B in period 1.

their funds to plan C. The table illustrates two components of naive behavior: whether naifs procrastinate in carrying out plan C, and if so, how long they wait before giving up on plan C and switching their money to plan B. $\beta^c$ is the critical self-control problem such that for smaller self-control problems naifs do not procrastinate, and thus choose plan C on day one; for larger self-control problems, $\beta < \beta^c$, naifs procrastinate. The last column states how much time must pass before plan B becomes as attractive as plan C.

Table 4-6 illustrates striking procrastination by naifs. In general, the magnitude of self-control problems required to induce procrastination is consistent with the examples in the preceding section. And when people procrastinate, they procrastinate for a very long time—almost twenty-six years in the first entry of table 4-6—at which point they do what they could have done for free at the start. For example, when people can transfer from 0 percent to 5 percent accounts for free, but can spend an extra $500 to find a 6 percent investment opportunity, even for a very small self-control problem ($\beta = 0.99$) naifs may do nothing for twenty-five years, and then transfer to the 5 percent account.

## The Bigger the Stakes, the Worse the Procrastination

Our calibrations in table 4-6 illustrate that whether people procrastinate depends on how costly the option is that they plan to pursue. Because as it becomes more important for people to prepare carefully for retirement, people plan to put in more effort, a paradoxical possibility emerges: the more important it is for people to invest wisely, the less likely they are to do so.[26]

To illustrate these principles, we consider a situation in which putting more and more effort into retirement preparation can yield a larger and larger return. Suppose that retirement savings are in some default plan, plan A, that has yearly rate of return $r_A$. As before, people can keep their money in plan A or can transfer it without cost to plan B, which yields return $r_B > r_A$. But now people can also choose from among several costly options, C, D, and E, with successively higher rates of return, $r_C < r_D < r_E$, entailing successively higher transfer costs, $C_C < C_D < C_E$.

---

26. O'Donoghue and Rabin (1999a) play out this theme in detail in a somewhat different and more abstract model; but investing for retirement is perhaps both the prototypical and the most important example of the general principles attained.

Table 4-6. *When People Transfer Funds: Choice of Alternatives*

| | | | | | | | Naïfs | |
|---|---|---|---|---|---|---|---|---|
| $r_A$ (percent) | $r_B$ (percent) | $r_C$ (percent) | C | $\delta^{365}$ | TCs | $\beta^c$ | If $\beta > \beta^c$ | If $\beta < \beta^c$ Move to plan B in (years) |
| 0 | 5 | 6 | 500 | .99 | | .986 | | 25.8 |
| | | | 500 | .96 | | .994 | | 25.3 |
| | | | 2,000 | .96 | | .999 | | 14.0 |
| 0 | 7 | 8 | 500 | .99 | Move to plan C on day 1 | .966 | Move to plan C on day 1 | 26.1 |
| | | | 500 | .96 | | .986 | | 25.7 |
| | | | 2,000 | .96 | | .997 | | 17.1 |
| 0 | 10 | 11 | 500 | .99 | | .892 | | 26.4 |
| | | | 500 | .96 | | .954 | | 26.1 |
| | | | 500 | .91 | | .991 | | 25.2 |
| | | | 2,000 | .96 | | .988 | | 19.7 |

In simple examples like those in tables 4-2 and 4-3, having a larger principal or a lower discount rate—two factors that make retirement preparation more important—make it *less likely* that people procrastinate in transferring money to a known alternative. Table 4-7 presents calibrations showing that when a person must choose from among alternatives, exactly the opposite can occur: having more money to invest or a lower discount rate can make people *more likely* to procrastinate. The calibrations shown in table 4-7 are based on the assumption that money is initially in a 0 percent interest account and that there is a thirty-year investment horizon. We also assume that $r_B$ is sufficiently smaller than $r_C$ to be irrelevant (as it was in table 4-6). For each case, the table shows which of the three costly plans—C, D, or E—TCs choose immediately and how large a self-control problem is required for naifs to procrastinate.[27]

The first three rows of table 4-7 show that having a larger principal can increase the likelihood of procrastination. To understand why, one should consider the outlook of naifs. In row three, for example, the best thing to do with a principal of $10,000 is to select plan C, the choice for TCs. Naifs would procrastinate in switching to plan C if $\beta$ < 0.949, but would switch immediately if $\beta$ > 0.949. With a principal of $50,000, naifs who intended to choose plan C would be less likely to procrastinate because an increased principal makes people less likely to procrastinate over any specific choice. But table 4-7 shows that plan D is now the best choice, as indicated by the fact that TCs now choose it, and naifs will procrastinate over moving this larger sum to plan D for any $\beta$ < 0.977. The increase in the critical value of $\beta$ means that even though the principal is larger, naifs are more likely to procrastinate because the transfer cost of moving to plan D is higher than the cost of moving to plan C. Similar logic applies when the principal increases to $100,000: people would be less likely to procrastinate if they stuck to plan D, but the more costly plan E becomes the best choice. As a result, people are more likely to procrastinate because of the larger transfer cost and despite the larger principal.

Rows four, five, and six of table 4-7 illustrate how becoming more patient, as expressed by a lower rate of discount (that is, having a larger $\delta^{365}$), can increase the likelihood of procrastination. The intuition is almost identical to that for an increased principal. Although becoming more

27. Unlike table 4-6, table 4-7 does not show how long naifs procrastinate because this characterization is more complicated here. For example, people might initially plan to choose plan D but procrastinate, and eventually complete plan C when it becomes optimal; or people might initially plan to choose plan D but procrastinate, later decide that plan C is optimal but still procrastinate, and eventually complete plan B when it becomes optimal.

Table 4-7. *When People Transfer Funds: Effects of Investment Amounts and Discount Rates (Thirty-Year Horizon, Plan A Yields 0 Percent)*

| | $r_C$ (percent) | $C_C$ | $r_D$ (percent) | $C_D$ | $r_E$ (percent) | $C_E$ | $P$ | $\delta^{365}$ | TCs | Naifs procrastinate when β is less than |
|---|---|---|---|---|---|---|---|---|---|---|
| 1 | 6 | 300 | 6.5 | 3,500 | 6.75 | 8,000 | 10,000 | .96 | Plan C | .990 |
| | | | | | | | 20,000 | .96 | Plan D | .998 |
| | | | | | | | 30,000 | .96 | Plan E | .999 |
| 2 | 8 | 300 | 8.25 | 3,500 | 8.35 | 9,000 | 10,000 | .96 | Plan C | .977 |
| | | | | | | | 30,000 | .96 | Plan D | .993 |
| | | | | | | | 60,000 | .96 | Plan E | .995 |
| 3 | 10 | 300 | 10.1 | 3,500 | 10.15 | 10,000 | 10,000 | .96 | Plan C | .949 |
| | | | | | | | 50,000 | .96 | Plan D | .977 |
| | | | | | | | 100,000 | .96 | Plan E | .983 |
| 4 | 10 | 100 | 10.5 | 2,500 | 10.75 | 9,000 | 10,000 | .91 | Plan C | .969 |
| | | | | | | | 10,000 | .96 | Plan D | .992 |
| | | | | | | | 10,000 | .99 | Plan E | .994 |
| 5 | 12 | 100 | 12.25 | 2,500 | 12.35 | 9,000 | 10,000 | .91 | Plan C | .934 |
| | | | | | | | 10,000 | .96 | Plan D | .985 |
| | | | | | | | 10,000 | .99 | Plan E | .989 |
| 6 | 15 | 100 | 15.1 | 2,500 | 15.15 | 9,000 | 10,000 | .91 | Plan C | .821 |
| | | | | | | | 10,000 | .96 | Plan D | .957 |
| | | | | | | | 10,000 | .99 | Plan E | .969 |

patient implies that people are less likely to procrastinate over any given plan, it also implies that the best plan is more costly, and as a result the likelihood of procrastination can increase.

The calibrations in table 4-7 clearly depend on the values we chose for the variables. We chose these values to be discrete representations of more continuous real-life choices, where there are decreasing returns to the effort exerted toward finding a better investment, but no upper bound on the amount of effort.[28] Although the calibrations involve large increases in the effort cost that yield only small increments to the rate of return, these are precisely the types of margins a person is likely to confront in finding investments with high returns.[29]

Consider again the rhetorical question from the introduction: "Given its immense importance, will people really harmfully procrastinate in preparing for retirement?" Economists often make the reasonable conjecture that people may make errors, but are less prone to do so when the stakes are high. Our calibrations in table 4-7 illustrate that this conjecture may be very wide of the mark when the error is *irrational* procrastination. Indeed, our answer to the rhetorical question is that people are likely to procrastinate in preparing for retirement precisely *because* retirement preparation is so important.

## Policy Implications

Our premise has been that people may err in one particular way in preparing for retirement: they plan to invest wisely but then procrastinate in carrying out these plans. Our formal model and calibrations illustrate this point for the simple decision to transfer funds from a low-interest account to a high-interest account. But we believe that the intuitions behind this model hold more generally. In response to changes in life circumstances, people often reassess their preparation for retirement. Many such situations have characteristics similar to those of our formal model: the decision is important and people would like to put in significant effort, but they would rather put in this effort tomorrow than today.

28. O'Donoghue and Rabin (1999a) show that the results illustrated in table 4-7 hold more generally when the choice set is continuous.

29. We suspect that procrastination might be mitigated by another type of error: people do not realize how much effort they ought to be willing to expend to find a slightly higher return. We conjecture that many people do not realize, for example, that earning 10.6 percent rather than 10.5 percent for thirty years on an initial $10,000 investment will cause their retirement savings to be $7,100 larger.

We now consider policy prescriptions suggested by our analysis. Because these policy prescriptions suggest ways to help people overcome errors, they are inherently paternalistic. But we focus on policies that reflect a kind of "cautious paternalism": they can be extremely valuable if people are making errors, but they have relatively small costs if people are fully rational. We believe that most people most of the time are better judges of what is good for them than government officials, economic theorists, and other social scientists are. But we also believe that people often make errors, that there is some discernible pattern to these errors, and that people can sometimes cause themselves significant harm by making the errors.[30] For this reason we think that it is worthwhile to explore the expected costs and benefits of different policies to correct the errors. Indeed, we believe that a program to *formally* explore cautiously paternalistic policies, where one carefully lays out precise conditions under which a proposed policy improves social welfare, would be a useful alternative to the rigidly antipaternalistic approach the field of economics has adopted. Such a disciplined approach would also constrain advocates of paternalistic policies by forcing them to examine carefully the costs and benefits of their proposals.

Our policy discussion also serves a second purpose. For many of the policies we consider—some of which already exist in some form or another—we explain how our model and calibrations predict that people should react. These predictions can serve as proposed tests of the descriptive validity of the model.

Our central finding is that people exhibit a strong bias for the status quo. They tend to leave their retirement savings wherever they now are, even when that is not the best thing to do, because they never get around to switching. This sluggishness suggests an obvious act of cautious paternalism: the government or employers could choose the default investment while allowing people to override this selection at minimal costs. For example, a portion of every worker's paycheck might be automatically deposited in some reasonable investment plan. If people are fully rational, the cost of such a policy would be small as long as workers can withdraw the funds inexpensively. For procrastinators, in contrast, wisely chosen default plans could have huge benefits.

Our model also suggests that people are very sensitive to short-term incentives. According to our model, people procrastinate in preparing for retirement unless the cost of a short delay overcomes their desire to put in

---

30. Another realm where people would seem to be making costly errors is the realm of addiction. See, for instance, Schelling (1992); and O'Donoghue and Rabin (1997).

the effort sometime in the future rather than now. Thus there is a role for policies that make the cost of a short delay loom larger, and for policies that reduce the effort required to take action and thereby reduce the desire to delay. As long as manipulations of short-term incentives do not significantly affect long-term incentives, they can be relatively innocuous to fully rational people while immensely benefiting procrastinators.

In this light, tax incentives that encourage people to invest in 401k plans, IRAs, and other retirement accounts may help overcome procrastination in preparing for retirement. The motivation for tax sheltering is not to improve the allocation of saving, but rather to raise the amount of saving, and our model sheds no light on whether tax incentives increase or decrease saving. But our model suggests that an unintended side effect of tax incentives is to increase the perceived cost of delay. If the default plan is taxable and the best likely alternative is tax exempt, the perceived cost of delay will include lost tax savings in addition to lost interest.[31]

A second way to make people perceive high costs of delay is to impose deadlines on financial decisions. A particularly simple way to do this is to allow less frequent transaction dates. If transactions can occur only on the first day of any given month, the first day of the month will loom as a deadline. People will be forced to recognize that if they do not transfer money before the deadline, they will be unable to make the transfer for at least thirty days. Such deadlines impose at most very small costs for fully rational people, namely the lost interest from having to wait until the first transaction date. But the deadlines can have a large impact in helping people overcome procrastination.

The government in fact imposes deadlines on certain financial decisions through tax incentives. Deposits in IRAs and Keogh plans must be made before the year's tax return is filed—April 15 for most people. We emphasize again that the motivation for tax sheltering is not to improve the allocation of saving. But this deadline is exactly the kind of "use it or lose it" proposition that can help overcome procrastination. Indeed for fully rational people, such a deadline ought to be irrelevant because they should maximize the advantages of tax sheltering by making maximum deposits at

---

31. A second beneficial side effect of tax incentives is that early-withdrawal penalties may provide commitment devices that induce people with self-control problems to avoid dissaving. Of course, if such commitment devices are useful, sophisticated people are likely to construct them by setting up a bank account with the desired restrictions; tax incentives for sophisticates would probably provide little commitment opportunity beyond what is already available. Naive people, in contrast, think they have no need for such commitment devices, and therefore tax incentives for naifs may have a large effect of providing commitment devices.

the earliest possible moment. But Lawrence Summers reports that 45 percent of 1984 IRA contributions were made in 1985. To reconcile this behavior with fully rational behavior, he attributes the timing to such reasons as "the advertising blitz that financial institutions put on every March and April."[32] We think our model provides a more plausible explanation. In fact, our model suggests that such deadlines may be exactly the right policy.

Our final proposed intervention, aimed at reducing the effort required to invest wisely, is to provide seminars in the workplace on retirement planning. These can potentially reduce the required effort in two ways: by providing helpful guidance and, if they are made part of a normal workday, by reducing the opportunity cost of focusing attention on investing wisely.[33] Such seminars might also help overcome procrastination by creating deadlines. If they are offered infrequently, people may perceive that not going to today's seminar means having to wait until the next one. Douglas Bernheim has in fact argued that organized retirement seminars can do a great deal to boost retirement savings.[34]

We present these policy prescriptions with caution. More analysis is required to determine under what conditions their benefits outweigh their costs. But because our model suggests that people may make major errors in retirement planning, we believe a careful consideration of cautiously paternalistic policies such as those discussed above is certainly called for.

## Appendix: Derivation of Tables

*Derivation of table 4-1.* The table merely presents $L(1)$ and $L(T)$ as defined in the text.

*Derivation of table 4-2.* As should be clear from the text, the critical cost for TCs is $\overline{C}^{tc} \equiv \delta^T L(T)$, and the critical cost for naifs is $\overline{C}^n \equiv [\beta/(1 - \beta\delta)] \delta^T L(1)$.

*Derivation of table 4-3.* We assume in table 4-3 that people can make the transfer on days 1, 8, 15, and so forth . Just as for table 4-2, on day 1 TCs

32. Lawrence Summers, "Summers Replies to Galper and Byce on IRAs," letter to the editor, *Tax Notes*, June 9, 1986, pp. 1014–16.

33. Offering employees a cash subsidy for attending the seminar on their own time may not be sufficient because the extra take-home pay may be perceived as a delayed reward.

34. Bernheim (1994).

directly compare making the transfer immediately to never making the transfer, and therefore the critical cost for TCs is unchanged. When TCs make the transfer immediately, naifs repeatedly *believe* they will make the transfer in seven days if they do not do so today. Given the lost retirement savings from a seven-day delay is $L(7)$ and the transfer cost is $C$, on day 1 naifs will prefer delaying seven days if and only if $C > \beta\delta^7 C + \beta\delta^7 L(7)$, and hence the critical cost for naifs is $C^n \equiv [\beta/(1 - \beta\delta^7)]\,\delta^7 L(7)$.

*Derivation of table 4-4.* If sophisticates delay for $\tau$ days, then on day 1 they must prefer to delay for $\tau$ days rather than to make the transfer immediately, which holds if and only if $C > \beta\delta^\tau C + \beta\delta^\tau L(\tau)$. Hence, the maximum delay for sophisticates is

$$\overline{\tau} \equiv \max\{\,\tau \in \{0,1,2,\ldots\} \mid \beta\delta^\tau L(\tau) - (1 - \beta\delta^\tau)\,C < 0\,\}.$$

*Derivation of table 4-5.* Let $\hat{\tau}_t(\hat{\beta})$ denote the delay *perceived* in period $t$ by a person with perceptions $\hat{\beta}$. To formalize a solution concept for partial naivete, we assume that $\hat{\tau}_t(\hat{\beta})$ is equal to the delay perceived in period $t$ by a completely sophisticated person with self-control problem $\hat{\beta}$ (which can be uniquely determined via backwards induction). If we then let $\overline{\tau}_t(\beta)$ denote the longest delay that a person with self-control problem $\beta$ would tolerate in period $t$, we can conclude that a person with self-control problem $\beta$ and perceptions $\hat{\beta}$ will never make the transfer if and only if $\hat{\tau}_t(\hat{\beta}) \le \overline{\tau}_t(\beta)$ for all $t$.

Unfortunately, both $\hat{\tau}_t(\hat{\beta})$ and $\overline{\tau}_t(\beta)$ will vary across $t$, making it computationally difficult to fully characterize the set of $\hat{\beta}$ that will induce procrastination. We can, however, arrive at sufficient conditions without too much trouble. First note that the longest delay a sophisticate with self-control problem $\hat{\beta}$ could perceive in period $t$ is $\overline{\tau}_t(\hat{\beta}) + 1$, and therefore a sufficient condition for a person to never make the transfer is $\overline{\tau}_t(\hat{\beta}) < \overline{\tau}_t(\beta)$ for all $t$.

Let $L_t(\tau)$ be the lost retirement savings from a $\tau$-day delay starting in period $t$ (and obviously conditional on not having made the transfer before period $t$). It is straightforward to derive

$$L_t(\tau) \equiv P(1 + r_A/365)^{t-1}[(1 + r_B/365)^{T-t+1} - (1 + r_A/365)^\tau(1 + r_B/365)^{T-t+1-\tau}].$$

It is convenient to define $A_t(\tau) \equiv \delta^{T+1-t} L_t(\tau) + \delta^\tau C$, and then

$$\overline{\tau}_t(\beta) \equiv \max\{\tau \in \{0,1,2,\ldots\} \mid C > \beta A_t(\tau)\}$$
$$\text{and}\ \ \overline{\tau}_t(\hat{\beta}) \equiv \max\{\tau \in \{0,1,2,\ldots\} \mid C > \hat{\beta} A_t(\tau)\}.$$

For any given $t$, $\overline{\tau}_t(\beta) < \overline{\tau}_t(\beta)$ if and only if $\beta A_t(\overline{\tau}_t(\beta)) \geq C$. By definition $\overline{\tau}_t(\beta)$ satisfies $A_t(\overline{\tau}_t(\beta) + 1) \geq (C/\beta)$. It is straightforward to show that if $\delta(1 + r_B/365)/(1+ r_A/365) \geq 1$ (which holds for all examples considered), then we have $A_t(\tau +1) - A_t(\tau) \leq A_1(1) - A_1(0)$ for all $t \geq 1$ and $\tau \geq 1$, which implies

$$A_t(\overline{\tau}_t(\beta)) \geq A_t(\overline{\tau}_t(\beta) + 1) - [A_1(1) - A_1(0)] \geq (C/\beta)$$
$$- [A_1(1) - A_1(0)] \text{ for all } t.$$

A sufficient condition for $\overline{\tau}_t(\beta) < \overline{\tau}_t(\beta)$ for all $t$ is then $\beta[(C/\beta) - [A_1(1) - A_1(0)]] \geq C$, and the condition used in table 4-6 is

$$\hat{\beta} \geq C/[(C/\beta) - [A_1(1) - A_1(0)]].$$

*Derivation of table 4-6.* As discussed in the text, on any given day naifs will consider three options: choose plan B today, choose plan C today, and (plan to) choose plan C tomorrow. First, consider the comparison of plan C today and plan C tomorrow. If we define

$$\tilde{L}(\tau) \equiv P[(1 + r_C/365)^T - (1 + r_A/365)^\tau (1 + r_C/365)^{T-\tau}],$$

then a sufficient condition for naifs to always prefer plan C tomorrow to plan C today is $C > \beta\delta^T \tilde{L}(1) + \beta\delta C$ or $\beta < C/[\delta^T \tilde{L}(1) + \delta C] \equiv \beta^C$.

Next consider the comparison of plan B today and plan C tomorrow. Define $t^*$ to be the first day on which the person prefers plan B today over plan C tomorrow. Assuming $r_A = 0$ percent,

$$t^* = \min\{ t \in \{0,1,2, \ldots\} \mid \beta\delta^{T+1-t} P(1 + r_C/365)^{T-t}$$
$$- \beta\delta C < \beta\delta^{T+1-t} P(1 + r_B/ 365)^{T+1-t}\}.$$

Note that $t^*$ is independent of $\beta$.

Table 4-6 then uses the following logic. If $\beta > \beta^C$, people either choose plan C on day 1 or plan B on day 1. In fact, for all examples we consider, they choose plan C on day 1 (which follows from $t^* > 1$). If $\beta < \beta^C$, then the person will choose plan B on day $t^*$.

*Derivation of table 4-7.* TCs clearly choose plan $K \in \{C,D,E\}$ that maximizes

$$\delta^T P(1 + r_K/365)^T - C_K.$$

For each $K \in \{C,D,E\}$, define

$$\tilde{L}^K(\tau) \equiv P[(1 + r_K/365)^T - (1 + r_A/365)^\tau (1 + r_K/365)^{T-\tau}],$$

and then a sufficient condition for naifs to always prefer plan $K$ tomorrow to plan $K$ today is

$$C > \beta\delta^T \bar{L}^K(1) + \beta\delta C \text{ or } \beta < C/[\delta^T \bar{L}^K(1) + \delta C] \equiv \beta^K.$$

Table 4-7 then reports the plan $K^{tc} \in \{C,D,E\}$ chosen by TCs, and the critical self-control problem $\beta^{Ktc}$ that will induce naifs to procrastinate on plan $K^{tc}$. To ensure procrastination for all $\beta < \beta^{Ktc}$, we must confirm that for each $K' \in \{C,D,E\}$ people do not prefer plan $K'$ today to plan $K$ tomorrow. For all examples we consider this condition holds.

# References

Ainslie, G. 1975. "Specious Reward: A Behavioral Theory of Impulsiveness and Impulse Control." *Psychological Bulletin* 82 (4): 463–96.

————. 1991. "Derivation of 'Rational' Economic Behavior from Hyperbolic Discount Curves." *American Economic Review* 81 (2): 334–40.

————. 1992. *Picoeconomics: The Strategic Interaction of Successive Motivational States within the Person.* Cambridge University Press.

Ainslie, G., and N. Haslam. 1992a. "Hyperbolic Discounting." In *Choice over Time,* edited by George Loewenstein and J. Elster, 57–92. Russell Sage.

————. 1992b. "Self-Control." In *Choice over Time,* edited by George Loewenstein and J. Elster, 177–209. Russell Sage.

Akerlof, George. 1991. "Procrastination and Obedience." *American Economic Review* 81 (2): 1–19.

Benartzi, S., and Richard H. Thaler. 1995. "Myopic Loss Aversion and the Equity Premium Puzzle." *Quarterly Journal of Economics* 110 (1): 73–92.

————. Forthcoming. "Risk Aversion or Myopia? Choices in Repeated Gambles and Retirement Investments." *Management Science.*

Bernheim, B. Douglas. 1994. "Personal Saving, Information, and Economic Literacy: New Directions for Public Policy." In *Tax Policy for Economic Growth in the 1990s,* edited by Charls E. Walker, Mark A. Bloomfield, and Margo Thorning, 53–78. Washington: American Council for Capital Formation, Center for Policy Research.

Fischer, C. 1997. "Read This Paper Even Later: Procrastination with Time Inconsistent Preferences." Chapter of Ph. D. dissertation. University of Michigan.

Gneezy, U., and J. Potters. 1997. "An Experiment on Risk Taking and Evaluation Periods." *Quarterly Journal of Economics* 112 (2): 631–45.

Goldman, S. M. 1979. "Intertemporally Inconsistent Preferences and the Rate of Consumption." *Econometrica* 47 (3): 621–26.

————. 1980. "Consistent Plans." *Review of Economic Studies* 47: 533–37.

Laibson, David I. 1994. "Essays in Hyperbolic Discounting." Ph.D. dissertation. Massachusetts Institute of Technology.

————. 1995. "Hyperbolic Discount Functions, Undersaving, and Savings Policy." Unpublished paper. Harvard University.

————. 1997. "Golden Eggs and Hyperbolic Discounting." *Quarterly Journal of Economics* 112: 443–77.

Laibson, David I., Andrea Repetto, and Jeremy Tobacman. 1998. "Self-Control and Saving for Retirement." *Brookings Papers on Economic Activity,* 1: 91–196.

Loewenstein, George, and Drazen Prelec. 1992. "Anomalies in Intertemporal Choice: Evidence and an Interpretation." *Quarterly Journal of Economics* 107 (2): 573–97.

Lusardi, Annamaria. 1998. "Information, Expectations, and Saving for Retirement." Working paper. Dartmouth College.

O'Donoghue, Ted, and Matthew Rabin. 1997. "Addiction and Self Control." Unpublished paper. Cornell University and University of California, Berkeley.

———. 1999a. "Choice and Procrastination." Unpublished paper. Cornell University and University of California, Berkeley.

———. 1999b. "Doing It Now or Later." American Economic Review 89 (1): 103–24.

———. Forthcoming a. "The Economics of Immediate Gratification." *Journal of Behavioral Decision Making.*

———. Forthcoming b. "Incentives for Procrastinators." *Quarterly Journal of Economics.*

Peleg, B., and M. E. Yaari. 1973. "On the Existence of a Consistent Course of Action When Tastes Are Changing." *Review of Economic Studies* 40: 391–401.

Phelps, Edmund S., and R. A. Pollak. 1968. "On Second-Best National Saving and Game-Equilibrium Growth." *Review of Economic Studies* 35: 185–99.

Pollak, R. A. 1968. "Consistent Planning." *Review of Economic Studies* 35: 201–08.

Prelec, Drazen. 1989. "Decreasing Impatience: Definition and Consequences." Working Paper 90-015. Harvard Business School.

Schelling, T. C. 1992. "Addictive Drugs: The Cigarette Experience." *Science* 255: 430–33.

Strotz, R. H. 1956. "Myopia and Inconsistency in Dynamic Utility Maximization." *Review of Economic Studies* 23: 165–80.

Thaler, Richard H. 1991. "Some Empirical Evidence on Dynamic Inconsistency." Reprinted in *Quasi Rational Economics,* by Richard H. Thaler, 127–33. Russell Sage.

Thaler, Richard H., and others. 1997. "The Effect of Myopia and Loss Aversion on Risk Taking: An Experimental Test." *Quarterly Journal of Economics* 112 (2): 647–61.

COMMENT BY
# Peter Diamond

Ted O'Donoghue and Matthew Rabin consider how people make decisions about whether to change retirement investments. The authors contrast three types of decisionmakers. Time-consistent agents rank various
alternatives the same way over time. They maximize the present discounted
value of a period utility function, with a constant discount rate.

The other two types of agent use a utility function that contains an extra
multiplicative factor with a value less than one. This multiplicative factor
reduces all utilities not experienced in the period when the decision is being
made. Such utility functions, like hyperbolic utility functions, lead to systematic changes in the rank ordering of outcomes with the passage of time.
The two types of "quasi-hyperbolic" discounters differ in their predictions
of their own future behavior. "Sophisticated" decisionmakers predict that
future decisions will be made to maximize the (future-based) same objective function being used currently. "Naive" decisionmakers predict that
future decisions will be made to maximize an objective function that does
not contain the multiplicative factor. Naive decisionmakers act as if they
could control their own future actions; sophisticated ones recognize that
their own future actions may not be what is currently preferred.

Psychologists have given us a pattern of responses as parameters change
in experiments where the context is held constant. The problem for economists is that the context of most economic decisions is endogenous and
may be changed as a result of past economic decisions. How should one
build models to capture such endogenous contexts? One answer is to do
comparative statics only for parameter changes that do not alter the context
and to be cautious about the implications for situations in which changes
in parameters may alter the decisionmaking context. For example, in the
cases O'Donoghue and Rabin analyze, one could consider the change in
the interest rate on either the higher or lower return alternative account
to be a parameter change that does not alter the context. But would adding
a third option also be just a parameter change that does not change the
context? With three choices, one of the options is not the larger or the
smaller, but is "intermediate." Does this new positioning have significance apart from the specific value of the interest rate? If so, applying the
model "fit" to data with just two choices to a setting with three choices may
be misleading. A similar question is whether the nature of a cost of imple-

mentation alters the context. That is, both the level of cost and "type" of cost may change.

Can varying a cost of implementation be treated simply as a parameter change when the source of the change in cost involved research on options and a decision? Is there some way of converting such contextual changes into quantitative form within a single model? If so, can one infer a cost-equivalent measure of the implementation action or must that be backed out from revealed preference?

With these warnings in mind, I note two preconditions for designing a model and presenting calculations of which parameters result in procrastination (and how much). First, one must accept the maximization model as being the appropriate one for this set of decisions. Second, one must accept the modelers' description of the set of alternatives over which the maximization is being performed.

The authors derive a "status-quo bias" for the naive and sophisticated agents. They show that the bias is likely to hold for a much larger range of parameter values for naive than for sophisticated agents. I am sympathetic to the idea that the issues modeled contribute to a status-quo bias and that procrastination can be reduced by the "cautious paternalism" the authors support. Yet, I wonder if the model of behavior has too few channels for behavioral effects. Human beings always ignore a vast array of potential decisions. At every moment, we might be thinking about changing every ongoing economic and noneconomic relationship. But we do not. What if there is an inertia about considering any decision, an inertia that might be overcome by factors that are not part of their maximization model? That is, the bases for choice, when one is confronted with a need to decide (as in an experiment) or when one has decided that "this is the time" to consider taking action may be different from the factors that trigger consideration of whether to think about taking action. I believe that such additional factors also matter. They do not contradict the O'Donoghue-Rabin analysis, but rather suggest a need to add to it (and so delimit it somewhat).

One possibility is that in some situations, people do not want to consider decisions or, possibly, do not want to make the calculations needed to evaluate alternatives for a decision. Some people avoid information that might be relevant for a decision, such as stopping smoking.[1] While the avoidance of information may come from a "cost of decisionmaking," I think the framework is too narrow. The avoidance of decisionmaking may come, instead, from the tendency of people to react differently to outcomes

1. Tamerin and Resnik (1972).

of acts of omission and of commission, a distinction that is not present in this paper's objective function. Some people might be willing to imitate the decisions of others but do not take actions because they are not willing to make a decision in the absence of a clear example to imitate. For example, telling people that their neighbors have purchased flood or earthquake insurance has a powerful effect on their willingness to buy insurance.[2] But if one hears that one's neighbor has bought flood insurance, has one received valuable information or just an example to follow? Similarly, some of the effects of employer-provided seminars on retirement planning may come not from the information they provide, but from the social process they set in motion. One is doing what others are doing—or doing something different from what others are doing—rather than simply making a decision.

Some public interventions may trigger decisionmaking that would not affect a maximizer of the type O'Donoghue and Rabin have modeled. Advertisements that remind people of an opportunity about which they are already aware might fall into this category.

An interesting part of the analysis in this paper is its focus on the implications of having two alternatives to the default option, not just one. The authors hold that procrastination is more likely when there are two alternatives to the status quo rather than one. Yet the choice set analyzed is restricted to a single decision among the two alternatives to the status quo at some point in time. They do not allow consideration of a two-move strategy, which would be superior for some parameters with the quantitative example they offer.

How people delimit their choices seems to me a central issue. The alternatives that the authors analyze do not explain how people make this critical decision. Yet, it is a critical part of the description of the behavior being considered.

A further issue in considering the objective function being characterized is how to date the benefits and costs in order to know how to evaluate them. Is dating to be done in terms of effects on consumption? That would be the natural approach for an economist, but I suspect that it is wrong. Just as most people do not integrate gambles into an evaluation of asset position, so too the benefits and costs of a particular decision about retirement investment are probably not based on an integrated calculation of consumption. If not, then how does one date the pieces that go with a deci-

2. Kunreuther and Slovik (1978); Kunreuther (1978).

sion? When buying mutual funds, for example, do people react differently to a front-load charge than to an annual fund management fee when each reduces the sum available at retirement by the same amount? We expect out-of-pocket fees to affect decisions differently from front-loads, but when the amount to be deposited is under the control of the saver, it is not clear how to draw such a distinction economically. Yet mental accounting suggests that such a distinction should be drawn.

In sum, this is an interesting paper. My comments highlight one of the great difficulties in formal modeling of the behavioral approach to choices. We know that how people make choices depends heavily on the context within which decisions are made. For that reason, the analyst needs to be very careful when using a mathematical formulation of a particular decision context not to carry the model over to a setting where the context has changed in a way that affects the accuracy of the model. Indeed, description of the relevant parts of the context is the critical first step in such modeling.

# References

Kunreuther, H. 1978. *Disaster Insurance Protection: Public Policy Lessons.* John Wiley.

Kunreuther, H., and P. Slovik. 1978. "Economics, Psychology, and Protective Behavior." *American Economic Review* 68 (May): 64–69.

Tamerin, J. S., and H. L. P. Resnik. 1972. "Risk Taking by Individual Option: Case Study—Cigarette Smoking." In *Perspectives on Benefit Risk Decisionmaking,* 73–84. Washington: National Academy of Engineering. Reprinted in *Uncertainty in Economics: Readings and Exercises,* edited by P. Diamond and M. Rothschild. San Diego: Academic Press, 1989.

ROBERT L. AXTELL
JOSHUA M. EPSTEIN

# 5 )

# Coordination in Transient Social Networks: An Agent-Based Computational Model of the Timing of Retirement

THOUGH MOTIVATED by a policy question, this work has theoretical dimensions. There are two related theoretical issues. One is the connection between individual rationality and aggregate efficiency—between optimization by individuals and optimality in the aggregate. The second is the role of social interactions and social networks in individual decisionmaking and in determining macroscopic outcomes and dynamics. Regarding the first, much of mathematical social science assumes that aggregate efficiency requires individual optimization. Perhaps this is why bounded rationality is disturbing to some economists: they implicitly believe that if the individual is not sufficiently rational, it must follow that decentralized behavior is doomed to produce inefficiency. The invisible hand requires rational fingers, if you will.

Experimental economics and psychology have produced strong empirical support for the view that framing effects, as well as contextual and other psychological factors, create a large gap between *homo economicus* and *homo*

Thanks are due George Akerlof, Chris Carroll, Bob Hall, Peyton Young, and participants in the Brookings Work-in-Progress seminar. Research assistance from Trisha Brandon and David Hines is gratefully acknowledged. This research was partially supported by the National Science Foundation, under grant IRI-9725302.

161

*sapiens.*[1] Individual rationality is bounded. The questions we pose here are: Does that matter? How does it matter?

To answer these questions, we have developed a model in which imitation in social networks can ultimately yield high aggregate levels of optimal behavior despite extremely low levels of individual rationality. The *fraction* of agents who are rational in such an imitative system will definitely affect the *rate* at which a steady state sets in. But the eventual (asymptotic) attainment per se of such a state need not depend on the extent to which rationality is bounded. Perhaps the main issue, then, is not how much rationality there is at the micro level, but how little is enough to generate macro-level patterns in which most agents are behaving "as if" they were rational, and how various social networks affect the dynamics of such patterns. Of particular concern are the puzzling dynamics of retirement.

In 1961 Congress reduced the minimum age at which workers could claim social security benefits from sixty-five to sixty-two. By any measure, this was a major policy shift. Yet it took nearly three decades for the modal retirement age to fall correspondingly. While various explanations are possible, we suggest that imitative behavior and social interactions—factors absent from traditional economic models—may be fundamental in explaining the sluggish response to policy.

For modeling purposes, one can represent retirement decisionmaking (and perhaps a range of other problems) in the following stylized terms. First, there is an initial state of the world in which the individually optimal age at which to take some action is $Y$. Suddenly, a policy is instituted exogenously. Given this policy, the individually optimal age at which to take the action becomes $Y^* \neq Y$. What one observes, however, is not the instantaneous shift from $Y$ to $Y^*$ that would be predicted assuming universal, fully informed, rational behavior. Rather, there is a long process of patchy social adjustments, in which different clusters of individuals migrate to $Y^*$ at different rates, with some groups perhaps not getting there at all.

In our model, the action in question is individual retirement, the exogenously instituted policy is the 1961 congressional reduction in the age of eligibility for social security, and $Y$ and $Y^*$ are sixty-five and sixty-two, respectively. The actual data are plotted in figure 5-1.[2] As noted above, it took nearly three decades for the response—a downward shift in the modal retirement age from sixty-five to sixty-two—to manifest itself. We develop

1. See the recent review in Rabin (1998).
2. We thank Gary Burtless for supplying these data.

Figure 5-1. *Male Retirement Rate by Age, 1960, 1970, and 1995–96*

Percent

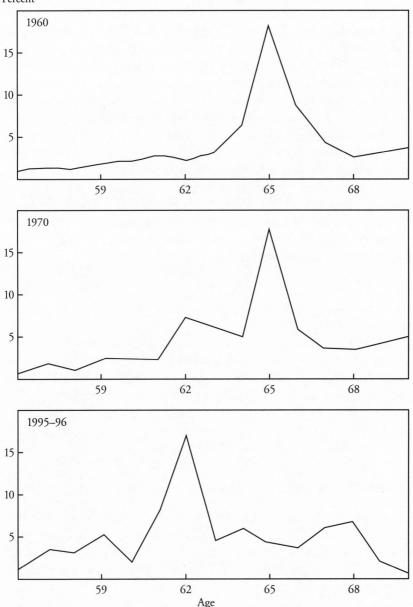

Source: Gary Burtless, personal communication.

a relatively general model, involving imitation in social networks, that generates such patchy and sluggish dynamics. It is not the only approach possible.[3]

One body of research has sought to explain the data with aggregate models in which a representative agent solves some life-cycle optimization problem.[4] If the goal is simply to fit the data, it is not unreasonable to attribute to agents the capacity to explicitly formulate and solve such dynamic programming problems. However, there is strong empirical evidence that humans do not perform well on problems whose solution involves backward induction.[5] For this reason, these models fail to provide a realistic microeconomic—that is, individualist—account of the phenomenon. We would like to provide such an account.

Our model does not invoke a representative agent but posits a heterogeneous population of individuals. Some of these behave "as if" they were fully informed optimizers, while others, indeed most, do not. Social networks and social interactions, clearly absent from the prevailing literature, play an explicit and central role.

# A Model of Retirement Age Norms

The agents in our model fall into three categories. One minority group of agents adopts the (presumably) optimal policy by a process we do not model. Another minority group is composed of randomly behaving agents who retire with a fixed probability once they reach retirement age. The majority of agents are imitators who mimic members of their social networks. For lack of better terminology, we designate these groups "rationals," "randoms," and "imitators," respectively.

## Agents, Cohorts, and Social Networks

The agent population is divided into age cohorts ranging from age twenty to age one hundred. Thus, there are eighty-one cohorts. Each contains $C$ agents for a total of $81C \equiv A$ agents. Each agent is assigned a random age of death drawn from $U[60, 100]$.[6] The average death age is thus eighty.

3. See, for instance, Burtless (1986).
4. See, for example, Rust and Phelan (1997); Laibson, Repetto, and Tobacman (1998).
5. See Camerer (1997).
6. Certain variables in our model are assigned random values. In all cases below, the random variables are assumed to be uniformly distributed. The uniform (that is, rectangular) distribution on the interval $[a, b]$ is denoted $U[a, b]$.

When an agent dies, it is replaced by a twenty-year-old agent.[7] In each time period each agent is activated exactly once, and if it is eligible to retire but has not yet done so, decides whether or not to retire.[8]

Agents are heterogeneous by social network; each has its own. A social network is simply a list of other agents, specified randomly and fixed over the agent's lifetime. The number of other agents is set by drawing a random network size, $S$, from $U[a, b]$. Some of these agents may be younger or older than the agent in question. The extent, $E$, represents how far the agent's social network extends above and below its own age cohort; $E$ is drawn from $U[0, c]$. Thus one agent might have a social network of seventeen others, ranging in age from five years younger to five years older than itself, while another agent might have a social network consisting of thirteen others who are all within a year of its own age. Any two networks may or may not overlap, that is, have agents in common.

At any given time, the set of all social networks constitutes a single random graph, with the agents as nodes and the network relations as directed edges.[9] Figure 5-2 shows a variety of social networks (see final color plate). Each rectangle represents an agent and each row represents an age cohort, with progressively older cohorts arrayed from top to bottom in the figure. Social networks are shown with X's for the three agents who are colored black, in the sixty, seventy-seven, and ninety-four age cohorts. The twenty-four members of the sixty-year-old agent's social network include thirteen younger agents and eleven older agents.

## Agent Types

As noted earlier, there are three broad types of agents. Rational agents retire at the earliest possible age allowed by government policy. Random agents retire with probability $p$ each period, once they reach the age of eligibility for retirement.

Imitator agents are the most heterogeneous and interesting. Each imitator has a unique social network. Within this individual network, there is some fraction $f$ of eligible agents who have actually retired. At each instant this is heterogeneous across agents, since the size and composition

7. The number of cohorts, number of agents per cohort, and distribution of death ages are all easily modified in the software that we have created for this model.

8. In the computational implementation of the model, the order of agent activation is randomized within cohorts in each period. It is commonly held that such randomization is necessary in order to suppress so-called simulation artifacts, that is, spurious correlation in the agent population.

9. For more on social networks, see Kochen (1989) and Scott (1991).

of networks are agent-specific. Agents are assigned an *imitation threshold*, $\tau$, representing the minimum proportion of members of the agent's social network who must be retired for that agent to retire. Each agent's behavioral rule then amounts to comparing $\tau$ with $f$.[10] If $f \geq \tau$, the agent retires; otherwise, the agent continues working until the following period, when it reevaluates its decision.

Notionally, the imitator agents play a simple coordination game within their social networks.[11] That is, agents derive utility from coordinating their behavior with the members of their social network. At every instant each agent in the population is either working or retired. Since $A$ is the number of agents, call $x \in \{working, retired\}^A$ the state of the population, and $x_i$ agent $i$'s state. Agent $i$'s social network is denoted by $N_i$. Then the utility that $i$ derives from interacting with the members of its social network in state $x$, $U_i(x)$, can be written

$$U_i(x) = \sum_{j \in N_i} u(x_i, x_j),$$

where $u(x_i, x_j)$ is the utility of $i$'s interaction with $j$.

The function $u$ can be thought of as the payoff function of a two-by-two symmetric game:

|  | work | retire |
|---|---|---|
| work | $w,w$ | $0,0$ |
| retire | $0,0$ | $r,r$ |

$U_i$ is then the payoff function of the social network game. Note that $\tau$ can be expressed in payoff terms. When an agent is young and none of its social peers are retired, $f = 0$, and the agent derives maximum utility from working. However, as its friends begin to retire ($f > 0$), the utility from retiring rises to $rf$, and the utility from working falls from $w$ to $w(1 - f)$. The agent will decide to retire if $f$ rises to a level such that $rf \geq w(1 - f)$, or equivalently, $f \geq w/(r + w)$; thus, the agent's imitation threshold $\tau$ in terms of payoffs is $w/(r + w)$.

In this social network game, then, how does the shift to earlier retirement diffuse through coupled heterogeneous networks? And how do the dynamics vary with key parameters, such as the number of rational agents,

10. It makes a difference to the numerical results whether an agent considers all agents in its social network or only those who are eligible to retire. The qualitative character of the results described below, however, does not depend on this distinction.

11. This development closely follows Young (1998, pp. 3–4).

the distribution of imitation thresholds, and the probability that a random player will retire when eligible? We resolve these questions quantitatively below by appeal to an agent-based computational model.[12] Before delving into detailed analysis of the model, however, a brief introduction to the general approach is in order.

## Agent-Based Computational Models

Compactly, in agent-based computational models, a population of data structures representing individual agents is instantiated and permitted to interact.[13] One then looks for systematic regularities—often at the macro level—to emerge from the local interactions of the agents. The shorthand for this is that macroscopic regularities "grow" from the bottom up. No equations governing the overall social structure are stipulated in multi-agent computational models, thus avoiding any aggregation or misspecification bias. Typically, the only equations present are those used by individual agents for decisionmaking. Different agents may have different decision rules and different information; usually, no agents have global information, and the behavioral rules involve bounded computational capacities—the agents are "simple." This relatively new methodology facilitates the modeling of agent heterogeneity, boundedly rational behavior, nonequilibrium dynamics, and spatial processes.[14] A particularly natural way to implement agent-based models is through "object-oriented" programming. Our object-oriented implementation of the present model is described in the appendix.

## Establishment of an Age Sixty-Five Norm: Two Realizations of the Model

We begin our analysis by describing in detail two particular realizations of our model, one with a relatively large fraction of rational agents and the other with relatively few. Because the model involves stochastic elements,

12. Coordination games on *fixed* social networks have been studied by Blume (1995) and Young (1998). But because our networks are transient, their analytical results do not apply.

13 For extended discussions of the agent-based computational approach, see Epstein and Axtell (1996); Axelrod (1997).

14. For more on the comparative advantages of this modeling technique, see Epstein and Axtell (1996).

each realization is essentially unique, even for fixed numerical values of all parameters. While we do characterize large numbers of realizations statistically below, we first focus on individual realizations, in order to build up some intuition about how the model works.

In all runs of the model described below, each cohort consists of $C = 100$ agents. Therefore the population size, $A$, is 8100. The size of each individual's social network is set by drawing a random number from U[10, 25]. Each agent's network extends up to five age cohorts above and below its own. Imitating agents have a homogeneous imitation threshold, $\tau$, of 0.5, meaning that 50 percent of the members of an agent's social network must be retired before that agent will retire. Random agents retire with probability $p = 0.5$ each period, once they are eligible. The government age of eligibility for retirement is sixty-five, and there is no age of forced retirement.

In the first realization, 15 percent of the agents are rationals, 80 percent are imitators, and 5 percent are randoms. Animation 5-1 portrays the evolution of retirement in this society and conveys a sense of how imitation propagates the retirement decision through social networks.[15] As in figure 5-2, each agent is a rectangle. Agents are arrayed across the page by cohort and down the page by increasing age. Retired agents are shown in red and dead agents are colored white. Among the unretired agents, the pink agents are rationals, the blue agents are imitators, and the few yellow agents are randoms.

It is worthwhile to explain exactly how to "read" an animation. At the start, there are one hundred agents in each of eighty-one age cohorts, of which the eldest forty-six are displayed. So, the top row of the animation represents one hundred agents of age fifty-five. Call the upper left-hand agent Tom. In matrix notation, at time $t = 1$, Tom is cell (1, 1). At $t = 2$, Tom is the cell immediately below: (2, 1). In general, at time $t$, Tom is cell $(t, 1)$. A change in color indicates that an agent has either retired or died.

In animation 5-1, notice that a uniform retirement age of sixty-five quickly sets in, despite the fact that only a fairly small minority (15 percent) of the population arrives at this decision rationally. Figure 5-3 gives a time-series plot of the fraction of agents eligible for retirement who actually are retired. Note that this trajectory is essentially monotone. Within the first six periods, essentially all of the eligible population retires.

15. QuickTime™ movies of this and subsequent animations in this chapter are available at ⟨http://www.brook.edu/es/dynamics/papers/retirement [July 1997]⟩.

Figure 5-3. *Fraction of Eligible Agents Retired over Time, Typical Realization, 15 Percent Rational Agents*

Fraction retired

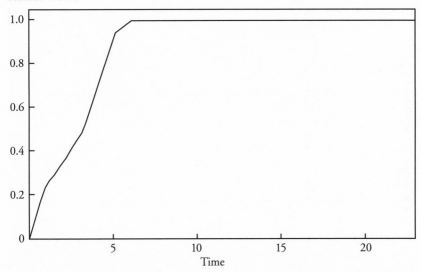

Time

In the second realization, the mix of agent types is changed: now only 5 percent of the agents are rationals and 90 percent are imitators. Animation 5-2 is a typical result. Note that the older cohorts show extensive fluctuation in retirement levels before the system converges to full retirement at age sixty-five. It is as if retirement "percolates up" from older to younger agents. Figure 5-4 gives the time series of the fraction of agents eligible for retirement who are retired. It takes a long time for the absorbing state to be achieved in this case. Notice that now the trajectory is not monotone.

## Some Sensitivity Analysis

Each of the realizations described above yields interesting qualitative information about the model. However, in order to characterize the model's overall behavior quantitatively, it is necessary to make many realizations for a particular set of parameters and progressively build up a statistical portrait of the solution space computationally. That is, the intrinsic stochasticity of the model can be approximately characterized through a sufficiently large number of realizations. Once this is done for a particular configuration, one can study the effect of varying parameters.

Figure 5-4.  *Fraction of Eligible Agents Retired over Time, Typical Realization,*
*5 Percent Rational Agents*

Fraction retired

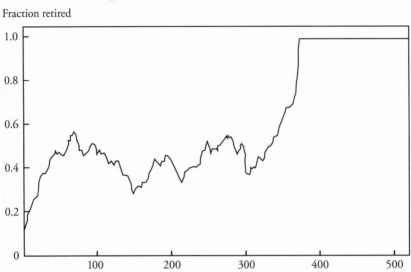

Time

We first define a base case configuration of the model:

| Parameter | Value |
|---|---|
| Agents/cohort ($C$) | 100 |
| Rational agents | 10 percent |
| Imitative agents | 85 percent |
| Imitation threshold ($\tau$) | 0.50 |
| Social network size ($S$) | U[10, 25] |
| Network age extent ($E$) | U[0, 5] |
| Random agents | 5 percent |
| $p$ | 0.50 |

We study the effect of each of these parameters on the time required for the age sixty-five retirement norm to emerge, the *transition time*. The first parameter, the number of agents per cohort ($C$), was found to have no effect on the average transition time for $C > 100$. So we begin our exploration of the model by varying the relative proportions of the three agent types—rationals, imitators, and randoms—keeping all other parameters as in the base case. We performed fifty realizations for each configuration of the model and estimated mean transition times along with standard deviations. Figure 5-5

Figure 5-5. *Effect of Fraction of Rational Agents on Transition to Age 65 Retirement Norm, by Fraction of Randomly Behaving Agents*

Transition time

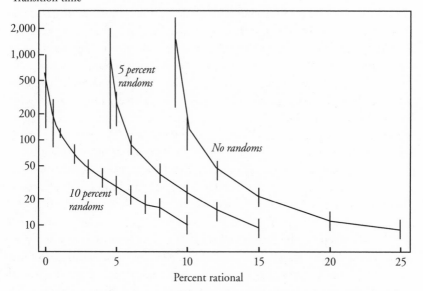

Percent rational

shows the average transition times for three levels of randomly behaving agents as a function of the fraction of rationals (and hence imitators). Note that the ordinate is in logarithmic coordinates; error bars are ±1 standard deviation and are asymmetrical, due to the logarithmic scale.

Reducing the proportion of rationals, while holding constant the proportion of randoms, increases transition time. When randoms comprise 0 or 5 percent of the population, certain minimum proportions of the population must be rational for a retirement age norm to arise. For a given fraction of rationals, the transition time decreases as the proportion of randoms increases. Notice that the variances increase rapidly with transition times.

Our next sensitivity analysis concerns the effect of the imitation threshold ($\tau$) on transition time. Since social networks are composed of individuals, the fraction of agents in a given network who are engaged in some behavior can only take on certain discrete values. That is, small changes in $\tau$ may have no effect on agent decisionmaking, and thus no effect on transition times. For example, imagine that all agents have social networks of size ten. Clearly, increasing $\tau$ from 0.55 to 0.58 has no effect; agents either have five or fewer retired agents in their network or they have six or more. Only when $\tau$ is moved across a discrete boundary, such as from 0.58 to 0.62, is there an effect.

Therefore instead of studying the dependence of transition times on the average imitation threshold—surely a very "lumpy" dependence—we investigate the effect of making the threshold progressively more heterogeneous in the agent population while holding the average value of τ constant. Figure 5-6 shows how transition times depend on the standard deviation in the imitation threshold, with the average threshold fixed at 0.50. Once again, the ordinate is in logarithmic coordinates. Increasing the variance in the threshold decreases the average transition time. The reason is that in high-variance populations there are relatively more agents with low thresholds, and these agents quickly retire, leading the rest of the population to retire quickly as well. Note that when there is low variance in the imitation threshold, there is significantly more variance in transition time.

The three panels of figure 5-7 explore the dependence of transition time on the size of agent networks (*S*). The separate (and opposite) effects of changing the average size and the size variance are presented in the first two panels. They are combined to produce the overall effect shown in the third panel. In particular, the first panel describes the effect of increasing network size, holding variance constant. Note that the time required to transit to a uniform retirement age increases very rapidly with increasing social network size; in large networks, it is difficult for a new norm to become established.

Figure 5-6. *Effect of Standard Deviation in Imitation Threshold on Transition to Age 65 Retirement Norm*

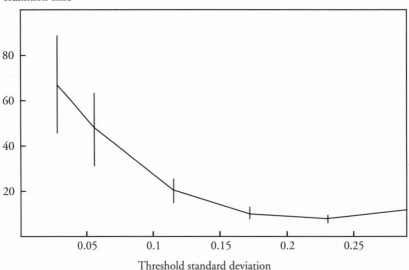

Transition time

Threshold standard deviation

Figure 5-7. *Effect of Size of Social Network on Transition to Age 65 Retirement Norm*

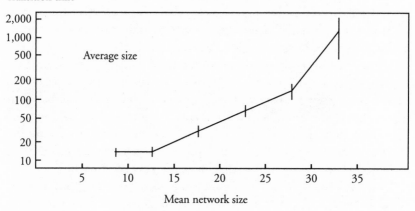

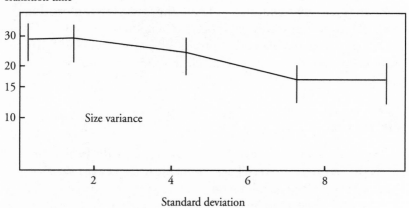

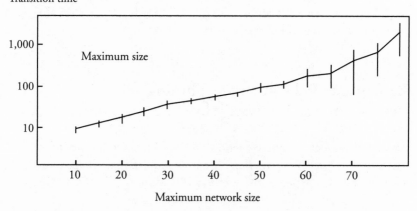

The second panel gives the dependence of the transition time on the dispersion (the population standard deviation) in social network size, holding the average size constant. In this case, as the variance increases the transition time decreases, although this is a relatively weak effect. The reason for this is that the small networks catalyze the transition to a new norm, and as the variance increases, there are more small networks.

These two effects are combined in the third panel, where the abscissa, call it $\overline{S}$, represents the maximum size of any social network; that is, the size ($S$) of an agent's network is set by drawing a random number from $U[10, \overline{S}]$. As $\overline{S}$ increases, both the average social network size and the variance rise, and the two competing effects on transition time given in the first two panels of the figure play out, yielding the third panel. Overall, the general effect is that the transition time increases very rapidly with $\overline{S}$.

Next, we consider the effect of increasing the extent of agent social networks in the age cohort dimension ($E$). Throughout the discussion above, the maximum extent of a social network has been five cohorts above and below an agent's own cohort. Figure 5-8 shows the effect of varying this parameter. Note that increasing the extent of agent social networks in the age dimension decreases transition times. The reason for this is that networks having greater extent include older agents, who are more likely to be retired.

*Dynamics and "As If"*

Notice that in figure 5-6 the only variable affected by the fraction of rationals is the transition time. The attainment, per se, of the age sixty-five retirement norm is compatible with any rationality fraction above a critical level. So while in establishing the social norm, the system does behave "as if" all agents are rational, it also behaves "as if" none are! However, in taking a long time to achieve the norm it does not behave "as if" all agents are rational; indeed, it behaves as if most are not.

# Response to Policy Change: Shifting the Retirement Age from Sixty-five to Sixty-two

Above, our model permitted agents to retire when they wished; no mandatory retirement age was in effect. We now require that all agents retire at age seventy. This increases the speed at which the age sixty-five retirement

Figure 5-8. *Effect of Extent of Social Network on Transition to Age 65 Retirement Norm, by Fraction of Rational Agents*

Transition time

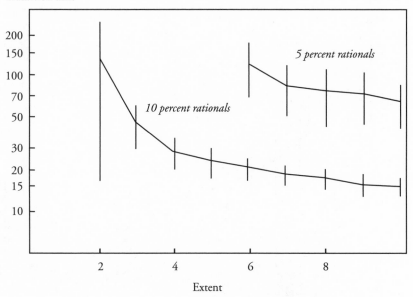

Extent

norm is established. We wish to investigate the effect of policy interventions on retirement age norms. Therefore once the norm of sixty-five is established, we throw a "policy switch" and lower the retirement age to sixty-two, mimicking the 1961 policy change by Congress. In our model, this switch means only that rationals claim benefits at age sixty-two and that randoms and imitators *may* receive benefits at age sixty-two. We measure how long it takes for a new retirement age norm to become established. Keep in mind that when the age of eligibility for social security benefits was lowered from sixty-five to sixty-two, it took nearly thirty-five years for a new norm to emerge (see figure 5-1). In animation 5-3, with rationals and randoms each constituting 5 percent of the population, $\tau$ distributed on U[0.5, 1.0], and the social networks as in the base case, a new norm emerges after some twenty periods. In short, the model replicates the sluggish adjustment that in fact occurred, at least qualitatively.

We have made many realizations of this model, varying the number of rationals in the population. The results are shown in figure 5-9. Note that the transition time to the age sixty-two norm falls as the fraction of rational agents increases. Based on this parameterization of the model, a new

Figure 5-9. *Effect of Fraction of Rational Agents on Transition to Age 62 Retirement Norm*

Transition time

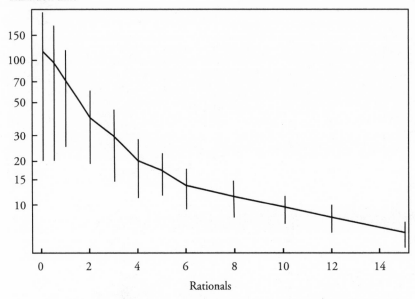

Rationals

norm is instituted in about thirty-five periods if between 1 and 4 percent of the population responds rationally—that is to say, immediately—to the new policy. The sensitivity analyses described in figures 5-6 through 5-8 indicate how the speed of adjustment depends on other parameters in the model. In particular, we expect the time required to adjust to a policy shock to rise for less variance in the imitation threshold ($\tau$) and for increases in the average size and extent of social networks.

This use of the agent-based computational model as a kind of laboratory in which alternative policies can be studied seems to us a fertile application of the technology, and one that has not been systematically exploited.

## Two Subpopulations, Loosely Coupled by Social Networks

Some subgroups in society may be better informed and educated than others. Such differences can affect the relative rates at which these communities adopt various norms. In animation 5-4 the agents have been divided into two distinct subpopulations of the same size: the agents on the left do not include any rational agents, while of the agents on the right, 10 percent are rationals. Other parameters are as in the base case configuration. The two subpopulations are coupled through their social networks as follows: 10 percent of each agent's network belongs to the other subpopulation, with the remainder belonging to its own group. We term this quantity—10 percent—the *coupling* between subpopulations. Even this rather loose coupling is sufficient for the group containing some rationals to pull the other into conformity with its retirement norm, as shown in animation 5-4.

We have studied this general effect by systematically varying the extent of coupling between subpopulations and measuring the times required for each group to reach a retirement norm of age sixty-five from an initially unretired state. The results are shown in figure 5-10; each point is an average of over fifty realizations. Note that very little coupling is needed for the nonrational subpopulation to be pulled into conformity with the more rational subpopulation.

## Conclusions

With social network interactions and imitative dynamics, very little individual rationality may be needed for society as a whole ultimately to exhibit optimal behavior. More pointedly, there is a large literature, experimental and theoretical, devoted to the question: how rational are individual humans? From the perspective of network imitation, it may not matter. Moreover, the nonequilibrium dynamics and the social patchiness of a response to policy will depend on both the size and the structure of networks. It is not clear how one would adapt the representative agent approach to study either of these dependencies. However, they are naturally explored within the agent-based computational framework.

This chapter has barely scratched the surface of a rich and promising area of study. Many fruitful avenues for future research suggest themselves, both analytical and computational. On the analytical side, it would be extremely useful to have—for the transient networks we describe—theorems analogous to those of Lawrence Blume and H. Peyton Young, which give conditions under which social norms will be established eventually for static networks.[16] Furthermore, it would be desirable to have formal expressions for the way in which transition time

16. Blume (1995); Young (1998).

Figure 5-10.  *Effect of Social Network Coupling on Transition to Age 65 Retirement Norm*

Transition time

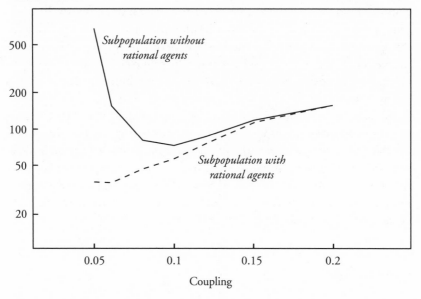

distributions depend on model parameters such as the fraction of imitators and size of social networks.

Computationally, it would be useful to extend our model of retirement age norms to include income shocks and imitative consumption behavior over the life cycle, as in the agent-based model of Christopher Carroll and Todd Allen.[17] We suspect that doing so would add more heterogeneity to the outcomes observed in our model. Furthermore, such a model would provide a useful laboratory in which to explore new theoretical ideas, like the effect of hyperbolic discounting, as well as to experiment with policy alternatives, like increasing the retirement age or privatizing social security.

While we have interpreted this model as applying to retirement, it could be applied to a wide range of settings in which social interactions mediate purely rational behavior. Obvious candidates include contagion behavior in markets, migration to different health plans, or the diffusion of technological innovations. In reality, these phenomena occur in social networks, while most existing models treat them either as occurring in "per-

17. Carroll and Allen (1997).

fectly mixed" environments or via local interactions on regular lattices or other highly specialized topologies. The agent-based computational approach is well suited to studying such processes with any topology of interactions.

## Appendix A
## Implementation of the Model: Agents as Objects

There are many ways to computationally implement agent-based models. This can be done in any modern programming language, or with any of several mathematical or simulation software packages. However, since the model is stated in terms of individual agents, there is one idea from modern computer science that renders the implementation both transparent and efficacious: object-oriented programming.

Objects are contiguous blocks of memory that contain both data (so-called *instance variables*) and functions for modifying these data (the object's so-called *methods*). This ability of objects to hold both data and functions operating on data is called *encapsulation*.[18] Agent-based models are very naturally implemented using objects, by interpreting an object's data as an agent's state information and the object's functions as the agent's rules of behavior. A population of agents who have the same behavioral repertoire but local state information is then conveniently implemented as multiple instantiations of a single agent object type or class.[19]

We have implemented the model described in the text using object-oriented programming. Not only are individual agents objects, but so too are cohorts, albeit objects of a different class than agents. In fact, it has proven convenient for the population of cohorts as a whole to be an object as well.

The agent object has a variety of state variables and behavioral methods. An agent's state information includes type (rational, imitator, or random), age, current employment status (working or retired), and the age at which it will die ("death age").[20] All of this information is stored locally, in the agent object. Each agent also keeps track of some number

---

18. Other features of the object model, such as inheritance and polymorphism, seem to be less relevant to agent-based computational models than encapsulation.

19. For a discussion of the distinction between object and agent, see Jennings, Sycara, and Wooldridge (1998).

20. The agent is assumed not to know its death age.

of other agents who are identified as its social network. These data are maintained in a social network object, described below. The agent's main decision in the present model is whether or not to retire: this is the agent object's basic *method*. This agent object specification is summarized as follows:

*Pseudo-code block 1: Agent object*

```
OBJECT agent;
  type;
  age;
  death_age;
  alive_or_dead;
  social_network;
  working_or_retired;
  next_agent_in_agent_list;
  FUNCTION initialize;
  FUNCTION retirement_decision;
  FUNCTION draw.
```

In practice, it makes sense to implement as private some of these data and methods—that is, accessible only to the agent to whom they belong—while others are public, although this is not essential.[21]

Each social network is also conveniently implemented as an object. The size of each social network is data local to that object, as is an array of pointers to (that is, memory addresses of) the agents who constitute the network. Methods associated with this object include routines for determining how many agents in the network are eligible to retire, and how many are actually retired. This social network object specification is summarized as follows:

*Pseudo-code block 2: Social network object*

```
OBJECT social_network;
  size;
  array_of_agents;
```

21. Private data and methods are accessible only to the agent to whom they belong, unless other objects are given special access privileges.

```
FUNCTION initialize;
FUNCTION number_eligible_to_retire;
FUNCTION number_retired;
FUNCTION fraction_retired_of_eligible;
FUNCTION draw.
```

Cohorts are also implemented as objects. The size of the cohort is kept as local data, as is an array of agents who constitute the cohort. The methods of this object are primarily data-gathering and statistical routines, useful in characterizing the behavior of the cohort overall. The cohort object is summarized as follows:

*Pseudo-code block 3: Cohort object*

```
OBJECT cohort;
  size;
  array_of_agents;
  FUNCTION initialize;
  FUNCTION average_social_network_size_among_
    agents_in_cohort;
  FUNCTION number_retired;
  FUNCTION fraction_retired_of_eligible;
  FUNCTION draw.
```

The population of cohorts is also an object. Similar to the cohort object, it is merely an array of entities (here, cohorts), together with data-gathering and statistical methods for discerning the state of the population overall.

Putting all of this together, the agent-based computational model amounts to

1. initializing all agents, social networks, and cohorts;
2. choosing an agent at random and incrementing its age;
3. checking to see if the agent has achieved its death age; if yes, then go to 2; else
4. having the agent decide whether to retire;
5. repeat 2 through 4 for all agents;
6. periodically gather and report statistics on the population.

This algorithm is summarized as follows:

*Pseudo-code block 4: Overall model*

```
PROGRAM retirement;
  initialize agents;
  initialize social networks;
  initialize cohorts;
  repeat:
    select an agent at random;
    increment its age;
    if age < death_age then do
      retirement_decision;
    get statistics on the agents and cohorts;
  until user terminates.
```

The object model is largely responsible for the relatively compact description of this code.[22]

# References

Axelrod, Robert. 1997. *The Complexity of Cooperation*. Princeton University Press.

Blume, Lawrence. 1995. "The Statistical Mechanics of Strategic Interaction." *Games and Economic Behavior* 5: 387–424.

Burtless, Gary. 1986. "Social Security, Unanticipated Benefit Increases, and the Timing of Retirement." *Review of Economic Studies* 53: 781–805.

Camerer, Colin. 1997. "Progress in Behavioral Game Theory." *Journal of Economic Perspectives* 11 (4): 167–88.

Carroll, Christopher, and Todd Allen. 1997. "Learning about Intertemporal Choice." Paper presented at the Santa Fe Institute Workshop on Local Interactions Models in Economics. Santa Fe, New Mexico.

Epstein, Joshua M., and Robert L. Axtell. 1996. *Growing Artificial Societies: Social Science from the Bottom Up*. Brookings.

Jennings, Nicholas R., Katia Sycara, and Michael Wooldridge. 1998. "A Roadmap of Agent Research and Development." *Autonomous Agents and Multi-Agent Systems* 1 (1): 7–38.

Kochen, Manfred, ed. 1989. *The Small World*. Norwood, N.J.: Ablex Publishing Corporation.

Laibson, David I., Andrea Repetto, and Jeremy Tobacman. 1998. "Self-Control and Retirement Savings: Do 401(k)'s Help?" Working paper. Harvard University.

---

22. The actual source code is less than 2,000 lines of C++ and compiles in the CodeWarrior environment for the Macintosh. A Java implementation is available at (http://www.brook.edu/es/dynamics/papers/retirement [June 1999]).

Animation 5-1. *Rapid Propagation of Retirement Behavior through Social Networks, No Mandatory Retirement Age*

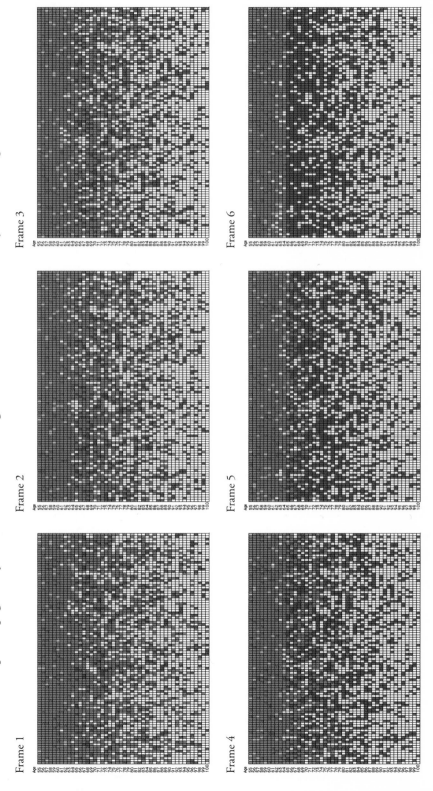

Frame 1

Frame 2

Frame 3

Frame 4

Frame 5

Frame 6

Animation 5-2. *Slow Propagation of Retirement Behavior through Social Networks, No Mandatory Retirement Age*

Frame 1

Frame 2

Frame 3

Frame 4

Frame 5

Frame 6

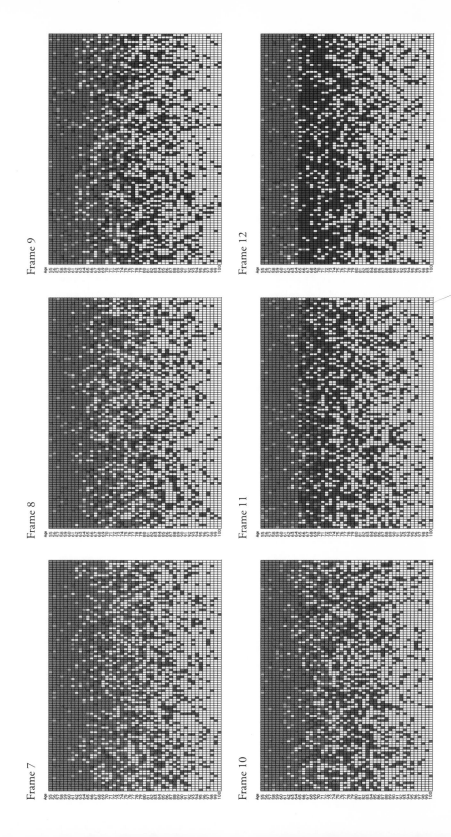

Animation 5-3. *Propagation of Retirement Behavior through Social Networks, Mandatory Retirement Age of 70 and Policy Change from Earliest Retirement Age of 65 to 62*

Frame 1

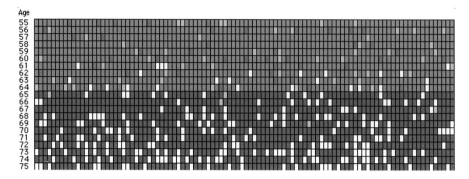

Frame 2

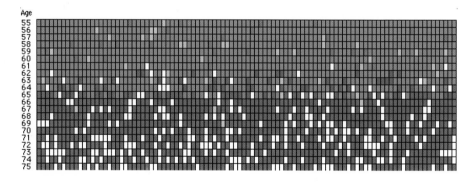

Frame 3

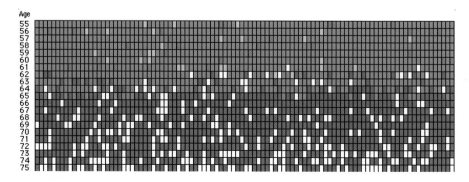

# Animation 5-3. *(continued)*

## Frame 4

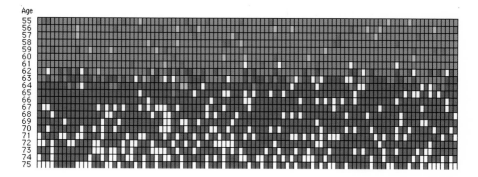

## Frame 5

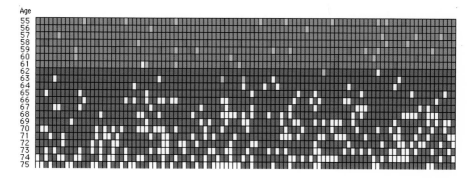

## Frame 6

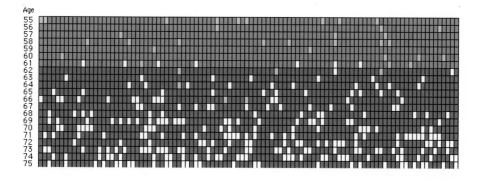

Animation 5-4. *Retirement Dynamics in Two Loosely Coupled Subpopulations*

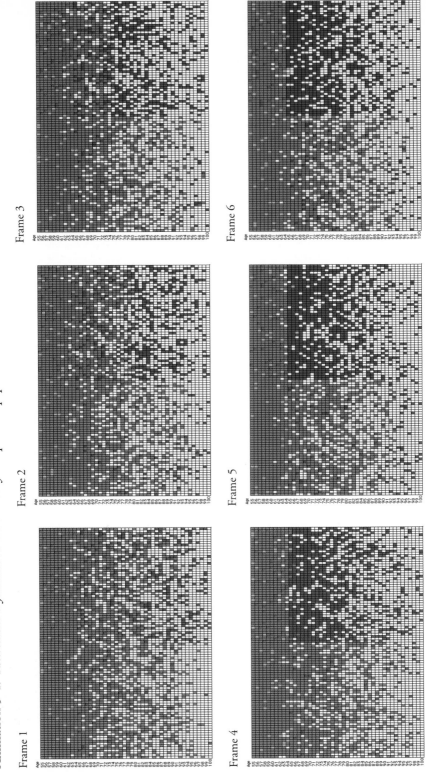

Frame 1

Frame 2

Frame 3

Frame 4

Frame 5

Frame 6

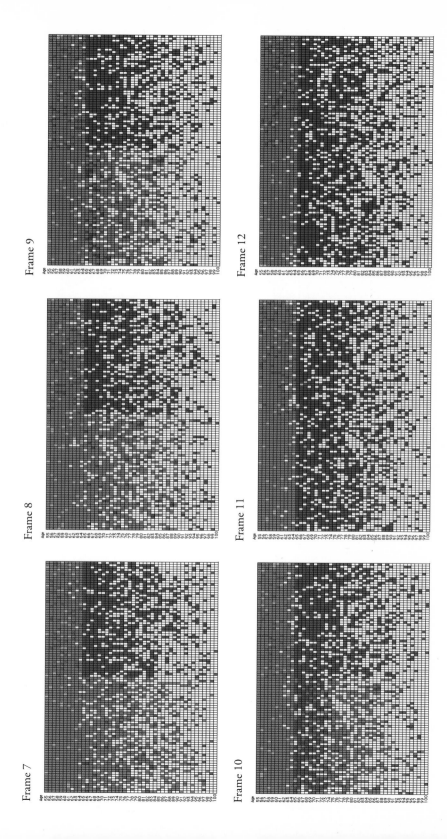

Frame 7

Frame 8

Frame 9

Frame 10

Frame 11

Frame 12

# Figure 5-2. *Typical Agent Social Networks*

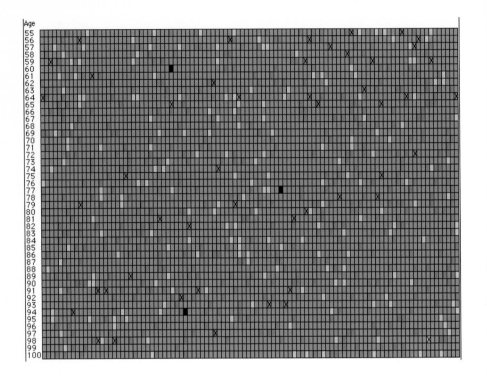

Rabin, Matthew. 1998. "Psychology and Economics." *Journal of Economic Literature* 36 (March): 11–46.

Rust, John, and Christopher Phelan. 1997. "How Social Security and Medicare Affect Retirement Behavior in a World of Incomplete Markets." *Econometrica* 65 (4): 781–831.

Scott, John. 1991. *Social Network Analysis.* Sage Publications.

Young, H. Peyton. 1998. "Diffusion in Social Networks." Working paper. Brookings.

COMMENT BY

# Robert E. Hall

The ideas in this chapter call to mind the central paradox of the human brain. On the one hand, the brain can perform in ways that go far beyond the abilities of the best existing computers. It can make sense out of images and sounds faster and better than any computer-based recognition system. Every time you take a step, your cerebellum solves a two-point boundary value problem that no computer can. And the human ability to solve the kinds of poorly specified problems encountered in daily life is unmatched.

On the other hand, people do stupid things. They pay 25 cents a minute for long-distance service they could buy for 9 cents. They invest in mutual funds with annual expense ratios of 2 percent when they could invest in better-performing funds with annual expenses of 0.3 percent. People believe in silly rumors, take advice from fake spiritualists, and some drink too much alcohol. A discouraging number fail to save anything for retirement. And my brain, which has no trouble remembering the first-order conditions for the optimal timing of consumption, cannot remember why I started up the staircase at home by the time I get to the top (I'm not getting Alzheimer's—this has been a lifetime problem). Large numbers of people neglect their problem-solving skills. Only a tiny fraction of the adult population can use the Amtrak schedule to find the latest train from Philadelphia that gets to Washington, D.C., before 5 p.m.

Robert Axtell and Joshua Epstein base their work on the observation that a significant fraction of the population copies the decisions of others rather than solving problems from scratch. In some circumstances, imitation is the result of hard-edged optimization: it is optimal to imitate people who have superior information. When I am driving in Massachusetts, I slow down as soon as anyone around me slows down, because I know that most drivers have radar detectors and I do not. But imitation surely extends beyond this example of on-the-spot rationality. Many people run their lives on the principle of imitation. Rather than rethink every problem from first principles, they do what other people do. The basic idea of the model in this chapter rings exactly true: human societies are made up of a few problem solvers and masses of imitators.

Almost all humans are born with amazing problem-solving capabilities. Those that we all require for daily life, such as the cerebellum's facility with three-dimensional two-point boundary value problems, flourish in all but the disabled. But specialization begins at an early stage. By the teenage years, only a small part of the population has honed their problem-solving skills to the point that they will be able to think through issues such as the best time to retire. Probably no more than one adult in a thousand is able to set up a spreadsheet that correctly measures the amounts of postretirement consumption possible with different retirement ages and different amounts of preretirement saving. Everybody else solves this problem by imitation and consulting experts.

There is a grand piece of sociobiology to be carried out here. Did humans evolve a mechanism for shutting down original problem solving in an optimal fraction of the population so that specialists could send everybody in the same desirable direction? In organizations such as armies, individual problem solving is constrained. Most soldiers just take orders from officers. And the scope for problem solving is limited for the more junior officers.

Axtell and Epstein's focus, however, is on just one aspect of imitative behavior—its dynamics. Their basic idea is that people cannot distinguish the true problem solvers from imitators. If they could, they would imitate right away and there would be no dynamics. Instead, people look around once a year and observe how others are behaving. The behavior of concern to Axtell and Epstein is retirement age. People take polls of their social circles and retire when the majority of other people the same age have retired. The dynamics arise from the choice to take the poll only once a year. If people looked around every day instead of at the beginning of each year, the dynamics would be 365.25 times as fast.

There is another rationalization for the same type of behavior: there may be externalities across individuals with respect to retirement. People may lose the benefits of socializing if some are retired and others are not. Retired people have much more flexible time schedules. Those still at work but near retirement may find that they want to retire when their friends do in order to synchronize their social activities. Models with this kind of local externality have been developed by Steven Durlauf and others.[1] The coordination model presented in this chapter could be interpreted along these lines, though the chapter does not explain the complementarity.

The data shown in figure 5-1 strongly support the view that the dynamics of change in retirement age are extraordinarily sluggish. First, they suggest—virtually conclusively in my view—that the age of initial eligibility for full social security benefits has a big effect on retirement age. As

---

1. Durlauf (1993, 1997). See, also, chapter 2 in this volume.

the three graphs show, much of the population retires at the point of first eligibility for full benefits.

Because the spike at the age of initial entitlement is so strong, the slow change in retirement behavior after the 1961 reduction in retirement age strongly supports the authors' hypothesis. If there had been a gradual downward shift in retirement age, it could be attributed to a multitude of factors other than the policy change—the increasing incidence of disability among men who survive past age 60, increasing wealth, and the like. But the disappearance of the old spike at age 65 and its gradual replacement by a spike at age 62 makes a pretty solid case in favor of the authors' particular explanation.

Numerical simulation has swept my own field of macroeconomics in the past decade as the standard way to understand models. Axtell and Epstein cling to what I would see as the older view that simulation is a little exotic and questionable and calls for an explicit defense as a research method. I think such defensiveness is unnecessary. There is no need to talk about "agent-based" models and certainly no need to discuss the actual programming methods employed. It is no more necessary to tell us that object-oriented C++ programming was used to produce the results than it is to say that the manuscript was prepared in Microsoft Word.

I think there is a lot to learn from this type of research. I look forward to additional insights from models of the random interaction of large numbers of individuals subject to interesting complementarities.

## Reference

Durlauf, Steven. 1993. "Nonergodic Economic Growth." *Review of Economic Studies* 60: 349–66.

———. 1997. "Statistical Mechanics Approaches to Socioeconomic Behavior." In *The Economy as an Evolving Complex System II,* edited by B. Arthur, S. Durlauf, and D. Lane. Menlo Park: Addison Wesley.

DAVID FETHERSTONHAUGH
LEE ROSS

# 6

# Framing Effects and Income Flow Preferences in Decisions about Social Security

DECISIONS ABOUT age of retirement and the public policy provisions that influence such decisions are important alike for wage earners, employers, and the social welfare system. We shall present preliminary evidence that the framing as well as the content of incentives available to older workers may influence their decisions on when to retire. That is, we shall consider policy changes that alter both the financial consequences of retiring and the manner in which financial consequences are described to, and understood by, the worker. Although we focus specifically on retirement decisions, our broader concerns involve theoretical issues regarding framing that are receiving increasing attention from economists, psychologists, and political scientists.

We present survey evidence suggesting that people's expressed intentions regarding age of retirement may depend on how variations in social security benefits that depend on the timing of retirement are described—that is, "framed." The relative attractiveness of retirement at age 68 or age 65 may be different, at least for some people, when the options are framed as financial *losses* from "early" retirement rather than the conventional formulation as financial *gains* from "late" retirement. In contrast, some preliminary evidence suggests that decisions about retirement at 65 versus 62 may *not* be subject to the same framing effects. We then present evidence that the willingness of wage earners to delay retirement from age 65 to 68 might be very different if the current incentive for doing so—an increment in yearly benefits—were replaced with a single, actuarially equivalent, lump-sum payment. Finally, we present the responses to survey questions that dealt with the solvency of the social security system and the prospect of choosing not to join the system. Responses to these questions shed some light on the basis for our participants' expressed preferences and set the stage for concluding reflections on the challenges that our findings pose for the social security system and for public policy more generally.

## Framing

It has long been clear that essentially identical propositions may evoke very different responses because of how they are presented, or framed. Opposing interest groups seek public support by presenting the issue of abortion access either as a matter of "a woman's right to choose" or "an unborn baby's right to live." Politicians talk about the need to support "freedom fighters" but stamp out "terrorists" or advocate "affirmative action" but oppose "reverse discrimination." Pollsters and survey researchers understand that the wording of a question can distort expressions of public opinion.[1] Likewise, the designers of social security knew that public support for "retirement funds" and "insurance" would be more warmly received than "wealth redistribution" or "intergenerational income transfers."

Despite intuition and experience suggesting that decisions may significantly depend on how the alternatives confronting people are presented, most economists give little attention to matters of framing. They maintain that economic preferences and choices depend (at least to a first approximation) on the expected utility of the alternatives. In recent years, however, this "objectivist" tradition has been challenged with increasing vigor by both psychologists and behavioral economists.[2] Daniel Kahneman and Amos Tversky in particular have offered compelling demonstrations that people are more averse to losses than they are attracted to gains of a given size. This attitude, labeled *loss aversion,* means that people are sus-

---

1. See Payne (1951); Sudman, Bradburn, and Schwarz (1996); Schuman and Presser (1981); Clark and Schober (1992); Fischhoff (1991); and Converse and Traugott (1986).

2. Psychologists include Daniel Kahneman, Amos Tversky, Eldar Shafir, Paul Slovic, Sarah Lichtenstein, and Baruch Fischhoff. Noted behavioral economists include George Loewenstein, Richard Thaler, Drazen Prelec, Matthew Rabin, and Colin Camerer.

ceptible to manipulations that reframe a given choice as a potential loss or a potential gain.[3]

## Choice and the Framing of Decisions

Imagine you just have learned that you are suffering from a treatable form of cancer. Your doctor gives you a choice between surgery and radiation therapy and informs you of the relevant mortality risks. You are told by your doctor that of those who choose surgery, 10 percent die during surgery and 66 percent die by the end of five years. By contrast, of those who choose radiation, 0 percent die during treatment and 78 percent die by the end of five years. (See summary of the two options in the upper portion of box 6-1.) Which treatment would you choose?

Now imagine, instead, that your doctor provided you with the same information in terms of survival rates. You are told that of those who choose surgery, 90 percent survive the surgery and 34 percent are alive after five years, while of those who choose radiation therapy, 100 percent survive the treatment and 22 percent are alive after 5 years. Given this alternative framing of the two options, which treatment would you *now* choose?

If you resemble clinic patients who were offered essentially these hypothetical choices, you would be more likely to elect radiation therapy over surgery if you were presented with the question in the mortality frame than in the survival frame. The logically inconsequential change from survival to mortality framing produced an increase from 18 percent to 44 percent in the portion of patients choosing the "safer" (in the short run) but seemingly inferior (in the long run) radiation option.[4] Even more startling was the finding that when practicing physicians were presented at a medical conference with the questions, the impact of the manipulation was as large as it was for the clinical patients. Expertise and experience apparently failed to shield these medical practitioners from the tendency to see a reduction of immediate mortality from 10 percent to 0 percent as more meaningful than an increase in immediate survival from 90 percent to 100 percent.

Consider another life-and-death decision, one that involves other people's fate rather than your own. Imagine that a small nation is preparing for the outbreak of a new and exotic disease that is expected to kill 600 people. Two programs to combat the disease have been proposed. If program A is

3. Kahneman and Tversky (1984).
4. McNeill and others (1982).

---

Box 6-1. *Framing Choices*

Mortality frame

Surgery: Of 100 people having surgery 10 die during surgery or the postoperative period, and 66 die by the end of five years.

Radiation therapy: Of 100 people having radiation therapy, none die during treatment, and 78 die by the end of five years.

Survival frame

Surgery: Of 100 people having surgery 90 live through the postoperative period, and 34 are alive at the end of five years.

Radiation therapy: Of 100 people having radiation therapy all live through the treatment, and 22 are alive at the end of five years.

---

adopted, you are told, 200 people will be saved. If program B is adopted, there is a one-third chance that 600 people will be saved and a two-thirds chance that nobody will be saved. Which program would you favor? Now consider the same threat and set of expected outcomes, but this time given options that are framed somewhat differently. You are told that if program A is adopted, 400 people will die. If program B is adopted, there is a one-third chance that nobody will die and a two-thirds chance that 600 people will die. Which treatment would you *now* choose?

Notice that the alternatives in both versions of the problem describe identical outcomes. What changes is the *reference point* that each version of the problem adopts. In one version the alternatives offer the prospect of a certain versus uncertain gain of lives; in the other version they offer the prospect of a certain versus uncertain loss of lives. The lives-saved version implicitly adopts the reference point of a death toll of 600 and offers the sure-thing prospect of saving some of those lives versus the risky prospect of trying to save them all. The lives-lost version implicitly adopts the reference point of a death toll of 0 lives and the sure-thing prospect of losing some of those lives versus the risky prospect of trying to reduce that loss to zero.

This framing manipulation once again produced dramatically different preferences among respondents in a classic study.[5] When the alternatives were framed in terms of number of saved lives, a majority (72 percent)

5. Kahneman and Tversky (1979).

favored the option that saved 200 people for sure over the option that gambled with all 600 people. When the alternatives were framed in terms of the number of lost lives, however, a majority (78 percent) favored the option that avoided the certain loss of 400 lives and gambled in hope of reducing that loss to zero. This opposing pattern of preferences even held when respondents answered both questions within a few minutes.

The results of these and other simple experiments illustrate that the subjective value of alternatives can depend on how they are framed and on the reference point used for comparisons among them. People hate losses more than they love objectively equal gains. They are also more willing to take risks or expend efforts to avoid or reduce losses than to produce or increase equivalent gains. This asymmetry makes people susceptible to manipulations that transform comparisons of losses into comparisons of gains or vice versa.[6] It is thus not by accident that the difference between the cash price and the credit price for gasoline has been universally framed as a discount for paying cash rather than as a surcharge for using a credit card. Many customers who would think it sharp practice and unfair for a merchant to impose a credit card surcharge regard it as fair, and even generous, for the same merchant to offer a discount for payment in cash.

The same asymmetry in response to prospective loss versus gain, we believe, has been important in public responses to social and political policy. Few Americans objected to rewarding World War II veterans with extra points on civil service placement exams. Many more, we suspect, would have rejected the objectively identical policy had it been framed as a penalty—a reduction in the test scores of all nonveterans—including almost all women and all disabled or middle-aged people—who had not served in the war. In analogous fashion, a tax table can offer an exemption for each child—the current practice—or, with complete equivalence, it could levy a surtax on the childless.[7] Many who are willing to embrace the former would be outraged by the latter.

The experiments and examples we have described all illustrate violations of the *invariance* axiom on which the standard economic model of rational choice rests—that different representations of the same alternatives should not yield different preference orderings.[8] If A is preferred to B, given one description of the relevant outcomes and probabilities associated with the two options, then B should not be preferred to A given some other

6. Thaler (1980); and Kahneman and Tversky (1988).
7. Schelling (1981).
8. Savage (1954).

(equally accurate) description of the same outcomes and probabilities. Unfortunately, a wealth of evidence calls this assumption into question and with it the standard economic model, at least as a description of actual behavior if not as a normative guide.

It was, in fact, observed violations of invariance and other assumptions of normative models of choice that prompted Daniel Kahneman and Amos Tversky to develop *prospect theory,* an account of human decisionmaking that emphasizes two empirically based principles that help to explain how people actually make choices. First, as the examples we discussed earlier suggest, people are assumed to evaluate alternatives not in terms of their consequences for total wealth, but rather in terms of gains and losses measured from some specified or naturally occurring reference point. Thus, when considering the difference between the cash and credit prices for gasoline, people do not base their decisions on how the alternatives will affect their bank balance or overall wealth. Instead, they attend to the prospect of an attractive gain for paying cash relative to the reference point, the "neutral" option of paying by credit card and receiving no discount. They normally do not attend to the prospect that would be posed by the alternative framing of their choice—paying a penalty for the use of credit relative to the "neutral" option of a cash transaction.

A second key assumption of prospect theory is that losses loom larger than gains, so that a given departure from the reference point exerts less impact when it reflects a bonus earned than when it reflects a penalty paid. This feature of the theory explains why forgoing a cash discount is less aversive than incurring a credit surcharge, and why so many people willingly buy gas with credit cards despite the added cost. It is these features of prospect theory, we shall argue, that make prospective retirees' decisions about social security options susceptible to simple framing effects.

## Framing and Social Security

Age 65 is the current "default" age or "reference point" for social security decisions, even though 65 is not, in fact, the modal retirement age (see chapter 1 by Gary Burtless).[9] Workers are permitted to claim reduced social security benefits before age 65, and nearly two-thirds choose to do so. At the same time, many wage earners, especially in academia and the profes-

---

9. Indeed, life expectancies, health prospects, and typical job demands have shifted dramatically since the current system was enacted. Furthermore, both public and private pension plans generally provide a variety of options regarding retirement dates and benefits.

sions, elect to continue working beyond this "normal" retirement age and to reap the various financial benefits, including increased social security and private pensions, available to those who choose to extend their working lives.

Nevertheless, age 65 continues to be referred to as the normal retirement age, and the age at which unreduced retirement benefits are available. Thus, in fact as well as in popular perception, monthly retirement benefits are increased for those who retire "late"—that is, after age 65—and decreased for workers who retire "early"—that is, before age 65. Our point is a simple one: other framings featuring earlier or later reference points for the calculation of benefits are possible, and these framings might produce different retirement preferences, intentions, and behavior, even if the financial consequences are unchanged.

It is worth emphasizing that the adjustments in monthly social security benefits are actuarially fair on the average for workers who retire between ages 62 and 65 and will become actuarially fair by 2008 for workers retiring between the ages of 65 and 70. An adjustment is actuarially fair if expected lifetime benefits are constant on the average whatever the age at which benefits begin. Workers who retire earlier receive smaller monthly social security checks than those who retire later, but early retirees receive them for a longer time. Until 2008 workers who start to receive benefits after age 65 will continue to pay a price for the "delay." This state of affairs, of course, does not mean that delaying retirement past age 65 is an unwise decision for all or even for most wage earners. The provisions of private investments and pensions, personal circumstances, and the social and other psychic benefits of continuing on the job may fully justify such a decision for many people.

What the current social security system offers, it should by now be apparent, is essentially a mix of gain and loss framings. Workers who anticipate retiring before age 65 are subject to loss framing. They expect their monthly benefits to be reduced relative to the full-benefit reference point because of their decision to stop working before the "normal" retirement age. Workers who anticipate working after age 65 are subject to gain framing. They expect to receive a benefit or credit relative to the full-benefit reference point because of their decision to continue working after the "normal" retirement age.

It is obvious that many factors influence when people retire. Some are financial—savings, private pensions, and investment opportunities, for example. Some are nonfinancial—job satisfaction, peer influence, family situation, the meaning attached to retirement by the worker and the worker's peers, for example. Our contention, based on prospect theory, is simply that the age 65 reference point and the current framing of early versus late retirement may play some role in this decision as well. More specifically, we argue that a reframing of options might lead at least some wage earners to make different retirement decisions. Outcomes framed in terms of prospective losses should make "late retirement" more attractive and "early retirement" less attractive than outcomes framed in terms of prospective gains.

## The Attractions of One-Time, Lump-Sum Payments

Although our interest with the framing of social security benefits has its origin in basic theory and laboratory research, the second concern of this chapter and of our survey is rooted in the observation that many people prefer a single, relatively large lump-sum payment to a series of smaller earlier or later payments that, by conventional reckoning, are of equal or even greater value. Economists sometimes attribute this preference to something they term the "wealth illusion," although in the case we shall discuss, it is not clear that any illusion is involved. Whatever its source, the existence of such a lump-sum preference suggests the prospect of a lump-sum payment might be more attractive to workers weighing the pros and cons of delaying their retirement than the prospect of a lifelong increase in monthly benefits provided by the current social security system.

One example of this lump-sum preference is seen in the perplexing institution of the once popular Christmas club, in which people seem willing to deposit small amounts from their weekly or monthly paycheck in accounts that pay little or no interest in exchange for a propitious lump sum at Christmas.[10] Of course, people also prove willing to commit themselves to a stream of future payments (with a high interest rate) to receive a lump sum immediately. Similarly, millions of Americans choose to "buy now and pay later." Late-night television commercials invite accident victims receiving damage settlements to convert a stream of future payments into a lump payment today; and contracts offered to professional athletes and other highly sought employees frequently are sweetened with a signing bonus that caters to the signer's preference for an immediate lump-sum payment rather than higher continuing payments.

Several factors seem to be involved in these cases of lump-sum preference. The first is simple temporal discounting. People generally prefer

10. Thaler and Loewenstein (1992); and Shefrin and Thaler (1992).

dollars today over dollars tomorrow. In some cases this preference may reflect a rational belief about the value of future versus present dollars. In other cases it may reflect a less rational inclination to choose immediate gratification rather than delay, even when the reward for such delay seems substantial. Second, people prefer certainty because the future is uncertain and the elimination of uncertainty is worth some sacrifice in terms of expected outcome. Third, people may reckon that pooling smaller payments into a single large sum might enable them to create or exploit an otherwise unavailable opportunity. Fourth, people may use the replacement of a payment with a single future payment as an instrument to control or regulate their own behavior.[11] They may want to commit themselves to automatic deductions from each paycheck, which they will not miss, to shield themselves from procrastination, impulse buying, and other related human failings. In other words, they may feel that they will spend a lump sum more wisely than a stream of smaller payments.

Christmas clubs involve several of these features. The saver gives up a portion of each paycheck, a sum small enough not to be missed, for a consequential single payment when the money will be especially welcome and needed. The deductions from salary, moreover, are automatic and thus not dependent on willpower or the vicissitudes of immediate financial demands. To enjoy these benefits, the saver is willing to forgo not only the advantages of flexibility in saving and spending, but also all or some of the interest that could be earned through other types of savings or investment plans.

In contrast to the Christmas club, replacing a portion of the social security annuity with a lump-sum payment would entail a trade of both present and future payments for the lump sum. That is, wage earners delay retirement, thereby putting off the date at which the stream of monthly social security payments begins, but at the same time they continue to amass additional employment earnings and savings. They receive a single payment on the date of retirement or at some fixed time thereafter instead of the stream of increments to yearly postretirement benefits that would otherwise have served as the incentive or reward for delaying retirement.

A lump-sum payment runs counter to the general philosophy underlying social security, which is to ensure a flow of real income for as long as the pensioner or the pensioner's spouse lives. We assume that the lump-sum payment would replace only the "extra" benefits paid to workers who remain economically active after the "normal" retirement age. With this

11. Elster (1979); Schelling (1984); and Thaler and Shefrin (1981).

qualification, a relatively large lump-sum payment could offer workers an incentive to remain economically active that is different from, and perhaps larger than, the incentive of the increment in yearly payments.

A lump-sum payment would offer the wage earner a variety of benefits not provided by an increment in yearly payments. First, it may appeal to those who harbor doubts about the durability of social security. Payment of a lump sum would reduce concerns that future solvency problems might cause benefit reductions, means tests, or income tests. Second, and perhaps more important, a lump sum could be used to finance a major purchase, such as a condominium in Florida, a new car, foreign travel, or paying off a mortgage. The delay of gratification called for in putting off the date of retirement would be rewarded with the gratification provided by a single marked event instead of a continuing stream of small incremental payments. If the lump sum were made available soon after retirement, such a payment would enable those with few liquid assets to borrow against what otherwise would have been a future income stream. Even more-affluent retirees might be subject to wealth illusion and value the lump sum more than a small increment in their total monthly income. We are making no judgment on whether borrowing against future income is wise or foolish but hypothesizing that many people will prefer to do so. This is the proposition we tested in our survey.

We asked survey respondents whether a one-time bonus or the current incentive—an increase in monthly benefits—would be more likely to cause them to delay retirement. We also posed a number of other questions designed to help us understand our potential retirees' responses both to the prospect of the one-time, lump-sum bonus, and to the more general pros and cons of early, on-time, or late retirement.

## Survey Findings: Loss versus Gain Framing

Our data are drawn primarily from two "convenience" samples, one drawn at the San Francisco International Airport and one at a San Francisco Giants baseball game. Together, the samples included 176 male participants over the age of 40, with a median age of 47 and median annual earnings of approximately $65,000. We shall also present results from a smaller airport sample of 82 respondents. Because these samples are not representative of the U.S. population, especially with respect to income, broad generalizations are hazardous. Nevertheless, the results we report indicate how framing and the option of a lump-sum bonus might influence retirement decisions and possibly other economic decisions made in anticipation of retirement.

## Framing of Retirement at Age 68 versus 65

The first item in our main survey presented participants with options relevant to their own retirement decision. Options I and II were substantively identical but were framed differently. Participants were assigned at random to one of the two framings. Option I framed the relevant alternatives in terms of prospective gain:

*Option I*

Under the *current* social security system, the *average* male American worker who is choosing to retire either at age 65 or 68 would have the following two choices:

A. He could retire at age 65 and begin receiving a social security pension of $10,000 a year.
*or*

B: He could retire *later,* at age 68 instead of 65, and begin receiving a social security pension of $12,500 a year, which is equal to $10,000 a year *plus a credit* of $2,500 a year for delaying retirement.

Given the two options above, which would *you* prefer?

(Note: amounts for *your* actual pension would depend, of course, on *your* earnings and contributions over the years, but the figures above essentially capture the type of choice to be made.)

Option II framed the choice as a prospective loss:

*Option II*

Under the *current* social security system, the *average* male American worker who is choosing to retire either at age 65 or 68 would have the following two choices:

A: He could retire at age 68 and begin receiving a social security pension of $12,500 a year.
*or*

B: He could retire *earlier,* at age 65 instead of 68, and begin receiving a social security pension of $10,000 a year, which is equal to $12,500 a year *minus a penalty* of $2,500 a year for retiring early.

Given the two options above, which would *you* prefer?

(Note: amounts for *your* actual pension would depend, of course, on *your* earnings and contributions over the years, but the figures above essentially capture the type of choice to be made.)

The difference in responses to the gain and loss framing proved dramatic (see table 6-1, upper panel). When a reward is offered for retiring later, only 38 percent of respondents chose the later of the two retirement ages, that is, age 68. When a penalty is imposed for retiring earlier, fully 57 percent chose that instead of the later retirement age. Older workers were notably more sensitive to the framing manipulation. Among those older than age 47, some 37 percent said they preferred the later retirement age when the options were described in terms of a prospective gain for late retirement and 63 percent when the options were described in terms of a prospective loss for early retirement. Among workers younger than age 47, the change from gain to loss increased the proportion preferring the later retirement age from 38 percent to 50 percent.

To test for the possibility that the atypical wage distribution in our sample may have distorted the framing effect, we separately analyzed the seventy-five members of our sample with earnings under $60,000 during the past year, a group for whom the relevant financial incentives or disincentives presumably would be most salient. The framing effect for these respondents proved to be even more pronounced than for the larger sample (table 6-1, lower panel). The 69 percent who indicated a preference for retiring at age 68 under the loss framing is notable because it greatly exceeds not only the percentage of our middle-income survey participants who expressed a preference for late retirement under the gain framing,

Table 6-1. *Preferred Retirement Age*

Percent

| | Retirement age | |
|---|---|---|
| *Framing* | 65 | 68 |
| *Age sixty-five versus age sixty-eight: all participants*[a] | | |
| Gain | 62 | 38 |
| Loss | 43 | 57 |
| *Respondents earning less than $60,000*[b] | | |
| Gain | 64 | 36 |
| Loss | 31 | 69 |

Source: Authors' survey.

a. This between-subjects difference in expressed preference was statistically significant, $\chi^2 = 6.62$, $p < .01$.

b. See text for explanation.

but also the percentage of middle-income workers who actually delay retirement under the current social security system, a system that presents a gain framing of the incentives for delaying retirement past age 65.

These results can be restated in terms of reference points for the retirement decision. The reference point under the current system is age 65. Although benefits are now payable as early as age 62 and most people claim benefits before reaching 65, the latter age is still called the normal retirement age. As a consequence, retirement at age 68 constitutes late retirement, and the delay results in a perceived gain. By setting the reference point or standard retirement age at 68, instead of 65, as we did for one group in the survey, we allowed people considering retirement between ages 65 and 68 to face the prospect not of a gain for late retirement, but of a loss for early retirement. We predicted that at least some people who deem the relevant gain as insufficient reward for late retirement would deem the corresponding loss as sufficient deterrent to early retirement. This prediction follows from prospect theory, according to which losses of a given magnitude loom larger than gains of the same magnitude. Our survey results confirm this prediction. They suggest that such a shift did in fact occur for a nontrivial percentage of the potential retirees, especially those who were relatively old or relatively less affluent.

## Framing of Retirement at Age 65 versus 62

We have presented results of framing the incentives for delaying retirement from 65 to 68 not in terms of gains but of losses. Might framing play a similar role in judgments about the current disincentives for retiring at age 62 instead of 65? To shed light on this question, we collected data from a smaller sample of eighty-two airport respondents. It would simplify our story if the gain-loss manipulation exerted the same effect on responses regarding retirement at age 62 versus age 65 as it did in on comparisons of the age 65 versus age 68 decision. Such were our expectations, but our results did not confirm them.

We presented equal numbers of subjects with each of the following two choices regarding retirement at age 62 versus age 65. For half of our respondents we framed the decision in terms of *delaying* retirement from a standard or reference age of 62—in other words, retiring late—to reap the financial gain of a larger yearly pension. For the remainder, we framed the same decision in terms of retiring *earlier* than 65, and accepting the loss involved in receiving a smaller yearly pension. The first option was framed as a prospective gain:

*Option I*

Under the current social security system, the *average* male American worker who is choosing to retire either at age 62 or 65 would have the following two choices:

1. He could retire at age 62 and begin receiving a social security pension of $10,000 a year.

*or*

2. He could retire *later,* at age 65 instead of 62, and begin receiving a social security pension of $12,500 a year, which is equal to $10,000 a year *plus* a *credit* of $2,500 a year for delaying retirement.

Given the two options above, which would *you* prefer?

(Note: amounts for *your* actual pension would depend, of course, on *your* earnings and contributions over the years, but the figures above essentially capture the type of choice to be made.)

A second group of respondents received the same option, but this time framed in terms of prospective loss:

*Option II*

Under the current social security system, the *average* male American worker who is choosing to retire either at age 62 or 65 would have the following two choices:

1. He could retire at age 65 and begin receiving a social security pension of $12,500 a year.

*or*

2. He could retire *earlier,* at age 62 instead of 65, and begin receiving a social security pension of $10,000 a year, which is equal to $12,500 a year *minus* a *penalty* of $2,500 a year for retiring early.

Given the two options above, which would *you* prefer?

(Note: amounts for *your* actual pension would depend, of course, on *your* earnings and contributions over the years, but the figures above essentially capture the type of choice to be made.)

The results failed to yield the predicted framing effect. Whether the decision was framed in terms of prospective gains or prospective losses, half the participants expressed a preference for the earlier retirement age (49 percent for gain and 51 percent for loss), and half expressed a preference for the later retirement age (51 percent for gain and 49 percent for loss).[12]

12. This lack of a framing effect, incidentally, seemed to apply to younger as well as older respondents and to relatively higher- and lower-wage earners alike (although there were too few of them in our sample to make comparisons meaningful).

These additional data, although based on a small sample of respondents, raise an obvious question about the robustness of our previously reported findings. Further survey work, with larger samples (and random assignment of respondents to answer either the 62 versus 65 or the 65 versus 68 retirement decision) might resolve the apparent discrepancy in results. But such seemingly inconsistent results might persist for the following reason.

The current social security system makes it natural for potential retirees to think of the age 65 versus age 68 decision as one hinging on the costs and benefits of late versus standard-age retirement, and the age 62 versus age 65 decision as one hinging on the costs and benefits of early versus standard-age retirement. What the wording of our survey questions attempted to do in each case was to reframe the relevant decision. Our results suggest that the relevant reframing attempt was effective in decisions about retirement at 68 versus 65, but ineffective in decisions about retirement at 62 versus 65.

The obvious question that arises is why the reframing attempt was unsuccessful in the age 62 versus age 65 case. The (admittedly post hoc) answer, we believe, requires a closer look at the trade-offs between financial considerations and life-style considerations. For most Americans, the increasingly prevalent decision to retire at age 62 represents a willingness to give up the prospect of slightly larger social security checks in order to begin their postretirement activities while they are still young and healthy enough to fully enjoy and exploit the opportunity. Electing not to retire at the earlier age accordingly entails the loss of that opportunity. In a real sense the gain-loss manipulation in our survey served to pit one combination of gain and loss (increment in pension coupled with the lost opportunity to "retire young") against another (a decrement in pension coupled with the gained opportunity to retire young). Again, what our survey results suggest is that the relevant trade-offs proved to be about equally attractive for the respondents considering age 62 versus 65 retirement in the two framing conditions.

There is, however, one obvious problem with this interpretation. We now need to account for why the same framing manipulation (with, presumably, a similar set of trade-offs) did prove effective in the case of the age 65 versus 68 decision. Why, the alert reader may wonder, were the prospective financial gains versus losses not offset by the losses and gains in leisure with which they were associated? Our tentative answer involves the symmetry or asymmetry created between the two elements in the decision. The issue of gaining or losing an early postretirement period, we suggest, does not arise naturally, saliently, or frequently, when the decisionmaker is weighing the costs and benefits of retiring later than the "standard" age of 65.

We are not sure how convincing readers will find such post hoc theorizing. Indeed, we would not be disappointed if subsequent, more comprehensive, survey work showed that appropriate framing can influence decisions about earlier-than-normal as well as later-than-normal retirement. But in any case the contrast in results for the age 68 versus 65 and the age 62 versus 65 surveys underscores the magnitude of the framing effect obtained in the former case. That is, while only about 50 percent of the respondents in our follow-up survey expressed a willingness to delay their retirement from age 62 to 65, regardless of framing, fully 57 percent of the respondents in our primary survey expressed a willingness to delay retirement to age 68, provided that doing so would allow them to avoid the loss of a yearly increment they would otherwise receive. Clearly, at least *some* of the participants who chose an age 68 instead of age 65 retirement to avoid loss would have chosen retirement at age 62 instead of 65 had those been the options presented.

## Survey Results: One-Time Bonus Payment versus Yearly Increment

Standard economic theory predicts that people will behave in the same way when confronted with options that are actuarially equivalent but structured differently, provided that they are not subject to liquidity constraints. If people discount the future at an interest rate of 10 percent, for example, and have liquid assets, they will behave the same whether they are offered $100 a year for ten years or a lump sum of $615 now. The findings in the preceding section raise some doubt about this prediction, as seemingly minor reframing of a choice elicits different responses. We turn now to survey findings that bear on the attractiveness of financial alternatives that are structured differently but are actuarially equivalent at a particular discount rate.

Following the framing question, we asked those participants in our primary survey who had been presented with the option of delaying retirement from age 65 to 68 to receive a more generous yearly pension to evaluate the attractiveness of two incentives for delaying retirement.[13] One

13. We tried but failed to find a way to compare the impact of a prospective loss of an increment in yearly pension with that of a prospective loss of a lump-sum bonus that could otherwise be earned. The questionnaire item we designed proved too complex and too hypothetical to be answered coherently or with conviction, as many of our respondents told us explicitly.

incentive, which was labeled the "current system," involved the same increase in postretirement income that they had considered previously. An alternative "bonus system" provided a one-time lump-sum payment instead of the increased annuity. We described the two alternatives as follows:

> Listed below are the two options that might become available to American workers who are deciding to retire at age 68 or age 65. The first option involves an increase in *yearly payment* and the second one involves a *one-time bonus*.
>
> 1. Under the current system he could retire three years *later* at age 68, and then begin receiving a social security pension of $12,500 a year, which is equal to $10,000 plus a *credit* of $2,500.
>
> *or*
>
> 2. Under the bonus plan he could retire three years *later* at age 68, and then begin receiving a social security pension of $10,000 a year, but he would also receive a one-time bonus of $25,000 when he retires.
>
> In which of the two systems described above would *you* be more willing to retire late?

From the standpoint of the social security program, $25,000 payable at age 68, together with an annuity starting at that age of $10,000 a year, has a present value, discounted at the 2.8 percent real interest rate social security reserves are projected to earn, of $125,740. In contrast, an annuity of $12,500 a year starting at age 68 has a present discounted value of $125,925.[14] In both calculations we ignore the effects of inflation because social security benefits are indexed and we use a real discount rate. Nevertheless, 76 percent of our survey participants chose the $25,000 bonus and $10,000 annuity, while only 24 percent chose the $12,500 annuity.[15] The apparent attraction of the one-time bonus was even more obvious when the same group was asked, in a subsequent question, about incentives for the *average American worker*. Approximately 80 percent of respondents reported that the one-time bonus would provide the greater incentive for workers to retire later; only 20 percent reported that the yearly increment provided the greater incentive.[16]

14. These calculations are based on the current average life span of 80 years.

15. The chi-squared test yields $\chi^2$ = 23.28, indicating a statistically significant difference likely to occur at random less than once in 1,000 times.

16. The chi-squared test yields $\chi^2$ = 32.29, a difference likely to occur at random less than once in 1,000 times.

## Survey Results: Reservations and Doubts about the Social Security System

The final section of the survey probed respondents' beliefs and feelings about the social security system. What doubts did participants harbor regarding the solvency of the current system and the wisdom of relying on it for future benefits?

For the question, "How confident are you that the social security system will be there for you when you retire, providing the full benefits you have been promised by the government?" (1 = "completely confident" to 5 = "not at all confident"), the mean response was 2.6. Roughly one-third of respondents checked the lowest point on the scale and 22 percent checked the adjacent point. Only 14 percent of respondents checked the highest point on the scale and only 15 percent checked even the adjacent point on the scale. Responses were similar from young and old and from affluent and less affluent participants.

An even more provocative item pointedly asked, "Suppose the government offered you now every dollar that you have ever paid into the social security system (but no interest) and then let you opt out of the system today (meaning that from now on you would not pay any more money into social security and not receive any money from social security in the future). Would you accept the offer?" The mean response was 1.87 on a 5-point scale, where 1 indicated "definitely accept offer." Fully 58 percent checked this response and 18 percent checked the next most extreme point. Only 7 percent of respondents indicated that they would definitely reject the offer, and only 3 percent checked the adjacent point indicating a somewhat less firm rejection.

We cannot tell whether these responses reflect the same lack of confidence regarding the solvency of the system that participants expressed more directly or the respondents' conviction that the current system offers today's middle-age workers a bad deal (or the more mundane conviction that they could make better use of their money now than in the future). These responses, however, may simply highlight the myopic preferences that make social insurance necessary in the eyes of its advocates. In any case, as with our data on the attraction of the one-time bonus, the provocative implication again is that such preferences could be exploited—either out of a willingness to take advantage of people's short-sightedness or irrational fears about solvency, or out of a "libertarian" sense that people should be allowed to make their own economic decisions.[17]

## Some Implications for Public Policy

For most Americans, retirement is one of the milestones of life. Because social security benefits will constitute a large portion of postretirement income for the majority of Americans, decisions about when to retire and the financial incentives and disincentives offered by the system are of critical importance. We have presented tentative evidence that framing retirement alternatives in terms of losses or disincentives for advancing retirement age instead of gains or incentives for delaying retirement age can systematically alter preferences. We also have presented evidence that potential retirees show a marked preference for a single, lump-sum, bonus payment as a reward for delaying retirement instead of the current incentive of increased monthly benefits.

### The Framing of New Incentives and Disincentives

In 1983 Congress voted to increase from 65 to 67 the age at which unreduced benefits are paid. The change is to be implemented gradually from 2001 through 2022. People will still be able to receive retirement benefits as early as age 62, although the reduction in monthly benefits will be even steeper than in the present system. Workers who claim benefits between the ages of 65 and 67 thus will face reductions in monthly benefits, relative to the new age 67 reference point, instead of increases relative to the age 65 reference point. If the implications of our present data and of the prospect theory analysis that prompted us to collect them are correct, this change in reference point may well prompt more workers to postpone retirement from 65 to 67 to avoid the relevant "penalty" or "loss." The manner in which this new policy is presented and comes to be understood by potential retirees will to some extent be under the control of government officials. Media pundits and various groups that offer advice to or lobby for older Americans will no doubt also exert some influence in this regard. Our survey suggests that, beyond the specific new set of financial incentives and

17. It would have been interesting to see how many participants would have been willing to accept an even less attractive "buyout"—for example, an offer of 50 cents for every dollar already "invested," or even the opportunity to simply leave the system, forgoing all their "investment," but gaining freedom from any future payments.

disincentives that will be stipulated, matters of framing are likely to exert a significant impact on the retirement decisions of America's work force.

## The Attractions of a Lump-Sum Bonus

The social policy implications of the preference for a lump-sum payment expressed by our respondents seem clear. Many, perhaps even the majority, of American workers would find such a lump-sum payment a more attractive inducement to stay on the job a few years longer than an actuarially equivalent or even a greater boost in monthly postretirement benefits. Indeed, our data suggest that many workers would trade not only the prospect of increased future pensions but their full entitlement to social security benefits for an actuarially inferior one-time payment. How much of a discount would be accepted by various percentages (or particular segments) of the population remains a topic for further research, preferably with a more representative sample of the U.S. population than airport and ballpark respondents and with questions that are less hypothetical than ours were. But even with these qualifications, our results call to mind the biblical story of Esau, who sold his patrimony for a mess of pottage.

Such research should address several possible explanations for our results. One is that the preference for a lump-sum payment arises from high discount rates—that is, the preference of respondents for smaller amounts of money soon over larger amounts spread into the distant future. Alternatively, respondents may believe that the utility of money for them personally will decrease as they age and have fewer and less attractive opportunities for enjoying it. Or they may believe that a lump sum coming soon after retirement would enable them to make large outlays—to purchase a condominium in a warmer part of the country, perhaps, or take the vacation of a lifetime—that might otherwise be unavailable to them. Another possibility is that our participants' deep-seated doubt about the solvency of the social security system makes them willing to accept a bird in the hand or that it would be wise to take the money and run while it is there for the taking.

Regardless of its source, the attraction of a lump-sum payment for so many respondents raises the question of whether retirees who are willing to work longer than their peers should be given a lump sum rather than an increased annuity. There are obvious adverse selection problems with offering such a choice because many people have good reason to believe they will enjoy longer or shorter lives (and thus receive a larger or smaller number of incremental payments) than the actuarial tables predict. However, once a worker has earned the basic pension payable at the age of initial entitlement, payment of a lump sum for deferring retirement has considerable attraction provided that public policy aims to encourage later retirement and people prefer lump sums to increased annuities. It should be noted, however, that the lump sum would most likely increase the chance that retirees who may supplement their pension with part-time work will find themselves with inadequate income at some future date when that work becomes impossible. We have no interest in encouraging schemes that exploit people's willingness to trade their entitlements unwisely or sell them more cheaply than would be in their enlightened self-interest. But we are loath to reject outright the possibility of offering retirees plans or options that could serve their objective interests, or even subjective preferences, better than the current system.

## Revealed versus Constructed Preference

Traditional economic models assume people have stable and logically consistent preferences. Confronted with choices, people order them according to their preferences and choose the best alternative. Behavior reveals the well-defined and stable preferences that reside within each person. However appealing this view may be, behavioral decision theory research has produced over the past several decades a growing body of evidence that people's preferences often are not simply *revealed*, but rather *constructed* in the process of elicitation. In particular, hundreds of studies have demonstrated that preference reversals can occur when different modes of preference elicitation are used. The most general message of our framing study thus is far from new. Our survey results break new ground primarily in demonstrating that even real-world decisions as consequential, and much discussed, as those involving retirement and benefit planning might be susceptible to the nonnormative influences encapsulated in prospect theory. Indeed, empirical results such as those reported in this chapter have led the distinguished decision theorist Paul Slovic to ask, "If different elicitation procedures produce different orderings of options, how can preferences be defined and in what sense do they exist?"[18]

This question takes on particular significance in contexts that are as important, complex, and relevant to public policy as those involving retirement. Policymakers whose job entails divining public will and implementing actions that purportedly honor it face an obvious dilemma if their job

18. Slovic (1995).

also entails framing the options and questions designed to discover that will. It is not an exaggeration to say that conventional ideas of the nature of democracy itself come into question.

Viewing preferences as constructed rather than revealed expressions of will is particularly problematic in situations for which no natural or neutral framing exists. Choice of a reference-point age for calculating social security benefits and the choice of gain or loss framing to describe the consequences of early or late retirement age is by no means the only case in point. To return to an example we used in opening, if people prefer surgery to radiation when the treatments are described in terms of survival rates, but prefer radiation to surgery when the treatments are described in terms of mortality rates, which statement of the problem constitutes the neutral description? Which is the one patients "ought" to be provided with and which is the one physicians "ought" to use in advising them? Is the problem solved by giving decisionmakers both framings and letting them choose the one they find most natural or useful? Policymakers cannot easily skirt the issue or the ethical problems these questions raise. Their decisions determine the status quo that in turn becomes the reference point used in evaluating new options. Once policymakers fully appreciate this state of affairs, the full extent of their power and the complexity of their ethical responsibilities cannot be ignored.

# References

Clark, H. H., and M. F. Schober. 1992. "Asking Questions and Influencing Answers." In *Questions about Questions,* edited by J. M. Tanur, 15–48. Russell Sage.

Converse, P. E., and M. W. Traugott. 1986. "Assessing the Accuracy of Polls and Surveys." *Science* 234 (4890): 1094–98.

Elster, J. 1979. *Ulysses and the Sirens.* Cambridge University Press.

Fischhoff, B. 1991. "Value Elicitation: Is There Anything in There?" *American Psychologist* 46 (August): 835–47.

Kahneman, D., and A. Tversky. 1979. "Prospect Theory: An Analysis of Decision under Risk." *Econometrica* 47 (March): 263–91.

———. 1984. "Choices, Values, and Frames." *American Psychologist* 39 (4): 341–50.

———. 1988. "Rational Choice and the Framing of Decisions." In *Decision Making: Descriptive, Normative, and Prescriptive Interactions,* edited by D. Bell, H. Raiffa, and A. Tversky, 166–92. Cambridge University Press.

McNeill, B. J., and others. 1982. "On the Elicitation of Preferences for Alternative Therapies." *New England Journal of Medicine* 306 (May 27): 1259–62.

Payne, S. L. 1951. *The Art of Asking Questions.* Princeton University Press.

Savage, L. J. 1954. *The Foundations of Statistics.* John Wiley.

Schelling, T. 1981. "Economic Reasoning and the Ethics of Policy." *Public Interest* 63 (Spring): 37–61.

———. 1984. "Self-Command in Practice, in Policy, and in a Theory of Rational Choice." *American Economic Review* 74 (2): 1–11.

Schuman, H., and S. Presser. 1981. *Questions and Answers in Surveys.* Academic Press.

Shefrin, H. M., and R. Thaler. 1992. "Mental Accounting, Saving, and Self-Control." In *Choice over Time,* edited by G. Loewenstein and J. Elster, 287–330. Russell Sage.

Slovic, P. 1995. "The Construction of Preference." *American Psychologist* 50 (5): 364–71.

Sudman, S., N. Bradburn, and N. Schwarz. 1996. *Thinking about Answers: The Application of Cognitive Processes to Survey Methodology.* San Francisco: Jossey-Bass.

Thaler, R. 1980. "Toward a Positive Theory of Consumer Choice." *Journal of Economic Behavior and Organization* 1 (March): 39–60.

Thaler, R., and G. Loewenstein. 1992. "Intertemporal Choice." In *The Winner's Curse,* edited by R. Thaler, 92–106. Free Press.

Thaler, R., and H. M. Shefrin. 1981. "An Economic Theory of Self-Control." *Journal of Political Economy* 89 (April): 392–410.

COMMENT BY

# Daniel Kahneman

In their chapter David Fetherstonhaugh and Lee Ross present preliminary evidence to support three conclusions: that the timing of retirement may be affected by the presentation, or "framing," of the financial consequences of this decision, that retirees may prefer a lump sum over a financially more advantageous stream of income, and that there is much skepticism about the future of social security. I will comment on the first two of these findings.

The authors' initial study investigates the effects of differential labeling of the difference between the social security benefits of an individual who retires at age 65 or at age 68. Following Richard Thaler's classic discussion of the effect of labeling the difference between cash and credit prices for gas as a credit surcharge or a cash bonus, the difference in benefits is framed either as a penalty for retiring at age 65 or as a credit for retiring at age 68.[1] As they expected, the authors found that the preference for late retirement is generally stronger when the difference in benefits is described as penalty than as a credit. What "does the work" in producing this effect? It is instructive to examine the wording of one of their questions (the italics are in the original):

> Under the current social security system, the *average* male American worker who is choosing to retire either at age 65 or 68 would have the following two choices: A. He could retire age 68 and begin receiving a social security pension of $12,500 a year, or B. He could retire *earlier,* at age 65 instead of 68, and begin receiving a social security pension of $10,000 a year, which is equal to $12,500 a year *minus a penalty* of $2,500 a year for retiring early.

In the alternative frame the order of the two options is reversed and the income difference is presented as a credit for delaying retirement. The authors focus on the framing of the cash difference as a credit or a penalty as an explanation of the different responses to the two versions, but they recognize that other interpretations are viable, a matter of some importance because different interpretations of the results could have different implications for policy.

What impresses me most as I read the question is that it implicitly designates retiring at 68 as *normal.* Option A is the default option, whereas option B is a permitted variant. Several cues point to this difference: option

---

1. For the classic account, see Thaler (1980).

A is presented first, its description is shorter, and option B is described as a variation ("He could retire *earlier* . . ."). Designating an option as a default is a potent manipulation. It is a commonplace of both common sense and social science that the probability of an action's being performed is greatly increased if it is perceived as the default action in given circumstances. Furthermore, this prediction holds even in the absence of any tangible incentives that favor the "normal" default action. It is therefore quite reasonable for survey respondents to infer that an individual's choice of retirement age will favor the default age. This inference would be reasonable even if postretirement benefits were independent of retirement age. I am therefore uncertain of whether the results obtained by Fetherstonhaugh and Ross are due to the implied retirement norm or to the framing of the difference in benefits.

The remarkable attractive power of a default action is nicely illustrated by an observation reported by E. J. Johnson and colleagues.[2] New Jersey and Pennsylvania allow car owners to give up the right to sue in exchange for reduced insurance premiums. In New Jersey motorists have to acquire the right to sue actively, at an additional cost. In Pennsylvania the full right to sue is the default. The effect of this manipulation is large indeed: 75 percent of Pennsylvanians but only 20 percent of New Jersey drivers retain the full right to sue. The ambiguity that I have noted in the interpretation of Fethersonhaugh and Ross's results is also present in this real-world case. Is the advantage of the default option due to loss aversion or does it reflect a more general behavioral inertia?

The advantage of default options is probably overdetermined. Staying with the default option is cognitively undemanding: this is what we do when we are not thinking very hard. Staying with the default is almost like doing nothing, whereas departing from it is an act of commission. As the famous distinction between killing and letting die illustrates, people are considered more responsible for the undesirable consequences of acts they commit than for the consequences of their omissions.[3] Increased responsibility is associated with greater threat of regret. Indeed, people experience stronger and "hotter" regret for the same consequence when it arises from something they did than from something they did not do. The default is also favored by a desire to conform and to do what most other people do. Finally, in the context of choices that are offered by a benevolent agency, the default is likely to be perceived as an implicit recommendation about what is best for most people.

2. Johnson and others (1993).
3. Baron (1993).

These observations have implications for both making policy and implementing it. The policy implication is that *any* factor that causes a change in the perception of the normal retirement age will have self-reinforcing effects on people's behavior. There are many ways of inducing such a change—most obviously by changing actual benefits. A change, even if it is initially resisted, is likely to be accepted eventually as a normal state of affairs and will define a set point that will attract the free choices of many individuals. This is also the conclusion that Fetherstonhaugh and Ross reached, perhaps on slightly different grounds. The implementation of policy is further complicated by the fact that there may be no neutral way of eliciting people's choices on important issues. The authors took on the challenge of showing that different formulations of the retirement age question could have a significant effect on preferences. The challenge of designing forms that do *not* bias choices by implicitly designating a default option could be even more daunting. The crucial point of the framing examples that Fetherstonhaugh and Ross discussed in their introduction may be that bias is unavoidable because it is not generally practical to present people with multiple frames. A frame must be chosen, and no frame is neutral. As they noted, the inevitability of framing effects raises subtle and difficult ethical issues for the implementation of policy.

Similar ethical issues are raised, even more obviously, by the second main finding of the chapter, the attractiveness of an actuarially inferior lump payment over a stream of retirement income. This finding would not be considered a problem in the standard intellectual framework of economic analysis, which takes agents to be fully rational and (in part therefore) encourages a norm of consumer sovereignty. Rational agents are supposed to understand the options they face and to consider the choice between lump sum and annuity in terms of coherent preferences for the trade-offs of wealth, risk, and time. More generally, it is assumed that people have good reasons for the choices they make and should therefore be free to apply any utility function and discount rate they please. The idea that citizens can be and should be assumed to be rational is a powerful argument against paternalistic concerns. Indeed, this idea has often been used to raise doubts about the need for the very institution of social security.

Life is much less tidy for those of us who think that the assumption of perfect rationality is not sufficiently realistic to guide policy in all situations. A belief that citizens are only boundedly rational imposes several burdens on policymakers. As the first studies of Fetherstonhaugh and Ross illustrate, the admission that people are susceptible to framing effects turns any choice of frame into an intervention, which almost inevitably biases choices one way or another. The lump sum question that the authors studied illustrates another type of dilemma: when is it appropriate to offer boundedly rational people options that they are likely to prefer for the "wrong" reasons?

The issues of bounded rationality and limited self-control arise with particular force in the context of time preferences. Contrary to standard rational theory, observed discount rates are susceptible to framing effects, and they also vary with the size of the stake, the nature of the event (gain or loss), and its immediacy.[4] The particular choice the authors studied between a lump sum and an annuity could also be affected by a cognitive bias, which has been called a "wealth illusion": the lump sum looks like a great deal of money when set against a periodic payment. This perception may bias intuitive beliefs about the mathematics of annuities in a direction that favors the lump payment. As Fetherstonhaugh and Ross note in their concluding comments, the acknowledgment of bounded rationality forces an uncomfortable choice between schemes that exploit people's mistakes and rules that restrict people's freedom to choose.

# References

Baron, Jonathan. 1993. *Morality and Rational Choice*. Dordrecht: Kluwer.
Johnson, E. J., and others. 1993. "Framing, Probability Distortions, and Insurance Decisions. *Journal of Risk and Uncertainty* 7: 35–51.
Loewenstein, George, and Richard H. Thaler. 1992. "Intertemporal Choice." In *The Winner's Curse,* edited by Richard Thaler, 92–106. Free Press.
Thaler, Richard H. 1980. "Toward a Positive Theory of Consumer Choice." *Journal of Economic Behavior and Organization* 1: 19–60.

4. Loewenstein and Thaler (1992).

GEORGE LOEWENSTEIN
DRAZEN PRELEC
ROBERTO WEBER

# 7

# What, Me Worry? A Psychological Perspective on Economic Aspects of Retirement

Elton Pasea is a mutual fund salesman's worst nightmare. . . . He lives quite nicely in Nederland, Texas, on $1,200 a month: $700 from Social Security and $500 from a union pension. He has never owned stocks, bonds, or mutual funds. His life savings of $33,000 are invested in certificates of deposit. . . . He doesn't have a million-dollar nest egg, and his income isn't at least 70 percent of his preretirement figure. . . . How can the poor wretch possibly be having such a good time?

"When Enough Really Is Enough," *New York Times*,
October 4, 1998

Economists and policymakers worry chronically that people are not saving enough for retirement. Many of the chapters in this volume exemplify that concern. The life-cycle model of saving and spending posits that people save when they are working and dissave during retirement so as to

This study was completed while the authors were visiting the Center for Advanced Study in the Behavioral Sciences. We are thankful for support from National Science Foundation grant SBR-960123 (to the Center) and for Loewenstein from NSF grant SBR-9521914 to the Center for Integrated Study of the Human Dimensions of Global Change at Carnegie Mellon University.

maintain a roughly constant level of consumption over their lifetime.[1] However, numerous studies report that consumption declines dramatically after retirement. Although economists have debated the cause of the drop in consumption, most are in agreement that the drop is unplanned, unexpected, and unintended.[2] For example, one recent article that tests a variety of explanations for the consumption drop concludes that "the only way to reconcile fully the fall in consumption with the life-cycle hypothesis is with the systematic arrival of unexpected adverse information."[3] In other words, these authors contend that people save too little for retirement, are surprised by their own postretirement poverty, and are forced to cut back on consumption. Concern about the insufficiency of retirement savings has led to calls for diverse interventions, such as new incentives to encourage saving, increases in social security benefits, and educational initiatives.

An implicit, and thus rarely tested, assumption underlies economists' concerns about the inadequacy of retirement saving: that the decline in consumption following retirement reduces the *well-being* of retirees.[4] If the drop in consumption were not assumed to reduce well-being, it would undoubtedly be viewed as not particularly disturbing—that is, as little more than an empirical challenge to the life-cycle model.

Although it might seem obvious that well-being depends greatly on consumption, research on the determinants of subjective well-being provides meager support for such a relationship. Studies employing diverse research designs and conducted on a wide range of populations have concluded that people adapt quickly to changes in income and that the relationship between happiness (or life satisfaction) and income is tenuous at best. This suggests that any effect of a postretirement drop in consumption on retiree well-being is likely to be small and transient. These predictions are reinforced by a chorus of critics (as highlighted in the *New York Times* article from which the opening quote was excerpted) who view economists' dire warnings as alarmist and as creating unnecessary angst among policymakers and savers.

1. Modigliani and Brumberg (1954).

2. Bernheim, Skinner, and Weinberg (1997).

3. Banks, Blundell, and Tanner (1998, p. 769).

4. In economics, consumption is not valued per se, but rather as a source of utility. Although many economists have disavowed any link between utility and well-being, it is difficult to draw many normative implications, such as those made by retirement researchers, without assuming that utility is at least strongly correlated with well-being.

# Income and Happiness

Most psychological research dealing with the relationship between happiness or subjective well-being (SWB) and economic variables has focused on income rather than consumption, probably because more information is available about income. There are many ways to measure this relationship, for example, across countries at one point in time, across time for one country, or across people within a country. Although each method tends to yield somewhat different results, the overall picture one gains from this diverse body of research is that the relationship between SWB and income is, at best, weak. Most people report that they lead satisfying lives, and measured well-being differs little even when material circumstances differ dramatically.[5] Thus, while a study of the well-being of 100,000 people from fifty-five countries in which average per capita income ranged from $120 (Tanzania) to $32,790 (Switzerland) did find a strong correlation (.58) between per capita GDP and subjective well-being, the correlation was completely eliminated once cross-national differences in respect for human rights were taken into consideration.[6] Studies of the relationship between SWB and income within a single country typically find positive but small correlations. For example, the correlation between wealth and reported happiness in the United States is only .12.[7] Finally, there is absolutely no evidence that the average reported SWB in a country increases as average real income increases.[8] For example, between 1958 and 1987 per capita real income in Japan rose fivefold, but there was no reported increase in subjective well-being.

Most of the research on how changes in income affect SWB has focused on *increases* in income, because incomes have generally tended to increase over time. Few studies have examined people's reactions to decreases in income, except for studies of job loss (which are difficult to interpret because job loss has many consequences that go beyond reduced income). However, other research has found that people adapt remarkably well in the long run to adverse outcomes, such as paralysis or the death of children or spouses, that intuitively seem more devastating than a decrease in income or consumption.[9] Not only do people adapt rapidly to such

5. Diener and Diener (1996); and Myers and Diener (1995).
6. Diener, Diener, and Diener (1995). See also Veenhoven (1991); and Diener and others (1993).
7. Diener and others (1993).
8. Campbell (1981); Diener (1984); and Easterlin (1974, 1995).
9. Frederick and Loewenstein (1999).

adverse outcomes, but they seem to underestimate their own powers of adaptation.[10]

If income accounts for little of the considerable variance in subjective well-being among persons, what factors *do* account for it? Genetic makeup seems by far the most important. According to a recent study of twins, genetic differences account for about 60 percent of the variation in SWB.[11] Other important determinants include nonmaterial aspects of life, such as one's social connectedness or whether one has children, and if so, their ages and how well they are functioning.[12] In sum, the psychological research provides little reason to expect a decline in consumption at retirement to have a strong or long-lasting effect on SWB.[13]

## Happiness in Retirement

Some research has examined how retirement affects subjective well-being. Are retirees really less happy, as one might expect given the observed decrease in consumption and the belief that consumption is an important

10. Gilbert and others (1998); and Loewenstein and Schkade (1999).

11. Lykken and Tellegen (1996).

12. Michalos (1987).

13. On the face of it, the finding that SWB does not depend much on income seems inconsistent with the great efforts that people make to improve their material circumstances. What might be the reasons for this apparent discrepancy? One possibility is that SWB actually does increase with income but the relationship is obscured by flaws in the measure of well-being. The greatest potential problem results from people's self-norming of SWB scales based on their own range of personal experiences. If people anchor SWB scales according to their own range of experience, then as their experiences change, the interpretation of the scale end points will change in the same direction. For example, although paraplegics rate themselves lower in SWB than people in perfect health, they nevertheless rate themselves higher (3.9 on a 1 to 5 scale) than most people would expect (Brickman, Coates, and Janoff-Bulman, 1978). These high ratings of SWB could mean that they are happy with their lives or it could mean that paraplegics, having experienced the intense misery of becoming paraplegic, have different notion of unhappiness. That is, a 1 on the 1 to 5 scale has a more negative meaning for paraplegics; and a 4 on a scale that is anchored on the bottom by the intense miseries of a paralyzing accident may reflect a much lower level of SWB than a 4 on a similar scale whose low point corresponds to more mundane misery. Such scale-norming would result in an underreporting of actual changes in happiness.

Another possible explanation for the discrepancy is that although people might eventually adapt to a change in income, the transition period could be pleasurable (when income rises) or painful (when it drops). People care a lot about brief periods of pleasure or pain (for example, they care tremendously about the last few minutes or even seconds of plane crash victims' lives), and these transitional periods of pleasure or pain could have considerable motivational force even if they are short-lived. Finally, it is possible that the lack of relationship between SWB and income is not artifactual and that the discrepancy results from people's erroneous belief that such a relationship exists. Many social critics (for example, Scitovsky, 1976) have argued that people overestimate the extent to which money buys happiness, and as a result exert too much time and effort on increasing their incomes relative to other activities that would bring them greater long-term happiness.

determinant of well-being? What factors in addition to differences in income account for differences in happiness? Analogous to the research showing little connection between income and SWB, research on happiness in retirement suggests that SWB drops little, if at all, in retirement, despite reduced income and deteriorating health.

A study of 310 Israeli male retirees, for example, found that 72 percent were satisfied or very satisfied with retirement, mostly because they were pleased to have given up work, they welcomed free time, and they enjoyed activities with family and friends.[14] Preretirement counseling and preparation for retirement had little effect. Satisfaction with free time was affected by level of education, work after retirement, and indoor recreational activities. Family influenced happiness mainly through shared leisure with spouse and contact with family, while rest and tranquillity were affected by state of health. Previous occupation had no effect on satisfaction.

A study of U.S. retirees found that retirement was associated with reduced reported happiness, but that this effect was statistically insignificant once the number of chronic health conditions and recent changes in health were included as controls.[15] The negative relationship between SWB and retirement was also partly due to changes in income, though the effect of income was smaller than for health. According to this study, divorce, separation, and widowhood also reduced SWB, as did unplanned retirement.

A subsequent study based on the same data set found that involvement in activities was important in determining the subjective well-being of retired men, and that poor health reduced well-being largely because it interfered with leisure activities.[16] Another study of the same data found no difference in reported happiness between retired and nonretired men. Voluntary retirees reported being happier than workers, while those who retired because of poor health reported the lowest SWB. Early retirement appeared to be unrelated to reported happiness.[17]

Another longitudinal study of 117 men found that well-being improved in the first year of retirement. Also, the factors responsible for overall well-being changed during retirement. Immediately following voluntary retirement, good health and adequate income were principally responsible for

14. Kremer (1985).

15. Beck (1982). This study is based on the National Longitudinal Survey (NLS) cohort of mature men.

16. Beck and Page (1988).

17. Crowley (1986). This study used a question directly asking about the respondent's happiness and a composite index scale measuring effect. Knesek (1992) confirmed the finding on early retirement using a different sample and a different measure of happiness.

high SWB. In later years, retirees with an "internal locus of control"—that is, those who felt that they were personally responsible for the events in their lives—had higher subjective well-being.[18] A study of 60 retired certified public accountants found that on the whole they were very satisfied with their activities and work, personal associations, health, and financial situation, the four areas on the Retirement Descriptive Index (developed to measure retirement satisfaction of professionals).[19] Volunteer work also correlated with retirement satisfaction, but length of retirement, reasons for retirement, education, and population of retirement community were not significant predictors of satisfaction. A majority responded that retirement was what they expected.

The research on postretirement well-being, therefore, tells a relatively coherent story. The decline in income associated with retirement reduces well-being modestly, but factors such as health, social contact and networks, preretirement planning, the timing of retirement, and whether retirement was voluntary are considerably more important. Moreover, perhaps because the increase in leisure time compensates for the loss of income, retirees are generally happy and satisfied with their lives both in absolute terms and relative to how they felt prior to retirement.

## Our Research

Our focus in this paper is on the impact of retirement on SWB, particularly insofar as retirement is accompanied by a decline in disposable income. If people have undersaved for retirement, and if income is in fact an important determinant of well-being, then one should expect to observe a significant downward shift in well-being among retirees—a decline that is mediated by decreases in income or consumption. Moreover, if the decline in consumption is not anticipated, as recent analyses suggest, then the resultant decline in well-being should also not be anticipated by the retirees themselves. Based on the literature just reviewed, however, we anticipated, to the contrary, that retirees would not experience an unanticipated drop in subjective well-being. We therefore extended our investigation to two additional questions. First, *why* does the decline in dispos-

---

18. Gall, Evans, and Howard (1997). Reitzes, Mutran, and Fernandez (1996) also found an increase in subjective well-being following retirement. They followed 757 older workers for two years and found lower depression scores and higher self-esteem scores for the part of their sample that retired.

19. Ward, Wilson, and Ward (1994). The index was developed by Smith, Kendall, and Hulin (1969).

able income not affect well-being? For example, do retired persons restructure their lives in ways that downplay the importance of the consumption of market goods? Second, and closely related, what factors *do* influence happiness in retirement? If consumption is not a very important determinant of happiness but other aspects of life are, there is a distinct possibility that non-income-based government interventions—for example, greater funding for senior citizen centers or recreational activities—could have a much greater impact (and at lower cost) than income-based interventions.

To address these questions, we conducted a survey of older male Americans who either were facing retirement or had retired in the previous few years. The survey included items intended to measure subjective well-being and potential financial and nonfinancial determinants of SWB in, and just before, retirement. We report evidence on how happy the retired are compared to people on the verge of retirement, what determines the well-being of both groups and how these determinants differ, whether nonretired persons correctly predict their own well-being in retirement, whether the retired recall their own preretirement happiness accurately, and what types of regrets the retired have regarding their own preparations for and timing of retirement. Even if the retired say that, despite lower levels of consumption, they are as happy as their not-yet-retired counterparts, it is still of interest to learn what they regret about their preparations for retirement, especially if they perceive themselves as having saved too little.

*The Survey*

The survey, which was self-administered by respondents, consisted of four legal-sized pages of questions. The first section asked nonretired respondents questions about their jobs—their occupation, work experience, and hours worked per week, and how much they liked their work—and about when, if ever, they planned to retire. Retired respondents were asked similar questions about their last job. They were also asked when they retired and why—for example, whether they were forced to retire and whether declining health was responsible.

Next, respondents were asked questions designed to measure various aspects of well-being. For nonretired persons, these questions addressed general happiness; happiness about five specific aspects of life—housing, local area, health, standard of living, and leisure-time activities; whether they expected to be happier or less happy after retirement; and happiness relative to their friends and acquaintances. For the retired, the questions were similar, except that instead of being asked how happy they expected to be, they were asked how happy they were in retirement relative to before they retired, and also how happy they were relative to their expectations before retirement.

Both groups were then asked to state whether they agreed or disagreed—on a scale from 1 (strongly agree) to 4 (strongly disagree)—with thirty-one statements, twenty-one of which were designed to measure feelings about time and money. Six of these items were taken from a widely used depression scale and were intended as an alternative measure of emotional well-being.

The next section asked respondents whether they agreed or disagreed with twelve statements dealing with possible regrets about preparing for retirement. Nine of these statements dealt with financial aspects of retirement, two with the timing of retirement ("I should have retired [made plans to retire] earlier" and "I should have tried [be trying] to delay my retirement"), and one with planning for free time ("I underestimated the importance of knowing how to use my free time in retirement" and "I believe that knowing how to use my free time will be important in retirement"). Finally, we asked respondents about interactions with family in and out of the area, about when they started to save for retirement (from "during their twenties" to "never"), and about income from various sources.

## The Sample

A consumer research firm, Market Facts, administered the survey. Market Facts sent surveys to 500 people aged 60 to 65 who had not retired as of their previous contact with Market Facts, and to 500 people aged 65 to 70 who had retired. The 1,000 people were drawn from Market Facts' Consumer Mail Panel, a sample of approximately 450,000 households nationwide that participate as survey respondents. The sample is meant to be demographically representative of the U.S. population based on such measures as household income, household size, age of head of household, geographic region, and urban-rural location, but it falls far short of being a probability sample of male Americans in these age ranges. As is evident in table 7-1, which presents selected demographic characteristics of the samples, and table 7-2, which presents a breakdown of income sources, respondents have higher mean family incomes than the U.S. average, the composition of that income differs, and minorities are substantially

Table 7-1. *Demographic Characteristics of Not Retired and Retired Samples*

| Characteristic | Not Retired (n = 204) | Retired (n = 275) | Significance of difference[a] |
|---|---|---|---|
| Age | 61.9 | 67.9 | 0.001 |
| Married (percent) | 81.1 | 78.8 | n.s |
| Live alone (percent) | 77.5 | 89.2 | 0.001 |
| Number of children | 2.60 | 3.10 | 0.01 |
| Type of work (percent) | | | |
| White collar, high status | 46.0 | 39.3 | n.s. |
| White collar, low status | 18.7 | 15.0 | n.s. |
| Blue collar | 22.7 | 25.5 | n.s. |
| Family income (dollars) | 66,628 | 43,392 | 0.001 |
| Recalled preretirement income (dollars) | . . . | 47,399 | . . . |
| Years since retirement | . . . | 8.20 | . . . |
| Plan to retire (percent) | 75.5 | . . . | . . . |
| Expected years to retirement (for those who plan to retire) | 3.34 | . . . | . . . |
| Age stopped working | | 59.7 | . . . |
| Geographic region (percent) | | | n.s. |
| New England | 6.4 | 5.5 | |
| Middle Atlantic | 15.2 | 12.0 | |
| East North Central | 19.6 | 17.5 | |
| West North Central | 9.3 | 5.8 | |
| South Atlantic | 19.6 | 20.0 | |
| East South Central | 3.4 | 7.3 | |
| West South Central | 8.3 | 9.1 | |
| Mountain | 3.9 | 6.9 | |
| Pacific | 14.2 | 16.0 | |
| Minority status (percent) | | | n.s. |
| Hispanic | 3.9 | 2.6 | |
| Asian | 1.5 | 0.0 | |
| Black | 1.0 | 1.8 | |

Source: Authors' calculations from survey.
a. n.s. indicates not significant.

underrepresented. Not surprisingly, the nonretired report much more wage income and less income from retirement plans, social security, and savings than do the retired.

Response rates among retirees were substantially higher than among workers—275 versus 204—largely because more than half of the "nonre-

Table 7-2. *Income by Source, for Not Retired and Retired Samples*[a]

Dollars unless otherwise indicated

| Income source | Not retired | Retired |
|---|---|---|
| Wages | 53,847 (99%) (23,440) | 6,721 (41%) (14,799) |
| Retirement plan | | 16,119 (88%) (14,879) |
| Social security | | 12,794 (97%) (6,759) |
| Income from savings | 11,918 (83%) (18,833) | 9,529 (75%) (14,622) |
| Government benefits | 28 (18%) (9,617) | 1,308 (17%) (4,256) |
| Income from relatives | 633 (3%) (6,200) | 58 (1%) (564) |

Source: See table 7-1.

a. Percentages in parentheses refer to fraction of group earning any income from this source. Dollar amounts in parentheses are standard deviations.

tirees" had retired since their last contact with Market Facts and returned the survey unanswered as they were instructed to do.

Our main sampling goal was to produce comparable samples of nonretired and retired men for comparison, not to produce a random sample of American men. Data in table 7-1 suggest that we achieved this goal. Other than expected age and income differences, the only significant differences between the two samples were in the percent living alone or with only their spouse (which was slightly higher for the retired sample) and the number of children (which was again higher for the retired). Both differences could potentially be explained by the more advanced ages of respondents in the retired sample.

## Findings: Happiness

Consistent with other recent research on subjective well-being both among retirees and in the general population, both nonretirees and retirees report high levels of happiness (table 7-3). While some differences between the

Table 7-3. *Happiness by Retirement Status*[a]

| Measure | Not retired (n = 204) | Retired (n = 275) | Significance of difference[b] (p<) |
|---|---|---|---|
| Feelings about life (1 = very unhappy to 4 = very happy) | | | |
| 1. Overall | 3.36 (0.65) | 3.46 (0.68) | n.s. |
| 2. Housing | 3.55 (0.65) | 3.66 (0.59) | 0.05 |
| 3. Local area | 3.45 (0.72) | 3.60 (0.62) | 0.05 |
| 4. Health | 3.27 (0.74) | 3.01 (0.94) | 0.01 |
| 5. Standard of living | 3.41 (0.63) | 3.36 (0.73) | n.s. |
| 6. Leisure activities | 3.12 (0.81) | 3.39 (0.74) | 0.001 |
| 7. Happiness relative to friends (1 = much less happy to 5 = much happier) | 3.63 (0.76) | 3.57 (0.88) | n.s. |
| Depression measures (−1.5 = less happy to 1.5 = happier) | | | |
| 8. I feel depressed | 1.05 (0.74) | 0.87 (0.87) | 0.05 |
| 9. I enjoy eating and have a good appetite | 1.11 (0.61) | 0.96 (0.72) | 0.05 |
| 10. I feel that everything I do is an effort | 0.78 (0.75) | 0.66 (0.88) | n.s. |
| 11. I feel happy | 0.82 (0.65) | 0.84 (0.77) | n.s. |
| 12. I feel lonely | 1.01 (0.76) | 0.89 (0.86) | n.s. |
| 13. I feel hopeful about the future | 0.60 (0.77) | 0.60 (0.82) | n.s. |
| 14. Aggregate depression measure (−9 = less happy to 9 = happier) | 5.41 (2.91) | 4.85 (3.59) | 0.1 |
| 15. Aggregate happiness measure (constructed variable) | 0.021 (0.905) | −0.009 (1.069) | n.s. |

Source: See table 7-1.

a. Standard deviations are in parentheses.

b. n.s. indicates not significant.

two groups are statistically significant, the average scores are remarkably similar. For example, both groups rate themselves approximately 3.4 on an overall happiness scale from 1 to 4 (row 1, table 7-3).

Although the two groups produce similar responses on overall measures of happiness (see also row 7, table 7-3), some differences are worth noting. The retired are slightly, but significantly, less happy as measured by the aggregate depression measure (row 14). The main causes of this difference are that retired respondents report being more depressed and enjoying eating less than do the nonretired. On measures of specific dimensions of happiness (rows 2 through 6), the retired group reports feeling better than the nonretired about housing, local area, and leisure, but worse about health. Despite a large difference in average incomes, the nonretired and retired groups report similar levels of satisfaction with their standard of living (row 5).

To facilitate analyses of overall well-being, we constructed an aggregate happiness index, which gives equal weight to overall feelings about life, happiness relative to friends, and the happiness measure derived from the depression items.[20] The aggregate happiness variable is normalized, with a mean of zero for the combined sample and standard deviation of one. We use the index as our central measure of happiness throughout the remainder of this chapter. Aggregate happiness of the nonretired and the retired (row 15) is almost identical.

In short, there is very little evidence in our sample of any serious drop in happiness following retirement. To the extent that happiness does drop, the cause seems to be a decline in health (row 4). Despite a 35 percent drop in family income, reported satisfaction with standard of living was remarkably similar in the two groups.

## What Determines Happiness?

In an attempt to explain happiness, we regressed the happiness index against the respondent's satisfaction with the six aspects of life: work, housing, local area, health, living standard, and leisure. These factors explain about half of the variance in the index—49 percent for the nonretired and 50 percent for the retired (table 7-4). For both samples, feelings about health and living standards are significant and equally important. Leisure is significant for both groups but more important for

---

20. These component measures are highly correlated ($r_{12} = .42$, $r_{13} = .65$, and $r_{23} = .44$).

Table 7-4. *Impact of Happiness Dimensions on Overall Happiness Measure*[a]

| Happiness dimension | Not retired | Retired |
|---|---|---|
| Satisfaction with (1 = very unhappy to 4 = very happy) | | |
| Work | 0.284*** | 0.046 |
| | (0.064) | (0.071) |
| Housing | 0.025 | 0.114 |
| | (0.095) | (0.102) |
| Local area | 0.118 | −0.060 |
| | (0.080) | (0.092) |
| Health | 0.381*** | 0.397*** |
| | (0.072) | (0.062) |
| Living standard | 0.262** | 0.225** |
| | (0.091) | (0.079) |
| Leisure | 0.211** | 0.465*** |
| | (0.070) | (0.080) |
| Constant | 4.222*** | 3.895*** |
| | (0.358) | (0.388) |
| *Summary statistic* | | |
| Number of observations | 194 | 254 |
| *R*-squared | 0.485 | 0.503 |
| Adjusted *R*-squared | 0.468 | 0.491 |

a. Dependent variable is aggregate happiness. $*p < 0.05$; $**p < 0.01$; $***p < 0.001$. Standard errors are in parentheses.

the retired. For the nonretired sample, feelings about work are also significant.[21]

Two main conclusions emerge from the analysis of the regressions presented in table 7-4. First, living standard does seem to matter—about as much as quality of leisure and feelings about work for those who are working, but less than feelings about health. Whether satisfaction with one's standard of living is correlated with one's income or consumption is, however, unclear. Second, following retirement, satisfaction from leisure

21. A pooled regression including interaction terms (not shown in the table) revealed significant differences between the two groups in the importance of feelings about work, which is more important for the nonretired, and in the importance of leisure, which is much more important for the retired sample.

increases markedly as a determinant of overall happiness. In fact, the difference in satisfaction from leisure between the retired and the nonretired almost exactly offsets the difference in satisfaction from work between the two groups. It is as if leisure was the job of the retired.

Consistent with earlier findings on SWB in the psychology literature, objective variables explain remarkably little of the variance in self-reported happiness (table 7-5). Drawing down on savings (which we thought might be a source of anxiety for people who are saving for retirement or are retired), homeownership (which we though might confer a sense of security), contact with family in or out of the respondent's local area, marital status, having children, level of education, and age all had insignificant effects on self-reported happiness.[22]

For the nonretired, respect on the job has a significant positive effect on happiness. The meaningfulness of this finding is clouded by the fact that "respect at job," the only subjective variable included in this regression, may be picking up differences in optimism or general outlook on life as well as actual effects of job respect on happiness. Contact with family in the area is marginally significant ($p < 0.08$). For the retired, the only statistically significant influence on the happiness index is whether respondents retired voluntarily. The coefficients on whether respondents have children are large but of opposite sign for the two groups and are statistically insignificant, suggesting that people have strong but highly varying reactions to their relations with their children.

We also examined the relationship between happiness and four job categories: white-collar high status, white-collar low status, blue-collar, and other. The overall effects were statistically insignificant. Blue-collar workers were less happy than low-status white-collar workers, who were less happy than high-status white-collar workers, but these differences were not significant. Low-status white-collar workers were the happiest group before retirement but the least happy following retirement, and the difference was statistically significant.[23]

*Predicted and Remembered Happiness*

In addition to asking respondents to report their current happiness, we also asked nonretired respondents to report how they expected their happiness

---

22. Of course, these regressions should be treated with caution because many of the variables are not truly exogenous but result from decisions. For example, perhaps children have little impact on happiness because those people who want them have them, and those who do not want them do not.

23. The difference was .41, significant at the 5 percent level.

Table 7-5. *Objective Determinants of Overall Happiness Measure*[a]

| Measure | Not retired | Retired |
|---|---|---|
| Income | −0.003 | 0.005 |
| (thousands of dollars) | (0.002) | (0.003) |
| Draw down savings | −0.259 | 0.053 |
| | (0.160) | (0.148) |
| Own home | −0.087 | −0.159 |
| | (0.275) | (0.276) |
| Contact with family | 0.015 | 0.001 |
| in area (visits per month) | (0.008) | (0.008) |
| Contact with family | 0.042 | 0.004 |
| outside area (visits per month) | (0.060) | (0.037) |
| Children (yes or no) | −0.395 | 0.275 |
| | (0.274) | (0.271) |
| Married | 0.231 | 0.077 |
| | (0.223) | (0.224) |
| Education (years) | 0.030 | 0.013 |
| | (0.027) | (0.029) |
| Age | 0.013 | 0.010 |
| | (0.044) | (0.040) |
| Hours worked per week | 0.000 | 0.001 |
| | (0.006) | (0.007) |
| Years at job | 0.001 | 0.002 |
| | (0.005) | (0.007) |
| Respect at job | −0.267** | 0.142 |
| (1 = strongly disagree to | (0.093) | (0.105) |
| 4 = strongly agree) | | |
| Retired voluntarily | . . . | 0.417** |
| | | (0.160) |
| Constant | −1.796 | −2.141 |
| | (2.716) | (2.746) |
| *Summary statistic* | | |
| Number of observations | 164 | 233 |
| *R*-squared | 0.11 | 0.08 |
| Adjusted *R*-squared | 0.04 | 0.03 |

a. Dependent variable is aggregate happiness. $*p < 0.05$; $**p < 0.01$; $***p < .0\ 001$. Standard errors are in parentheses.

to change following retirement, and we asked retired persons how their happiness had changed and how their happiness differed from what they had expected. Response options ranged from "much less happy," which we coded as –2, to "much happier," which we coded as +2. The retired report themselves as substantially happier than they were before they retired: 55 percent say that they are happier (31 percent say *substantially* happier) and only 14 percent claim that they are less happy than they were before they retired (table 7-6).[24] They also report that the increase in happiness was not anticipated. Those who are not retired anticipate that they too will be happier in retirement, and to approximately the same extent.

Unless those who are not yet retired are destined to be considerably happier when retired than the currently retired are, these results clash with the findings reported in table 7-3, which show, if anything, that the retired are slightly *less* happy than the nonretired. Retired people report experiencing a .68 increase in happiness, and a .67 increase in actual happiness relative to expected happiness. It follows that they do not remember having expected any increase in happiness. The retired think that the change was unanticipated. Nonretired persons, however, do anticipate a .60 increase in retirement happiness.

While the increase in happiness reported by retired persons is inconsistent with the similar levels of happiness reported by the nonretired and retired respondents, neither of these ways of examining changes in happiness following retirement points to a *decrease* in happiness. If retirees have saved too little and are surprised by their own postretirement poverty, this shortfall either has no impact on their self-reported happiness or is compensated for by other benefits of retirement.

# Income

Although both nonretired and retired respondents report high levels of happiness, they may be dissatisfied with their economic situation. Such discontent would be noteworthy even if it had little effect on overall happiness.

## Money Anxiety

Our survey contained four questions designed to measure respondents' assessments of the adequacy of their own income. Respondents were asked

24. This finding is consistent with research by Ross and Newby-Clark (1998) showing that people generally think that their lives have gotten better over time.

Table 7-6. *Predicted and Recalled Change in Happiness for Not Retired and Retired Persons*[a]

| Measure | Not retired: expected change | | Retired | | | |
|---|---|---|---|---|---|---|
| | | | Experienced change | | Experienced relative to expected change | |
| Much less happy (–2) | 8 | (4%) | 9 | (3%) | 9 | (3%) |
| Somewhat less happy (–1) | 8 | (4%) | 29 | (11%) | 21 | (8%) |
| About the same (0) | 81 | (40%) | 86 | (32%) | 87 | (32%) |
| Somewhat happier (1) | 64 | (32%) | 65 | (24%) | 90 | (33%) |
| Much happier (2) | 41 | (20%) | 84 | (31%) | 65 | (24%) |
| *Summary statistic* | | | | | | |
| Number of observations | 202 | | 273 | | 272 | |
| Mean | 0.60*** | | 0.68*** | | 0.67*** | |
| Standard deviation | (0.98) | | (1.12) | | (1.03) | |

a. Mean significantly different from zero: ***$p < 0.001$.

Table 7-7. *Feelings about Adequacy of Income*[a]

| Measure | Not retired (n = 204) | Retired (n = 273) | Significance of difference[b] (p<) |
|---|---|---|---|
| (−1.5 = strongly disagree to 1.5 = strongly agree) | | | |
| 1. I have plenty of money to do the types of things that I enjoy | −0.14* (0.96) | 0.05 (1.04) | 0.05 |
| 2. With my current income I have no trouble making ends meet | 0.41*** (0.90) | 0.45*** (0.93) | n.s. |
| 3. I have sufficient income for my wants and needs | 0.38*** (0.83) | 0.51*** (0.91) | n.s. |
| 4. I feel anxious about money | −0.32*** (0.91) | −0.47*** (0.94) | 0.10 |
| 5. Money Anxiety Index: items 4–1–2–3 (−6 strongly disagree to 6 strongly agree) | −0.99*** (2.77) | −1.48*** (3.23) | 0.10 |

a. Standard deviations in parentheses. Mean significantly different from zero: *$p < 0.05$; ***$p < 0.001$.

b. n.s. indicates not significant.

to indicate whether they agreed or disagreed—on a four-point scale from −1.5 (strongly disagree) to +1.5 (strongly agree)—with the following statements: "I have plenty of money to do the types of things that I enjoy"; "With my current income I have no trouble making ends meet"; "I have sufficient income for my wants and needs"; "I feel anxious about money." From the responses to these questions, we created a money anxiety index by subtracting the numerical values of answers to the first three questions from the response to the fourth. The index can vary between −6 and +6.

Means and standard deviations of responses appear in table 7-7, separately for nonretired and retired respondents. The mean response to the first question is close to the midpoint of the scale, though nonretired respondents tend to disagree slightly more that they have plenty of money. The means of the second and third items are significant and positive, indicating that respondents on the average are satisfied with their finances, although some are not. Respondents on average also disagree when asked whether they feel anxious about money. Overall, they disagree with the

Table 7-8. *Determinants of Anxiety about Money*[a]

| Measure | Not retired | Retired |
|---|---|---|
| Income | –0.018*** | –0.039*** |
| (thousands of dollars) | (0.005) | (0.007) |
| Age start saving | 0.408** | 0.682*** |
| (1 = twenties to 7 = never) | (0.134) | (0.119) |
| Own home | –0.848 | –0.715 |
| (1 = yes, 0 = no) | (0.668) | (0.639) |
| Drawing down savings | 1.298** | 0.459 |
| (1= yes, 0 = no) | (0.422) | (0.360) |
| Constant | –0.748 | –1.978* |
| | (0.893) | (0.834) |
| *Summary statistic* | | |
| Number of observations | 195 | 257 |
| *R*-squared | 0.16 | 0.27 |
| Adjusted *R*-squared | 0.15 | 0.26 |

a. Dependent variable is Money Anxiety Index. $*p < .05; **p < .01; ***p < 0.001$. Standard errors are in parentheses.

view that their income is inadequate. The retired are, if anything, more content about their income and less anxious about money than the non-retired. There is certainly no evidence of a sudden increase in financial anxieties following retirement.

To determine whether people's money anxiety was related to specific circumstances, we regressed the money anxiety index on a variety of variables: respondents' incomes, the age at which they began saving, whether they are homeowners, and whether they are drawing down savings (table 7-8). This analysis produced two clear findings. First, we were able to identify some statistically significant relationships. People with relatively high incomes or who started saving at a relatively early age are less anxious than others. People who are drawing down savings are more anxious, and the effect is particularly striking for those who are not yet retired, presumably because saving is the norm for older workers and dissaving is more acceptable for retirees. The second clear finding is that these variables account for only a small share of the variation in the money anxiety index.

Table 7-9. *Mean Values of Regret Variables*[a]

| Regret variable | Not Retired (n = 204) | Retired (n = 273) | Significance of difference[b] (p <) |
|---|---|---|---|
| (−1.5 = strongly disagree to 1.5 = strongly agree) | | | |
| **I should have made the sacrifices necessary to earn more money for retirement** | −0.069 (0.926) | −0.174** (0.989) | n.s. |
| **I should have become more knowledgeable about different savings and investment options** | 0.153 (0.930) | 0.071 (0.941) | n.s. |
| **I should have talked more with my spouse about our financial plans** | −0.222*** (0.947) | −0.348*** (0.939) | n.s. |
| **I should have restrained my spending on luxuries and nonessential items** | −0.569*** (0.838) | −0.511*** (0.933) | n.s. |
| **I should have gotten more professional help in planning for retirement** | −0.216** (0.935) | −0.419*** (0.955) | 0.05 |
| **I should have spent more time with my family, even if it meant earning less** | −0.304*** (0.897) | −0.301*** (0.955) | n.s. |
| **I should have started saving earlier** | 0.240*** (1.001) | 0.221*** (1.022) | n.s. |

| | | | |
|---|---|---|---|
| **I should have calculated how much money I would need to save in order to have an adequate retirement income** | 0.145*<br>(0.935) | −0.125*<br>(0.995) | 0.01 |
| I underestimated the importance of money for being happy in retirement | . . . | −0.147*<br>(0.987) | . . . |
| I underestimated the importance of knowing how to use my free time in retirement | . . . | −0.328***<br>(0.994) | . . . |
| I should have retired earlier | . . . | −0.888***<br>(0.806) | . . . |
| I should have tried to delay my retirement | . . . | −0.924***<br>(0.810) | . . . |

a. Terms in bold are included in composite financial regret variable. Mean significantly different from zero: $*p < 0.05$; $**p < 0.01$; $***p < 0.001$. Standard deviations are in parentheses.

b. n.s. indicates not significant.

*Financial Regrets*

Whatever their current happiness or financial anxiety may be, do retirees have regrets about past financial or other decisions? Do retirees and non-retirees differ in this way? To find out, we asked respondents questions designed to identify regrets (table 7-9). We were particularly interested in differences between nonretired and retired respondents in regrets about savings behavior. If retirees had not predicted how poor they would be following retirement, we might expect to observe greater regrets about saving for retirees than for people who are not yet retired.

Neither group expresses much regret. The mean responses tend to be significantly negative, indicating disagreements with the regret statements. Both groups believed that they should have become more knowledgeable about savings and investment options and were significantly more likely to agree that they should have started saving earlier, but both groups also significantly disagreed (on average) that they should have restrained their spending, talked more with their spouse about retirement, or gotten more professional help. Taken together, these opinions indicate some regret about how well the retirement savings strategy was executed but not about how much was saved or about the planning of the strategy.

The most significant difference between the two groups emerged from responses to the statement, "I should have calculated how much money I would need to save in order to have an adequate retirement income." It is startling that the nonretired endorse this statement, but the retired do not. Apparently, the nonretired fear they will have too little wealth when retired, but the retired find they can manage.

The final two rows of table 7-9 show that retired persons also have few regrets about the timing of retirement. They strongly disagree with the statement, "I should have retired earlier" (86 percent disagree or strongly disagree). And 86 percent also disagree with the statement, "I should have tried to delay my retirement."

Why do respondents experience the few regrets they express? To answer this question we used four financial variables—age at which respondents began saving, household income, homeownership, and a dummy variable indicating whether they had drawn down their savings during the previous year (table 7-10)—to explain variations in a financial regret index, equal to the sum of responses to the seven statements in bold in table 7-9. For both nonretired and retired persons, the age at which the respondent began saving has a significant impact on the financial regret index—later onset of saving means greater regrets. Income has a small impact for the

Table 7-10. *Objective Determinants of Financial Regret*[a]

| Measure | Not retired | Retired |
|---|---|---|
| Age started saving | 1.091*** | 1.049*** |
| | (0.241) | (0.209) |
| Income | –0.020* | –0.044*** |
| (thousands of dollars) | (0.009) | (0.012) |
| Own home | 0.568 | –1.055 |
| | (1.236) | (1.125) |
| Draw down on savings | 1.711* | 0.783 |
| | (0.753) | (0.634) |
| Constant | –3.862* | –2.811 |
| | (1.656) | (1.472) |
| *Summary statistic* | | |
| Number of observations | 184 | 236 |
| *R*-squared | 0.158 | 0.196 |
| Adjusted *R*-squared | 0.139 | 0.182 |

a. Dependent variable is financial regret. $*p < 0.05$; $**p < 0.01$; $***p < 0.001$. Standard errors are in parentheses.

nonretired and a larger and more statistically significant effect on the retired: greater income means less financial regret.[25] Once again, drawing down savings is associated with increased regret among the nonretired, but the effect on the retired is smaller and not statistically significant.[26]

# Individual Differences

The retired and the nonretired are similar on the average, but they are not identical in their attitudes; and within each group respondents vary widely in their specific attitudes. In this section we examine how respondents divide into groups that share similar opinions about retirement and life satisfaction. We employ "cluster analysis," a technique that finds different

25. Note that the composition of household income is very different before and after retirement (see table 7-2). When we regressed financial regrets against the different income sources, for retirees higher income from retirement plans and from savings significantly reduced financial regrets, but wage and social security income showed no such effects.

26. The differential effect of drawing down savings for the nonretired and retired groups is similar to that observed for the inadequacy of money variable.

groups that give similar answers to specific questions. These responses suggest explanations for observed variations in reported happiness.

We focused on a block of twenty-nine survey questions that deal with subjective beliefs and self-assessments and were presented in exactly the same form to both retired and nonretired respondents.[27] Respondents were divided into five clusters, as shown in table 7-11. Each cluster is characterized by a set of diagnostic statements taken from the original list of twenty-nine statements used for the clustering.[28] We also obtained a list of significant objective demographic measures, which are displayed below the "subjective" diagnostics. Below these, table 7-11 also provides summary statistics on relative cluster size, mean income, and mean overall happiness index, broken down for the retired and nonretired subgroups in each cluster. None of these "objective measures" determined the clusters; they are listed here only to make the cluster easier to interpret.

The five clusters divide into two "very happy" groups (A and B) and three less happy groups (C, D, and E). However, even the less happy clusters are reasonably happy, averaging about 3 on a scale of 1 through 4. This finding is consistent with the high self-reported happiness level that prevails in the sample. The happiness profile across the clusters is about the same for retired and nonretired respondents, while retirement and the interaction of retirement and happiness are not statistically significant determinants of cluster membership.[29] Income is a strong predictor of cluster membership, but only after controlling for retirement.[30] Among the nonretired, the highest-income cluster (E) has 35 percent more income than the lowest-income cluster (B), while among the retired the highest (A) has 138 percent more income than the lowest (D).

There is no simple relationship between income and happiness across clusters. Indeed, the cluster with highest overall income (E) is also the least happy. However, the *difference* in income between the retired and

27. The method of clustering is Ward's algorithm. This technique creates clusters so as to maximize variance explained by cluster membership. Looking at how average within-cluster distance measure varies with the number of clusters, we observed a sharp break between the fifth and sixth clusters, which pointed to a five-cluster solution, displayed in table 7-11.

28. These statements are selected by a stepwise linear regression of cluster membership (indexed by a dummy variable) against all twenty-nine individual attitude items, eliminating variables until only the variables with a criterion significance level remain (here the criterion level is .01). This process eliminates statistically redundant predictors and sifts out only those that have independent predictive validity, "holding constant the levels on the other items."

29. A nominal logit analysis shows happiness to be highly significant predictor of cluster membership ($p < .0001$).

30. Specifically, income is a significant predictor of cluster membership among retired respondents ($p < .003$) and marginally significant among the nonretired ($p < .09$).

nonretired subgroups in each cluster is associated with happiness: the "happy" clusters, A and B, exhibit the smallest disparity in income between preretirement and postretirement groups. Of course, the preretirement and postretirement groups are made up of different individuals, so one cannot interpret the difference as a drop in income. Still, the pattern is consistent with the evidence from tables 7-5 and 7-8, which suggests that income is a more important determinant of well-being for the retired than for the nonretired.

Clusters A and B belie Tolstoy's statement that "all happy families are alike." Members of cluster A have the most positive average rating on virtually every question presented in the survey. Two distinct sources of self-reported happiness stand out—no financial regrets and a vigorous enjoyment of life. The lack of regret about financial decisions is consistent with their relatively high income levels, both before and after retirement. Members of cluster B have much lower average income, yet report an almost an equally high happiness rating (in both cases it is close to the 4.0 scale maximum). They do acknowledge being "tight with money" and not having sufficiently investigated saving and investment options, but these signals of financial strain do not interfere with their happiness or with their ability to enjoy whatever consumption they can afford. Comparing clusters A and B, one could say that a high income contributes to a certain smugness in a self-report, but modest income is also compatible with happiness.

The three less happy clusters—C, D, and E—have similar overall happiness ratings but, again, very different "personalities." It is hard to avoid the impression that cluster C is in much better shape than the remaining two. People in this cluster are unhappy about their financial self-control: they believe they should have sacrificed more in the past and are loose with money, and these financial problems interfere with their enjoyment of consumption. Only the fact that they started saving relatively late in life distinguishes them from the rest of the population. Nonetheless, they are especially hopeful about the future and are not depressed. Perhaps careless in the past, they are carefree now.

People in cluster D seem to have been caught unawares by (actual or imminent) retirement. They score lower on most specific measures of happiness and higher on every regret measure than any other group. They alone agree that retirement is unpleasant to think about. They have invested least in learning how to use their time in retirement. The nonretired in this cluster claim not to have a clear idea about how they will spend their time; the retired claim that before they retired they did not have a clear idea of how they would spend their time in retirement.

Table 7-11. *Analysis of Individual Differences for Five Clusters of Respondents*[a]

| | Cluster A | Cluster B | Cluster C | Cluster D | Cluster E |
|---|---|---|---|---|---|
| Key diagnostic statements ($p < 0.01$) | −I should have become more knowledgeable about savings and investment options | +I feel happy about life | +I should have made the sacrifices necessary to earn more money for retirement | −I am happy with my standard of living | +I am depressed |
| | −I am anxious about money | +I am enjoying my free time | +I am hopeful about the future | +Spending money is painful for me | −I feel happy about life |
| | +I am happy with my leisure time activities | −I don't enjoy activities like eating out or travel, because I think about how much they cost | −I feel depressed | −I am happy with my housing | +I feel lonely |
| | −I should have spent more time with my family, even if it meant earning less | +I should have become more knowledgeable about savings and investment options | −I am happy with the local area in which I live | −With my current income I have no trouble making ends meet | −I should have become more knowledgeable about savings and investment options |
| | +I enjoy eating and have a good appetite | +I am tight with money | +I don't enjoy activities like eating out or travel, because I think about how much they cost | +I have plenty of time during the day to do the things I need and want to do | +I feel happy with my standard of living |

| Significant demographics (p < .05) | −I should have talked more with my spouse about our financial plans | −I am tight with money | +Retirement is an unpleasant thing to think about | +With my current income I have no trouble making ends meet | −I feel happy about my health |
| --- | --- | --- | --- | --- | --- |
| | *retired, married, didn't draw down savings, higher education* | *drew down savings, less urban, more children* | *started saving later* | *blue collar, started saving later* | *white collar, live alone, high income* |
| Percent of not retired | 16 | 38 | 25 | 7 | 14 |
| Percent of retired | 26 | 31 | 19 | 11 | 13 |
| Income, not retired (dollars) | 79,218 | 60,065 | 70,954 | 65,682 | 81,547 |
| Income, retired (dollars) | 49,750 | 35,625 | 28,076 | 20,893 | 42,058 |
| Happy, not retired (1–4) | 3.70 | 3.70 | 3.16 | 2.82 | 2.91 |
| Happy, retired (1–4) | 3.91 | 3.86 | 3.02 | 3.00 | 2.65 |

a. + = agree; − = disagree.

Members of cluster E show that even the affluent can be miserable. They are lonelier and less happy about their health than is any other group. The statement "I am depressed" is their single most diagnostic characteristic. The fact that they are satisfied with their standard of living and have few financial regrets does not save them from having the lowest average score on the benchmark "feel about life" question.

## Conclusions

Our main conclusion is that the retired people in our sample discovered, on average, that their income is sufficient to meet their needs. At the same time, the importance of adequate income increases during retirement. These two aspects of our findings are not inconsistent. Before retirement, one has largely adapted to one's current income, and therefore its impact on well-being is slight. Moreover, one is not yet sure whether savings will be sufficient for retirement. All of this may increase overall money anxiety and, simultaneously, disconnect that anxiety from objective financial circumstances.

After retirement, the uncertainty is resolved and one encounters a different financial environment. For most people, the uncertainty is resolved favorably, and they can relax and enjoy their wealth. This is why the happiest and most self-congratulatory of the five clusters (A) is overpopulated by retired people. The minority of retirees who discover that their income is inadequate, by contrast, face new discomforts to which they have to adapt.

These general conclusions should, however, be treated with caution. First, although we tried to collect a sample representative of the general population, timing and financial constraints prevented us from doing so. The sample is more affluent than the general population, and minorities are significantly underrepresented. We do find pockets of unhappiness, such as cluster D, that are associated with blue-collar occupations and very low income in retirement. Our sample is also self-selected to some extent; it consists of people who have agreed to answer surveys sent to them by a firm that collects data mainly for marketers. People who agree to being surveyed may be more content with their lives than those who refuse. But such a bias would probably apply to both the nonretired and the retired.

The second reason for caution in interpretation is that the data were collected at one point in time that reflects one set of nonrepresentative historical circumstances. There may be good reason to suspect that an unusual confluence of events that have favored current retirees: record increases in housing prices, stock markets, and the most sustained economic boom in postwar history, may affect both their income and their reported happiness.[31]

Third, although we employed diverse measures of subjective well-being, all the measures are vulnerable to scale self-norming and other problems. There is clearly a compelling need for studies that employ such new and diverse measures of subjective well-being as suicide rates, facial measurements, clinical incidence of depression, and rates of psychosomatic ailments. We suspect, however, that such measures will reveal a similar picture of the relationship between SWB and income, and more specifically that these measures will not reveal a postretirement drop in well-being.

Putting aside these caveats, our data, at a minimum, raise the question of whether the furor over the adequacy of retirement savings might possibly be exaggerated. In our sample, we see no evidence of pervasive undersaving; indeed, as noted, the retired were less likely than the not-yet-retired to endorse the statement "I should have calculated how much money I would need to save in order to have an adequate retirement income." If anything, people seem to anticipate greater financial woes than they actually end up experiencing.

Although we failed to observe a significant decline in happiness following retirement, our analyses do show large and significant changes in the *determinants* of that happiness. For the not-yet-retired, job satisfaction and the quality of leisure are the major determinants of reported happiness. Not surprisingly, job satisfaction (at their last job) is not a significant determinant of happiness for retired people, while the quality of leisure becomes an extremely important determinant. This increased importance of quality of leisure is worth keeping in mind when thinking about policies that affect the elderly. Although income maintenance is important, it is only one of many policies (and possibly not the most important or effec-

---

31. A new study could survey a representative sample over a longer time and incorporate other innovations. We would suggest including more questions about nonfinancial determinants of well-being, such as family relations, interactions with friends, hobbies, and travel, as well as questions about physical functioning. On the financial side, we would also include more questions about wealth as opposed to income. It would also be interesting to ask retired persons to recall not only their earlier well-being, but also earlier values of explanatory variables (we only asked about past income). If we sampled nonretired persons again, we would ask them to predict postretirement values of explanatory variables. Finally, we would ask respondents to evaluate directly the relative desirability of different policies involving retirement, such as those to promote savings or to enhance the quality of retirees' lives through nonfinancial policies.

tive) that could augment the well-being of retirees. In addition to policies that maintain incomes, other effective policies might seek to improve the quality of leisure directly. For example, the mother of one of the authors is retired and living by herself in the suburbs. Currently, she plays Ping-Pong regularly in the town hall, takes subsidized yoga classes at the public school, and spends hours in the public library. Later, when she becomes too old to drive, she may use the shuttle service offered by the town for its senior citizens. It seems likely that these types of services increase her well-being far more than would an increase in income equivalent to the marginal cost of the services. Further research on the financial and nonfinancial determinants of well-being in retirement could help inform such initiatives.

In closing, it may be worth mentioning that the story of Mr. Pasea in the epigraph to this chapter seems to have struck a responsive chord in at least some readers. A Daniel Smith, for example, wrote in response that "I chose to live in Manhattan rather than in Nederland, Texas, so my retirement income requirements are obviously higher than Mr. Pasea's. But the same basic rules apply. You can get by on a lot less when you're retired, without really depriving yourself of anything important. . . . If I had known earlier how much 'wealth' derives from such simple pleasures, I would have retired a lot sooner."[32]

# References

Banks, J., R. Blundell, and S. Tanner. 1998. "Is there a Retirement Savings Puzzle?" *American Economic Review* 88: 769–88.

Beck, S. H. 1982. Adjustment to and Satisfaction with Retirement. *Journal of Gerontology* 37 (5): 616–24.

Beck, S. H., and J. W. Page. 1988. "Involvement in Activities and the Psychological Well-Being of Retired Men." *Activities, Adaptation & Aging* 11 (1): 31–47.

Bernheim, B. Douglas. 1991. "How Strong Are Bequest Motives? Evidence Based on Estimates of the Demand for Life Insurance and Annuities." *Journal of Political Economy* 99 (5): 899–927.

Bernheim, B. Douglas, J. Skinner, and S. Weinberg. 1997. "What Accounts for the Variation in Retirement Wealth among U.S. Households?" Unpublished manuscript.

Brickman, P., D. Coates, and R. Janoff-Bulman. 1978. "Lottery Winners and Accident Victims: Is Happiness Relative?" *Journal of Personality and Social Psychology* 36 (8) 917–27.

32. *New York Times*, October 25, 1998, p. 14.

Brostoff, S. 1997. "Survey: Most Annuity Buyers Mid-Income." *National Underwriter* 35 (September 1): 30.

Campbell, A. 1981. *The Sense of Well-Being in America: Recent Patterns and Trends.* McGraw-Hill.

Crowley, J. E. 1986. "Longitudinal Effects of Retirement on Men's Well-Being and Health." *Journal of Business and Psychology* 1 (2): 95–113.

Diener, E. 1984. "Subjective Well-Being." *Psychological Bulletin* 95 (3): 542–75.

———. 1994. "Assessing Subjective Well-Being: Progress and Opportunities." *Social Indicators Research* 31 (2): 103–58.

Diener, E., and C. Diener. 1996. "Most People Are Happy." *Psychological Science* 7 (3): 181–85.

Diener, E., M. Diener, and C. Diener. 1995. "Factors Predicting the Subjective Well-Being of Nations." *Journal of Personality and Social Psychology* 69 (5): 851–64.

Diener, E., and others. 1993. "The Relationship between Income and Subjective Well-Being: Relative or Absolute?" *Social Indicators Research* 28 (3): 195–223.

Easterlin, R. A. 1974. "Does Economic Growth Improve the Human Lot? Some Empirical Evidence." In *Nations and Households in Economic Growth*, edited by P. A. David and M. W. Reder, 89–125. Academic Press.

———. 1995. "Will Raising the Incomes of All Increase the Happiness of All?" *Journal of Economic Behavior and Organization* 27: 35–47.

Frederick, S., and George Loewenstein. 1999. "Hedonic Adaptation." In *Well-Being: The Foundations of Hedonic Psychology*, edited by Daniel Kahneman, Edward Diener and Norbert Schwarz. Russell Sage.

Gall, T. L., D. R. Evans, and J. Howard. 1997. "The Retirement Adjustment Process: Changes in the Well-Being of Male Retirees across Time." *Journals of Gerontology: Series B* 52 (3): 110–17.

Gilbert, D., and others. 1998. "Immune Neglect: A Source of Durability Bias in Affective Forecasting." *Journal of Personality and Social Psychology* 75: 617–38.

Hausman, J. A., and L. Paquette. 1987. "Involuntary Early Retirement and Consumption." In *Work, Health, and Income among the Elderly*, edited by Gary Burtless, 151–81. Brookings.

Hurd, M. D. 1987. "Savings of the Elderly and Desired Bequests." *American Economic Review* 77 (3): 298–312.

———. 1989. "Mortality Risk and Bequests." *Econometrica* 57 (4): 779–813.

Karoly, L. A., and J. A. Rogowski. 1994. "The Effect of Access to Postretirement Health Insurance on the Decision to Retire Early." *Industrial and Labor Relations Review* 48 (1): 103–23.

Kremer, Yael. 1985. "The Association between Health and Retirement: Self-Health Assessment of Israeli Retirees." *Social Science and Medicine* 20 (1): 61–66.

Knesek, G. E. 1992. "Early versus Regular Retirement: Differences in Measures of Life Satisfaction." *Journal of Gerontological Social Work* 19 (1): 3–34.

Loewenstein, George. 1996. "Out of Control: Visceral Influences on Behavior." *Organizational Behavior and Human Decision Processes* 65 (3): 272–92.

Loewenstein, George, and D. Schkade. 1999. "Wouldn't It Be Nice? Predicting Future Feelings." In *Well-Being: The Foundations of Hedonic Psychology*, edited by Daniel Kahneman, Edward Diener and Norbert Schwarz. Russell Sage.

Loewenstein, George, and N. Sicherman. 1991. "Do Workers Prefer Increasing Wage Profiles?" *Journal of Labor Economics* 9 (1): 67–84.

Loewenstein, George, and R. Thaler. 1989. "Anomalies: Intertemporal Choice." *Journal of Economic Perspectives* 3 (4): 181–93.

Lykken, D., and A. Tellegen. 1996. "Happiness Is a Stochastic Phenomenon." *Psychological Science* 7 (3): 186–89.

McGoldrick, A. E. 1994. "The Impact of Retirement on the Individual." *Reviews in Clinical Gerontology* 4 (2): 151–60.

Michalos, Alex C. 1987. "German Social Report: Living Conditions and Subjective Well-Being, 1978–1984." *Social Indicators Research* 19 (1): 171.

Modigliani, Franco, and Richard Brumberg. 1954. "Utility Analysis and the Consumption Function: An Interpretation of Cross-Sectional Data." In *Post Keynesian Economics*, edited by Kenneth K. Kurihara, 388–436. Rutgers University Press.

Myers, David G., and E. Diener. 1995. "Who Is Happy?" *Psychological Science* 6 (1): 10–19.

Palmore, E. B, G. G. Fillenbaum, and L. K. George. 1984. "Consequences of Retirement." *Journal of Gerontology* 39 (1): 109–16.

Prelec, Drazen, and George Loewenstein. 1998. "The Red and the Black: Mental Accounting of Savings and Debt." *Marketing Science* 17 (1): 4–28.

Reitzes, D. C., E. Mutran, and M. Fernandez. 1996. "Does Retirement Hurt Well-Being? Factors Influencing Self-Esteem and Depression among Retirees and Workers." *Gerontologist* 36 (5): 649–56.

Reitzes, D. C., E. Mutran, and H. Pope. 1991. "Location and Well-Being among Retired Men." *Journal of Gerontology* 46 (4): 195–203.

Robb, A. L., and J. B. Burbidge. 1989. "Consumption, Income and Retirement." *Canadian Journal of Economics* 22 (3): 522–42.

Ross, Michael, and Ian R. Newby-Clark. 1998. "Construing the Past and Future." *Social Cognition* 16 (1): 133–50.

Scitovsky, T. 1976. *The Joyless Economy: The Psychology of Human Satisfaction*. Oxford University Press.

Smith, P., L. Kendall, and C. Hulin. 1969. *The Measurement of Satisfaction in Work and Retirement*. Chicago: Rand McNally.

Strack, F., L. L. Martin, and N. Schwarz. 1988. "Priming and Communication: Social Determinants of Information Use in Judgments of Life Satisfaction." *European Journal of Social Psychology* 18 (5): 429–42.

Veenhoven, Ruut. 1991. "Is Happiness Relative?" *Social Indicators Research* 24 (1): 1–34.

Wallace, M. 1956. "Future Time Perspective in Schizophrenia." *Journal of Abnormal Social Psychology* 52 (1): 240–45.

Ward, Suzanne P., Thomas E. Wilson, and Dan R. Ward. 1994. "Perceptions of Retirement Satisfaction: Data from Retired Certified Public Accountants." *Perceptual and Motor Skills* 78 (2): 525–26.

COMMENT BY
# Matthew Rabin

This chapter raises some important issues for retirement research, using evidence from a new survey. Noting that economists should and do care about retirement saving because of its welfare implications, the authors investigate the regrets and satisfactions people derive from their saving decisions, rather than investigating only the behavior. This focus on hedonics is welcome, and asking people how satisfied they are with their current activities and with their past preparation for retirement is itself a useful complement to other modes of retirement research.

The focus on psychological factors is also more generally welcome. Formal economics has traditionally assumed that people plan for retirement with perfect rationality, under the constraints of significant uncertainties, and do so with accurate forecasts of what contributes to their subjective well-being. If there is a single realm where economists ought to be wary of the rationality assumption, it is retirement planning. One of the arguments used persistently by economists to dismiss research exploring the limits of the rationality assumption—that through feedback from repeated decisions people (eventually) get things right—is not much of an argument in the context of retirement planning, because no 30-year-old decides how much to save twice. A second common argument is that people pay more attention to things that actually matter, and are therefore more likely to get things right on important issues, and hence one should ignore departures from rationality in these contexts. It makes perfect sense to conjecture that people spend a lot of time planning for their retirement and hence come closer to fully rational choice than they do on less important matters. Nonetheless, evidence in this chapter (though downplayed by the authors), in other chapters in this volume, and elsewhere, indicates that people spend remarkably little time thinking about retirement.

Three interconnected themes lie at the heart of the chapter. First, the authors identify some determinants of subjective well-being experienced by retirees and compare these determinants to those of nonretirees. They find, for example, that retirees are typically more concerned about their health than their lack of spending money, and that they enjoy leisure activities.

I thank Erik Eyster for research assistance and helpful comments, and the Russell Sage Foundation, the National Science Foundation, the MacArthur Foundation, and the Sloan Foundation for financial support.

Second, the authors' findings suggest that people err in their predictions about their happiness in retirement. Largely because people underestimate how well they will adjust to a lower material standard of living, they think they will be less happy in retirement than in fact they are. Third, the authors argue that all the fretting by economists and policymakers that Americans are saving too little might be overdone, since retirees seem to be as happy as nonretirees; and in contrast to the worrying by academics on behalf of retirees, retirees show little regret about having saved too little.

I believe that this chapter is a valuable contribution to the economic study of retirement planning and behavior. The survey produced some interesting findings, and the chapter promotes a useful reorientation of the focus of the economics of retirement. The detailed analysis of the sources of satisfaction among retirees and nonretirees and the development of profiles of different classes of individuals according to the levels and sources of their satisfaction are especially intriguing. The economics of retirement could be much improved by following through on some of the authors' suggestions for future research.

For several reasons, however, I think that their findings should be viewed as quite tentative. I also feel that many of the authors' interpretations of and inferences from their evidence are unwarranted. Because I hope such research will continue—and because the positive aspects of the chapter speak for themselves—my remaining comments focus on criticisms of these interpretations and inferences.

The authors' main conclusion is that despite substantial falls in spending at retirement, "the retired people in our sample discovered, on average, that their income is sufficient to meet their needs." The authors reach this conclusion using an array of arguments. First, they present survey evidence on how retirees differ from nonretirees in their spending patterns and preferences. In this context, the authors imply that standard economics assumes that people's spending patterns do not change with retirement, and in particular, that economists have mistakenly identified the substantial observed drop in consumption spending at retirement with evidence of undersaving, whereas it could be a sensible adjustment to the fact that less spending is needed in retirement.

The common assumption that the utility derived from consumption is separable from available leisure time is often a useful simplification. But it is a pretty bad simplification when comparing the well-being of those who are and those who are not retired. Economists are aware of that point, and introductory economics textbooks routinely explain that leisure time and consumption spending may be either substitutes or complements. Few economists would be surprised to discover that retirees have different tastes than nonretirees about how much to spend and what to spend it on. It is my impression that researchers discount the hypothesis that the drop in spending derives from a shift in preferences on *empirical* grounds. I think that the psychological sophistication and the survey evidence that the authors bring could help answer this question, but I do not find their evidence compelling that a precipitous drop in spending at retirement corresponds to changes in preferences.

The authors provide more direct evidence that retirees do not mind having lower levels of spending by asking both retirees and nonretirees how satisfied they are with their spending levels, whether they are anxious about money, and related questions. I find it hard to interpret the survey finding that spending does not matter a lot, and hence that the drop in spending is unlikely to lead to much lower well-being. I cannot really see how to get a handle on whether the observed modest effect of financial worries on well-being passes the threshold of concern among policymakers and researchers.

I am puzzled by the authors' inference that one should not be much perturbed by the reduction in well-being associated with the decline in income because it is small relative to the effects of such other factors as social contact and networks and the timing of retirement. I am most puzzled by the comparison of spending concerns with health concerns among retirees. That health concerns preoccupy many retirees is hardly surprising. Health problems—especially those that cannot be solved by increased spending—are a fact of life for all of us. They are particularly prevalent among retirees. As people age, bad health becomes an ever-increasing determinant of the loss of well-being. Indeed, the survey responses of those with serious health concerns may mean something quite different from those of healthier people. If so, the interpretation of these responses will be problematic, because even people with substantial impediments to subjective well-being in other domains might not register such dissatisfactions as intensely if they are preoccupied with their health. In any event, the argument that one should not focus on consumption satisfaction among retirees because it is a small concern relative to others seems analogous to downplaying concern about consumer protection in the funeral industry because bereaved families care less about being ripped off by undertakers than about the death of their loved ones. This is not a useful benchmark for deciding if regulation is needed, nor for assessing whether consumer rip-offs are a lesser problem for bereaved families than for other families.

It also bears emphasis that one component of the measure of satisfaction employed by the authors to conclude that retirees are satisfied is "happiness relative to their friends and acquaintances." But because retirees, on average, have more retired friends and acquaintances than do nonretirees, this measure by definition runs the risk of declaring that the two groups are equally satisfied. While there is surely substantial overlap among the acquaintances of the two groups, and while some degree of subjective well-being is derived from comparison with those around one, this is clearly an unsatisfactory measure of satisfaction for the question at hand.

Moreover, the authors call attention to the fact that their survey respondents are wealthier than the general population, and that one should therefore be cautious about generalizing from this evidence. I would reiterate this concern, and I worry even more than the authors do that this fact diminishes the legitimacy of inferences from the survey. While the evidence in this chapter shows that financial anxiety is not a dominant consideration among retirees who are not poor, it would surely be a bigger consideration among poorer retirees.

All said, however, while the hypothesis that a drop in spending may not yield a drop in subjective well-being may be somewhat surprising to economists, the authors are quite convincing that this hypothesis accords with a great deal of psychological evidence. To give context to the proposal that retirees adjust to their reduced standard of living, the authors review broad evidence that subjective well-being is often based on *relative* levels of consumption—relative either to a person's previous consumption or to the consumption of those around him. Although economists are beginning to investigate this possibility, most research has assumed that well-being is determined only by absolute levels of consumption. But even granting the hypothesis that people habituate to lower spending, this speaks more to the argument (with which I suspect the authors would agree) that spending levels in general do not matter as much in subjective well-being as economists suspect, for either the retired or the nonretired. One would therefore conclude that there is no need to worry about standards of living for nonpoor retirees simply because there is no need to worry about standards of living for any of the nonpoor.

A second reason why retirees might be fairly satisfied with their lives despite a drop in consumer spending is that they may perceive their needs incorrectly. The drop in consumption may represent underpreparation in terms of what people perceive ahead of time will be their spending needs after retirement; but it may be that these perceptions of future needs are exaggerated. Hence the drop in spending will not do much harm to retirees' well-being because there may be a systematic bias, one that reflects a general phenomenon as well as showing up in this chapter's survey data, that people anticipate needing more savings than they do in fact need.

I believe there is a great deal of truth in this observation, and that it is an important point. But I am quite concerned about the authors' inferences here. For instance, they note that people express little regret about not having saved enough or thought enough about their saving decisions. This finding is hard to interpret. It is, in fact, not clear why *anybody* should express regret about spending too little thought on retirement. Retirement planning is immensely important, and so people should rationally spend a lot of time on it. Moreover, because of various factors, such as cognitive dissonance, it is not obvious that people who have made big errors in saving would express great regret at these errors. Perhaps a benchmark from questioning degrees of regret expressed by people in other domains would help one to see whether this is a lot of or a little regret. Or perhaps more could have been inferred if the survey had asked whether anybody regretted spending too *much* time thinking about retirement. Given that rational behavior should be to spend a lot of time thinking about retirement, if significant numbers of people regret doing so, this would be more compelling evidence of the surprising contention that there is no systematic bias toward spending too little thought on retirement.

Finally, I feel that for the question of whether people experience more or less anxiety about money at retirement than they should, the authors' choice of comparison group is a poor one. The authors convincingly argue that people forced to decrease expenditures are pleasantly surprised by how painless it is to do so. Presumably this pleasant surprise occurs between the years immediately preceding retirement and the years immediately following retirement, which is exactly the comparison that the authors are making. But the problem behavior that is the focus of retirement research—that people undersave and underprepare for retirement—happens much earlier. A 60-year-old with too little money who has not yet retired will realize that he has too little money, and hence feel just as anxious as the 65-year-old who has just retired. Indeed, if those who feel the most anxiety delay retirement, there would be a selection bias in this survey suggesting that retired people feel less anxious about finances than those on the verge of retirement. If one wishes to infer the extent to which people are prepared for retirement by examining financial anxiety, the appropriate comparison group should be 30-year-olds, not 60-year-olds. To address this and other questions, it would have been useful to have gathered comparable evidence from people who are far away from retirement.

SHELLY LUNDBERG

# 8 | *Family Bargaining and Retirement Behavior*

W HEN THE social security system was established in 1935, women made up less than 25 percent of the work force and only a third of female workers were married. Economists' treatment of the retirement decision has been persistently influenced by this demographic fact, although the U.S. labor force is now 46 percent female and most working women are married. A traditional family model in which a single decisionmaker, the (usually male) household head, chooses an optimal lifetime path of work and consumption provides the implicit framework for almost all economic analysis of retirement. Other family members, including wives, are ignored in both theoretical modeling and empirical studies of retirement timing. In fact, the enigmatic but key variable "age of the household" employed in many retirement studies can be reliably translated as "age of the male household head."

A married couple faces a retirement problem very different from that of an individual worker. The work and consumption behavior of the couple will be the outcome of joint decisionmaking and will differ in both constraints and objectives from individual decisionmaking. Pooling resources within the family eases the time and income constraints facing any one worker and reduces the risk associated with changes in individual-specific factors such as health. Husbands and wives have distinct prefer-

253

ences, and their objectives may not coincide in either the short or the long run. Many of the important empirical issues in retirement behavior involve circumstances in which the needs and goals of married men and women may differ. For example, extensive poverty among elderly widows is the outcome of the consumption and savings decisions made by a married couple with different life expectancies. Recent discussions concerning individual control of social security assets and the fate of the spouse benefit bring into sharp relief the possible conflict of interest between elderly husbands and wives.

Analysis of these and other issues must begin with a model of saving and labor supply decisions that allows for the independent preferences of husbands and wives and for the eventual end of a marriage through death or divorce. Increases in market work among married women and decreases in marital stability during the past forty years have undoubtedly changed the retirement patterns of both men and women, but analysis of these influences will be difficult without a conceptual framework that incorporates the family context of retirement decisions. In recent years, models of collective family decisionmaking, including cooperative and noncooperative bargaining models, have been developed and have received considerable empirical support but have had little influence on the study of retirement.

I shall summarize alternative models of family behavior, including standard unitary models and the newer collective models, and speculate on how our understanding of retirement behavior might be improved by recognizing possible conflicts of interest between husbands and wives in family decisions concerning work, savings, and pensions. I show that marital bargaining models have important implications for policy. Distribution of well-being in marriage can be affected by who controls resources, so that policies affecting retirement ages or the allocation of retirement assets can affect the relative well-being of husbands and wives in elderly couples and possibly the efficiency with which resources are allocated. I explore the implications of bargaining models for some aspects of retirement behavior and suggest that some observed facts may be more consistent with a bargaining framework than a unitary one. Finally, I suggest elements of a research agenda for analyzing retirement in a game-theoretic context.

## Husbands, Wives, and Retirement

The typical model of retirement behavior examines the behavior of one person who faces alternative streams of utility over the remainder of his or her life. Retirement consists of leaving a career job and thereby losing most or all labor income. Each worker chooses the best retirement date by comparing the expected present value of future utilities associated with retirement at different ages, where these depend on market wages, accumulation of pension assets, the value of leisure, and the rate of time preference.[1] In general, however, retirees are not alone; most have a spouse whose future consumption (and leisure) will be affected by the retirement choice. We might expect a marital partner, whether she is a worker, retiree, or homemaker, to have some influence on her spouse's retirement decision, but this interdependence has been almost universally suppressed in theoretical modeling of retirement and receives little attention in empirical studies.

The one-person retirement decision is consistent with the "traditional family" model that is the basis of many empirical labor supply studies.[2] In the traditional family the husband is the primary earner and his work hours are assumed to depend on his wage rate and nonlabor income, but not on the work behavior or attributes of his wife. The wife, in turn, treats her husband's earnings as though they were property income. This specification, in which the husband's behavior affects his wife, but the wife's behavior does not influence her husband, is convenient for estimation but cannot be justified as the outcome of an optimizing model. As the lifetime labor force participation of women has increased in the United States, studies of retirement by male household heads have been augmented by studies of female retirement behavior that are also consistent with the traditional family model. The results of recent research on the labor supply of older men and women are not in general consistent with this framework because the work behavior of men does appear to be affected by the employment of their wives.[3] Only a few studies have treated the retirement decisions of husbands and wives as mutually dependent.[4]

---

1. Structural models of retirement behavior are relatively abundant. A few recent examples are Lumsdaine, Stock, and Wise (1992), Berkovec and Stern (1991), Stock and Wise (1990), and Gustman and Steinmeier (1986).

2. Lundberg (1988).

3. Honig (1998) finds that although older women's retirement expectations are influenced by their husband's income and retirement plans, they are influenced more strongly than in the past by their own expected wage, employer-provided benefits, and pension income. Blau (1998) finds that both husbands and wives are more likely to continue working if their spouse does so and to retire if their spouse has retired, a result that indicates preferences for sharing leisure.

4. The principal recent exception is Gustman and Steinmeier (1997), who construct a noncooperative model of retirement in two-career families as the basis for an empirical examination of coordinated retirement decisions. The joint retirement of husbands and wives has also been examined empirically by Hurd (1990), and by Clark and Johnson (1980).

These results suggest that a joint decisionmaking framework is needed. One possibility is to reject the traditional family model in favor of a joint utility or "unitary" model that assumes the family acts as though it were maximizing a single utility function that incorporates the preferences of all members, subject to a pooled budget constraint. In this model the sharing of resources between spouses implies that the earnings opportunities of both should affect the retirement behavior of each. For example, the health insurance coverage of an employed wife will affect the marginal value of medicare, which affects the husband's retirement decisions. A joint model also allows for interdependence of husband's and wife's consumption through household public goods and complementarity between the husband's and wife's leisure time.

An increasingly important alternative to the unitary model of family decisions is a game-theoretic or "collective" model that incorporates the separate interests of two or more family members. The original contributions to this literature were cooperative bargaining models, but a variety of noncooperative models and others employing a collective framework that does not rely on any explicit bargaining have appeared in recent years. One advantage of such models over the unitary model is that they permit analysis of an individual's life cycle—allowing for marriage, divorce, and the death of a spouse—rather than the life cycle of a married couple. For example, the effect of the social security spouse benefit on the lifetime work incentives of women must depend on the risk of divorce and the treatment of the benefit in the event of divorce. These models also allow for a conflict of interest between the husband and wife within the marriage and provide a mechanism by which family behavior emerges from disparate individual objectives.

Bargaining models widen the range of rational family behavior and can explain departures from the simple life-cycle model without abandoning the economist's standard assumption of forward-looking, purposeful individuals. In some games there is an explicit role for social norms in providing a couple with a fallback position or a focal point that affects the bargained outcome. This approach provides an explanation for the bunching of retirement ages that is related to, but not identical with, the direct effect of peer influence. Finally, a number of empirical puzzles concerning retirement behavior and the well-being of the elderly cannot be usefully addressed with models that assume a married couple acts as one. Most dramatic is the sizable reduction in the proportion of men who choose single-life annuity pensions rather than joint-and-survivor pensions following changes in regulations that should not have altered the choices of a single-utility married couple.[5] A 1974 amendment to the Employment Retirement Income Security Act required that a joint life annuity be the default provision, but did not restrict choices in any way. The 1984 Retirement Equity Act required notarized spousal approval before an employee could choose a single-annuity pension. The responses to these changes cannot be explained by a traditional family or unitary family model, but suggest that self-interested and strategic behavior by husbands and wives needs to be considered in explaining economic behavior relevant to retirement.

## Modeling Family Behavior

Alternatives to the traditional family model fall into two basic categories: unitary models in which a single utility function is maximized, and collective models, which include cooperative and noncooperative bargaining models. In a unitary model, outcomes are necessarily efficient and questions of distribution between husbands and wives do not arise in any meaningful way. Decisions depend on total family income and relative prices, and policies will influence behavior only through the overall family budget constraint or through direct restrictions on behavior. Outcomes are efficient in cooperative bargaining models, but distribution between individual family members will depend on bargaining power as reflected in the value of the "threat point" or alternative to cooperation. Individual welfare will therefore depend upon individual control of resources and an additional avenue for policy influence is provided. In noncooperative models the relative well-being of family members also depends on individual resources, but outcomes may be inefficient.

### Unitary Models

In the archetypical unitary model a husband and wife agree to maximize a social welfare function based on their individual utilities, subject to a joint budget constraint that pools their income.[6] This model allows the couple's expenditures to be analyzed as though the spouses were a single agent maximizing a utility function that depends on their joint consumption, subject to a joint budget constraint. This optimization problem generates "family" demands for goods and leisure that depend on prices and total

5. Diamond (1997).
6. Samuelson (1956).

income.[7] Extension to a life-cycle setting is straightforward, and the results are analogous to those in the individual model.

Unitary models have provided a simple and powerful framework for examining the consumption behavior and labor supply of families but have been subjected to increasing criticism on both theoretical and empirical grounds. A unitary family model cannot be used to analyze the formation and dissolution of marriages, nor can family decisions depend on conditions external to the marriage. This shortcoming is particularly important in analyzing retirement because the long-term decisions of an elderly couple must take into account the probability of widowhood. For example, since wives are typically younger than their husbands and women typically live longer than men, women have more incentive than men to save for old age. At middle age a wife can expect a retirement period that is, on average, 50 percent longer than her husband's.[8] Much of the criticism of unitary models has arisen from difficulties in reconciling a model in which a married couple maximizes a single utility function with the analysis of decisions to marry and to divorce, in which agents must compare their expected utilities inside marriage with their expected utilities outside marriage. The decisions of elderly couples require a different sort of external view—a return to the single state with widowhood.

Recent empirical evidence that is inconsistent with the unitary model has been an even more influential prod to the development of collective models of the family. A unitary model generates family demands that depend on prices and total family income, not the distribution of income among family members. Several empirical studies have shown that distribution does matter. The most provocative result is that the larger is the share of family income controlled by the mother, the greater is the well-being of the children.[9] For example, a recent policy change in the United Kingdom effectively transferred ownership of the universal child allowance from fathers to mothers. Although the size of the allowance did not increase, household spending on women's and children's clothing rose relative to spending on men's clothing.[10]

---

7. These demands have standard properties if the individual utility functions are well behaved.

8. This example comes from Browning (1994) and is based on Canadian life-expectancy data.

9. See Thomas (1990,1994), Haddad and Hoddinott (1994), and Rose (1999). Three recent surveys of changes in theoretical and empirical modeling of family behavior are Behrman (1997); Bergstrom (1996); and Lundberg and Pollak (1996).

10. Lundberg, Pollak, and Wales (1997).

## Collective Models

Evidence that distribution of income within the family influences consumption has stimulated the development of game-theoretic and other collective models of family behavior.[11] A typical cooperative bargaining model of marriage begins with a family that consists of only a husband and a wife. Each has a utility function that depends on his or her consumption of private goods ($U^h$ for the husband and $U^w$ for the wife). If agreement is not reached, then the payoff received is represented by the "threat point" ($T^h$, $T^w$), the utilities associated with a default outcome. The Nash bargaining solution is the allocation that maximizes the product of the gains to cooperation, given by the function $N = (U^h - T^h)(U^w - T^w)$, subject to the constraint that the family's joint income equals joint expenditure ($px = I^h + I^w$).[12] The utility received by husband or wife in the Nash bargaining solution depends on the threat point; the higher one's utility at the threat point, the higher one's utility in the Nash bargaining solution. So if the interests of husband and wife conflict over saving for old age or other matters, the observed outcome in these models depends on each spouse's threat point utility.

The threat point in a cooperative bargaining model is determined by the marital partners' best alternative to a cooperative marital equilibrium. In divorce-threat bargaining models the threat point is the maximal level of utility attainable outside the marriage. If divorcing partners maintain ownership of income received separately within marriage, the outcome of marital bargaining will depend not on total family income, but on how much income the husband and wife receive separately. The divorce threat point is also likely to depend on factors such as the probability of remarriage and the income available to divorced men and women, including eligibility for social security spouse benefits.[13]

In the "separate spheres" bargaining model the threat point is assumed to be internal to the marriage, not external as in divorce-threat bargaining models.[14] The alternative to agreement is an inefficient noncooperative equilibrium within marriage in which each spouse voluntarily provides household public goods, choosing actions that maximize utility, given the actions of their partner. This alternative is a gender-specialized equilibrium,

---

11. Most of these have been cooperative bargaining models, following the tradition established by Manser and Brown (1980) and McElroy and Horney (1981).
12. Solution concepts other than Nash bargaining yield similar results.
13. McElroy (1990) calls these "extrahousehold environmental parameters."
14. Lundberg and Pollak (1993).

where social norms assign responsibility for some household public goods to wives and others to husbands. Individual well-being in the noncooperative solution, and thus in the cooperative equilibrium as well, depends on individual control of income and other resources by the husband and wife. A noncooperative marriage, in which the spouses receive some benefits due to joint consumption of public goods, may be a more plausible threat in day-to-day marital bargaining than divorce, especially for elderly couples whose divorce rates (and remarriage prospects, given divorce) are low. Noncooperation need not involve overt conflict or hostility; the husband and wife simply fulfill socially accepted spousal responsibilities with minimal negotiation. Because the noncooperative solution depends on a gender-specific division of household responsibilities established and enforced by social norms, the model provides a route by which such norms can affect family outcomes.

Bargaining models of marriage widen the range of rational family behavior by removing some restrictive assumptions of unitary models, such as the pooling of individual incomes and the irrelevance of extramarital conditions for marital outcomes. Many variants of these models imply that who controls resources, both within and outside the marriage, can influence the distribution of resources within the marriage, and empirical evidence supporting this result is accumulating. For couples approaching retirement, bargaining power will be influenced by individual control of labor earnings and retirement timing, and by control of pension and other retirement assets and their disbursement. Wives with a history of market work and pension assets in their own name are likely to have a stronger bargaining position within marriage than wives who have stayed home. However, market work by wives is itself an outcome of the bargaining process. Jeffrey Gray finds that the labor supply of a married woman is an increasing function of her bargaining position within marriage, as measured by state divorce and marital property laws.[15] Men, it appears, bargain for their wives to stay home, and the outcome of this negotiation will affect the long-term distribution of family resources.

The high poverty rate of elderly widows and possible explanations for their relatively low incomes raise important issues for economic analysis as well as for public policy. Concerns about selfish or myopic decisions by deceased husbands seem to arise from a traditional model of family decisionmaking, with the husband making unilateral decisions about savings and retirement in line with his own preferences and

15. Gray (1998).

expected life span. However, the relative poverty of widows could also emerge from cooperative household bargaining in which the wife's bargaining power is insufficient to ensure a consumption profile that would keep her above the poverty line at the end of a long life. If a cooperative bargaining model with either an exterior or interior threat point correctly characterizes household relations, one can expect the increasing relative market income of women to improve their economic position as surviving spouses.[16] Bargaining models therefore suggest that policies that improve the labor market opportunities of women, as well as policies that restrict the annuitization of retirement income, will improve the status of elderly widows.[17]

Although the life-cycle equivalent of the one-period unitary model is well known, most bargaining models have been restricted to a static, one-period game. To analyze the retirement decision, it is important to recognize that period-by-period family decisions must be embedded in a forward-looking dynamic program in which each person recognizes the future implications of his or her current actions. Models of this decision require at least two periods, work and retirement, and for many issues a third period of possible widowhood must be added. Game-theoretic modeling of marriage requires a choice between cooperative and noncooperative frameworks. Cooperative bargaining models assume that binding, costlessly enforceable agreements between the players (concerning, for example, consumption paths and retirement dates) are possible, but agreements concerning distribution within the household are in general not legally enforceable. Social norms may provide some external reinforcement of spousal obligations, but it will be difficult for a husband or wife to credibly commit to future actions that will not be privately optimal. For this reason a noncooperative framework, which focuses on self-enforcing agreements, may be preferred for the study of family bargaining over time. In this case both distribution within the family and the efficiency of family behavior may depend on social or private mechanisms that help enforce intertemporal agreements, such as social norms or pressure from friends and extended family.

16. The only empirical evidence I am aware of on this point is provided by Browning (1995), who finds that the wife's share in household income has no significant effect on household saving rates in Canadian data.

17. This approach to influencing the intrafamily distribution of resources is a commonplace in the development literature and the recent initiatives of development agencies but has not been prominent in domestic policy discussions.

## Retirement and Bargaining

Retirement as an event in lifetime decisionmaking has three important characteristics. First, retirement from career employment has an element of irreversibility. Retirees can return to work, but typically at reduced wages because they lose the value of specific human capital associated with their career job or because they have stepped off a deferred-compensation, rising-wage profile. This decrease in the wage will reduce the retiree's potential control over income, and may decrease bargaining power within the household. Second, retirement reduces market work, increasing the time available for leisure and, especially for women, household work. Finally, retirement influences the retiree's assets and feasible consumption.

When a husband is the primary earner, he and his wife are unlikely to agree on when he should retire. Retirement substantially increases the husband's leisure, but not that of his wife, and the wife may have more interest in accumulating wealth for her longer expected period of retirement. Aside from the annoyance of women who suddenly find their retired husbands underfoot all day, we might expect wives to prefer a later retirement for their husbands than the men themselves would choose. However, the reduction in the retiree's potential income threatens his future control over family resources, and this will tend to delay his preferred retirement.

Several studies have documented a pronounced decline in consumption at retirement.[18] This pattern cannot be explained with a standard life-cycle model, and factors such as the end of work-related expenses and the substitution of leisure or home production for market goods cannot reconcile the theory with the facts. A discrete drop in consumption is consistent with a story in which individuals are surprised at retirement—"they take stock of their finances only to discover that their resources are insufficient to maintain their accustomed standards of living . . . and they revise their expectations downward in the light of this realization."[19] A model of intrafamily bargaining can provide an alternative explanation. With retirement comes a shift in the husband's marital threat point. When his control over market income falls, the consumption profile of the couple should shift toward the preferred profile of the wife, who expects to live longer and, therefore, prefers to maintain savings. This shift will, of course, have been anticipated, but the inability of the couple to make binding

18. The drop in consumption has been documented in the United States by Hamermesh (1984) and Mariger (1987); in Canada by Robb and Burbridge (1989); and in Great Britain by Banks, Blundell, and Tanner (1998).

19. Bernheim, Skinner, and Weinberg (1997, p. 5).

commitments with respect to future allocations will prevent the smoothing of consumption that a life-cycle model would predict. If marital bargaining is important in the observed consumption decline, we would expect it to occur only among married couples and to be more pronounced when the husband is much older than the wife.

Husbands and wives tend to retire together. In a unitary model, strong complementarity between the husband's leisure and the wife's leisure can explain simultaneous retirement. Other possible explanations include correlations in the retirement preferences of husband and wife, or correlations in their pension accrual profiles. Alan Gustman and Thomas Steinmeier find that the coordination of retirement is due to preferences, not budget sets, and that although the wife's retirement decision is not strongly affected by her husband's, the husband's retirement decision is strongly (positively) affected by his wife's.[20] This pattern is inconsistent both with the primary earner–secondary earner paradigm, which implies that the wife's behavior does not affect her husband's, and with the unitary model, which implies symmetry in the cross-spouse effects of retirement. Gustman and Steinmeier speculate that this result may arise from strategic behavior by the husband, who is reluctant to face the house and attendant responsibilities alone.[21]

## Research Agenda

Only a few of the many potential applications of game theory to retirement and related issues have been explored. Several recent studies have examined the joint labor supply of older husbands and wives. We know that the retirement decisions of men are, perhaps increasingly, dependent on their wives' labor supply behavior, and that the retirement decisions of married women are more strongly influenced by their own market opportunities than they were in the past. These facts are inconsistent with the traditional family paradigm that has motivated most retirement analysis. However, a number of empirical gaps concerning the marital context of retirement decisions inhibits the development of bargaining models. We know very little about how marital status and the *relative* earnings, ages, health status, and other characteristics of husband and wife affect decisions about

20. Gustman and Steinmeier (1997).
21. Gustman and Steinmeier's application of noncooperative models to retirement (see also Hiedemann, 1995) is in contrast to most marital bargaining studies.

savings and consumption. Characteristics of the extended family, particularly parents and children, may influence the potential resources and
responsibilities of mature men and women and may also serve as indicators
of the enforceability of long-term contracts between husband and wife. A
bargaining perspective on the well-being of widows requires longitudinal
or extensive retrospective data with which one can track not just total
resources of the former couple but also the wife's relative control over
resources throughout the marriage.

A model of marital bargaining that will have interesting implications for
retirement must be a multiperiod model, and the implications of current
consumption and labor supply decisions for future household resources are
key to all the issues I have discussed. So far, most game-theoretic models
of marriage have focused on issues that concern younger couples: the allocation of resources to children and investments in market and household
human capital. Bargaining between older couples will be simply one part
of a lifetime sequence of negotiations with one or a series of partners, but
in analyzing retirement behavior it may be useful to take as given investments in market and home human capital and to focus on issues more inte-
gral to the elderly and the retirement period.

Three modeling issues are of particular interest: how control over
resources is distributed between working and retired husbands and wives;
the role of risks and uncertainty concerning income, health status, and
death; and how commitments are to be enforced.

## Resource Control

The relative control of husband and wife over family resources is not easily measured.[22] The most straightforward indicator is relative income, but
this will also affect consumption and time use through its dependence on
wage rates, which are the prices of husband's and wife's time. In addition,
effective control depends not only on potential market income and asset
ownership, but also on the knowledge and abilities of each partner and on
custom. In a model of bargaining between elderly husbands and wives, it
may be reasonable to assume some asymmetry in market wages and returns
to household activities. Husbands will typically have higher wages and
more years of market work than their wives. As a result, they will be entitled to larger pensions, public and private. Their wives will have borne
the bulk of household responsibilities. Work histories interrupted by years

22. There is an extensive discussion of this point in Lundberg and Pollak (1996).

of raising children will have left them with relatively low earnings and pension accumulations, although perhaps with greater claims on the resources of children when widowed. This discrepancy in the market opportunities and pension accumulation of husbands and wives will decrease as recent cohorts of married women with more labor force experience grow older.

## Risk

Life-cycle models often incorporate uncertainty about life span or returns on assets, but marital bargaining models must also deal with the risk of disability in old age. This risk affects husbands and wives asymmetrically because husbands are usually older than their wives and likely to become disabled earlier. If the husband requires care, therefore, it is likely to be provided by his younger wife. Substitutes such as care by daughters or other relatives or institutional care may be available, but spousal care is likely to be preferred. The anticipation of disability, the need for care, and the alteration in bargaining power and the ability to bargain often associated with disability will influence the earlier strategic choices of husband and wife. The inadvertent bequests left by couples who have maintained asset positions as insurance against eventual disability testify to the perceived importance of this risk.

## Enforcing Commitments

Cooperative models of marital bargaining assume that a husband and wife can make binding, costlessly enforceable commitments. Together with the assumption that information is relatively good (or at least not asymmetric), the ability to make binding agreements ensures the efficiency of cooperative agreements.[23] Because legal institutions do not provide for external enforcement of contracts regarding allocation within marriage, the assumption of a binding agreement requires some motivation. Repeated noncooperative games have multiple equilibria, and an efficient equilib-

---

23. Most models of the family either assume or conclude that family behavior is Pareto optimal. Unitary models ensure Pareto optimality by assuming a family social welfare function that is an increasing function of the utilities of all family members: no member can be made better off without making another worse off. Cooperative bargaining models characterize the equilibrium distribution by means of a set of axioms, one of which is Pareto optimality. Pareto optimality is also the defining property of the collective model of Chiappori (1988, 1992). Rather than applying a particular cooperative or noncooperative bargaining model to the household allocation process, Chiappori assumes only that equilibrium allocations are Pareto optimal, and so his collective model contains cooperative bargaining models and common preference models as special cases.

rium can often be sustained by the threat of punishment. In essence, each spouse realizes that the one-period gain from deviating from an agreement will be less than the loss associated with being punished by the spouse in the periods that follow. It can be argued that marriage possesses characteristics—a long-term relationship, relatively good information, and a stable bargaining environment—that are known to promote efficient outcomes in a repeated noncooperative game.[24]

The assumption of a stable bargaining environment is questionable in models that examine the life-cycle behavior of a married couple. Theodore Bergstrom has noted that "this stationarity is lacking in a model where children grow up and leave the family and where the probability of death increases with age."[25] If the bargaining environment is not stationary, dynamic inefficiencies can arise if the husband and wife are unable to enter binding lifetime contracts. Few bargaining models have considered dynamic effects, but Robin Wells and Maria Maher present a dynamic model of marital time allocation that focuses on the specialization of husband and wife.[26] In their model the efficient equilibrium requires that the wife specialize in household production and the husband in market work. With period-by-period renegotiation of the marital contract, specialization results in a deterioration of the wife's relative bargaining strength. The threat point is a noncooperative equilibrium in which the partner who specializes in the production of income, a private good, will have an advantage over the partner who produces public goods at home. This discrepancy will increase over time because of learning in the market and home production. Therefore the wife will refuse to engage in an efficient degree of specialization unless her husband is wealthy enough to make an up-front wealth transfer that compensates her for her future loss in bargaining power and marital surplus. Wells and Maher predict, therefore, that household specialization and fertility will be inefficiently low because of strategic considerations in repeated marital bargaining.

Older couples are likely to face a changing bargaining environment. Retirement usually occurs just once and permanently reduces the available market wage of the retiree. The timing of this decision is under the control of the worker himself, who must consider two effects on subsequent family bargaining and the allocation of resources within a marriage. First, retirement will permanently change the household's trade-off

24. Browning and others (1994).
25. Bergstrom (1996, p. 1929).
26. Wells and Maher (1996).

between income and his leisure. Even if period-by-period decisions are made cooperatively, the husband who prefers more leisure and less income than his long-lived wife may be tempted to take a one-time action to increase his leisure that alters the prices the family faces in subsequent bargaining. Second, retirement may reduce the husband's threat point, so that he receives a smaller proportion of total family resources.[27] The first of these effects will probably lead to premature retirement, the second to delayed retirement. Both rely on the inability of the husband and wife to enter into binding lifetime contracts concerning consumption and time allocation.

Other changes in the marital bargaining environment may result from aging rather than retirement. As couples age, the probability of death and of incapacitation from ill health increases. In repeated games, cooperation between the players becomes more difficult to sustain as the end of the game approaches; elderly couples may be less able to reach efficient cooperative solutions.

If a married couple is able to agree on, and enforce, an efficient lifetime path of work and consumption, these decisions must be conditioned on the expected needs and life expectancies of both husband and wife. If only the husband engages in market work and only the wife produces household public goods, one would expect the husband to work longer and the wife to produce more household goods than they could in a noncooperative equilibrium. The folk theorem concerning efficient outcomes in repeated noncooperative games is often invoked to explain the maintenance of such an agreement. Whether an efficient equilibrium can be maintained if retirement is a one-time decision is less clear. If the husband would prefer to retire earlier than his wife would prefer, because she expects to live longer than him, it is difficult to see how an efficient commitment to retire later, say at age 65 rather than 62, could be enforced. The decision is made only once and, following a premature retirement, the wife would be better off agreeing to restore a period-by-period cooperative outcome under the new, postretirement circumstances rather than maintaining a noncooperative stance as punishment. The repeated-game folk theorem does not apply in this situation, nor is it likely to apply in the case of other infrequent decisions that are irreversible and can be made unilaterally by one spouse, such as quitting a job or becoming pregnant. A

---

27. The extent to which retirement is associated with a loss of control over income depends, of course, on the allocation of pension assets and associated control over their disbursement. I am assuming here formal joint control over assets in contrast to individual control over market income.

married couple's inability to enter into binding lifetime agreements concerning these matters may lead to inefficient outcomes. Social norms concerning appropriate retirement ages can help support only those agreements that conform with conventional behavior.[28]

If the distribution of household resources between a husband and wife depends on their individual control over market income, retirement can be a strategic tool in marital bargaining. Workers may retire too late in order to keep control of a larger fraction of total household resources or retire too early to reduce the price of their own leisure.[29] If retirement timing is not part of a binding lifetime agreement between marital partners, the outcomes of bargaining need not be efficient. Repeated bargaining between husband and wife can maintain efficiency as long as each has less to gain by behaving selfishly in the short run than he or she expects to lose from spousal punishments in the future. This discipline may erode as the end of the game—in this case, death—approaches. Finite life need not interfere with efficient outcomes if the probability of ending the game is constant. In fact, the probability of death increases with age, so that the repeated game of marriage becomes less likely to generate efficient solutions as the spouses age.

As they grow older, men and women will continue to want to have things their own way. Therefore, efficient outcomes can be maintained only if commitments can be enforced and opportunistic behavior limited. A husband who is the primary earner may be willing to work longer than he would prefer in exchange his wife's promise of care should he become disabled. However, the wife cannot credibly commit to provide such care in the final period of life unless it is privately optimal for her to do so because the husband's ability to punish her for abandonment is restricted to the terms of his will.[30] The effect of end-of-life noncooperation on the retirement date is not clear. The husband's inability to offer his wife an

28. For many years, retirement rates at age 65 were higher than would be predicted by standard models. Lumsdaine, Stock, and Wise (1996), although unable to explain the spike at age 65, found that married men were significantly more likely to retire at age 65 than single men and thus were bound longer than single men or women to a customary rule of thumb concerning the appropriate age to retire. One could speculate that within marriage social norms about retirement might serve as commitment devices that help maintain efficient work levels by older men and their wives.

29. It should be noted that control over labor income can be effectively replaced by control over assets and that any decisions regarding the allocation of pension income made at the time of retirement will also be important for subsequent bargaining and distribution.

30. Legal restrictions on the husband's ability to disinherit his spouse may therefore affect the range of possible bargains the couple can enter into as well as the default allocation. An empirical study of whether these restrictions, which vary across states and types of assets, are associated with differences in retirement behavior and caretaking arrangements would be informative.

enforceable income-care trade suggests an earlier retirement, but if assets can provide the husband with the means to purchase substitute care in old age, he may prefer later retirement and greater asset accumulation.

Important mechanisms exist for ensuring that marital commitments can be maintained late in life despite the erosion of threats of retaliation. Altruism or love for a partner can make taking care of them when they are old and disabled privately optimal, as can strong social disapprobation of spousal abandonment or mistreatment. Adult children can monitor parental behavior and punish a parent who fails to take care of the other. Children will also prefer to avoid becoming the sole support of a widowed parent, but punishing a dead parent who has failed to provide for the survivor will be more difficult than punishing a living one. The role of children provides some potentially testable hypotheses; for example, if the presence of children promotes cooperation between parents, one might expect to see more spousal care of disabled partners rather than market care or institutionalization among elderly couples with children.

Other features of family bargaining could lead to inefficiencies in the lifetime allocation of time and goods. Cooperative bargaining with internal, noncooperative threat points may be consistent with inefficient outcomes if bargaining itself is costly. The negotiation, monitoring, and enforcement of a cooperative agreement gives rise to transaction costs that are likely to vary among husband and wife pairs. Some couples may therefore prefer to remain at a separate-spheres equilibrium that is maintained by social enforcement and does not involve bargaining costs. Asymmetric information may also be important. Marriage, although a long and intimate relationship in shared accommodation, is unlikely to lead to complete revelation of preferences and all other important information. Misrepresentation of preferences, strategic incompetence, and maintenance of proprietary information about one's own sphere (the functioning of the household or financial status) are features of marital bargaining that could be formally modeled. The consequences of the 1974 ERISA provision that made joint life the default pension option suggest that asymmetric information within married couples may be an important feature of marital decisionmaking.

## Conclusion

Analyses of retirement behavior have typically employed a traditional family model in which all decisions are made by one agent: the household head. The joint utility or unitary model of the family allows for interactions between the time allocation and budget constraints of husband and wife, but assumes that the married couple acts as though they are one agent with a single utility function. Bargaining models of marriage, in contrast, allow us to consider separately the actions and intentions of the husband and wife and the prospect of dissolution of the marital unit through divorce or death.

Game-theoretic models permit a broader range of rational behavior than joint utility family models. They may help solve some empirical puzzles, such as the failure of consumption profiles to correspond to the individual life-cycle model. If marital partners are unable to make enforceable commitments concerning the future allocations of time and money, strategic motives may lead to discrete changes in family behavior. For example, retirement from a career job, if it is irreversible and its timing is not determined by a binding marital agreement, will lead to a change in the relative control over family resources by husband and wife.

Bargaining models also have potentially important implications for retirement policy: First, control over resources and the power to make independent decisions increase the ability of the husband or wife to negotiate household outcomes that are in their own private interest. The principal implications of this result are distributional. The existence of large numbers of poor widows may not demonstrate that the allocation of household resources over time was inefficient, but rather that the bargaining power of wives was too weak to guarantee them a large enough share to prevent poverty in old age. Second, marital bargaining may produce inefficient outcomes. Two cases in which inefficiencies may result are strategic responses to anticipated future changes in bargaining power, and an endgame reversion to noncooperative behavior as the end of life approaches. If an efficient lifetime contract between husband and wife involves specialization and the wife expects to live longer than her husband, then without binding commitments the husband may retire "too early," and the wife provide too few household services in the last years of life.

Models of bargaining by elderly married couples can be expected to generate varied results, depending on the exact specification of the utility functions, the nature of interdependencies between the spouses, and the ability of the couple to enforce intertemporal agreements. In general, however, some of the results generated by a unitary model of the household will not hold, and factors that did not affect unitary outcomes, such as individual control over income and assets, will become important in determining family behavior. More empirical research on the marital context of consumption and retirement could help establish whether bargaining issues are sufficiently important to explain some aspects of the behavior of older American couples.

# References

Banks, James, Richard Blundell, and Sara Tanner. 1998. "Is There a Retirement Savings Puzzle?" *American Economic Review* 88 (September): 769–88.

Behrman, Jere R. 1997. "Intrahousehold Distribution and the Family." In *Handbook of Population and Family Economics,* edited by Mark R. Rosenzweig and Oded Stark. Amsterdam: North-Holland.

Bergstrom, Theodore C. 1996. "Economics in a Family Way." *Journal of Economic Literature* 34 (4): 1903–34.

Berkovic, James C., and Steven Stern. 1991. "Job Exit Behavior of Older Men." *Econometrica* 59 (1): 189–210.

Bernheim, B. Douglas, Jonathan Skinner, and Steven Weinberg. 1997. "What Accounts for the Variation in Retirement Wealth among Households?" Working Paper 6227. Cambridge, Mass.: National Bureau of Economic Research.

Blau, David M. 1998. "Labor Force Dynamics of Older Married Couples." *Journal of Labor Economics* 16 (3): 595–629.

Browning, Martin. 1994. "The Saving Behaviour of a Two-Person Household." Working Paper 94–06. McMaster University.

———. 1995. "Saving and the Intra-Household Distribution of Income: An Empirical Investigation." *Ricerche Economiche* 48: 277–92.

Browning, Martin, and others. 1994. "Income and Outcomes: A Structural Model of Intrahousehold Allocation." *Journal of Political Economy* 102 (6): 1067–96.

Chiappori, Pierre-Andre. 1988. "Rational Household Labor Supply." *Econometrica* 56 (1): 63–89.

———. 1992. "Collective Labor Supply and Welfare." *Journal of Political Economy* 100 (3): 437– 67.

Clark, Robert, and Thomas Johnson. 1980. "Retirement in the Dual Career Family." Final Report to the Social Security Administration. Washington.

Diamond, Peter. 1997. "Macroeconomic Aspects of Social Security Reform." *Brookings Papers on Economic Activity,* 2: 1–87.

Gray, Jeffrey S. 1998. "Divorce Law Changes, Household Bargaining, and Married Women's Labor Supply."*American Economic Review* 88 (3): 628–42.

Gustman, Alan L., and Thomas L. Steinmeier. 1986. "A Structural Retirement Model." *Econometrica* 54 (3): 555–84.

———. 1997. "Retirement in Dual-Career Families: A Structural Model." Dartmouth College (April).

Haddad, Lawrence, and John Hoddinott. 1994. "Women's Income and Boy-Girl Anthropometric Status in the Côte d'Ivoire." *World Development* 22 (4): 543–53.

Hamermesh, Daniel S. 1984. "Consumption during Retirement: The Missing Link in the Life Cycle." *Review of Economics and Statistics* 66 (1): 1–7.

Hiedemann, Bridget. 1995. "A Stackelberg Model of Social Security Acceptance Decisions in Dual Career Households." Seattle University.

Honig, Marjorie. 1998. "Married Women's Retirement Expectations: Do Pensions and Social Security Matter?" *American Economic Review Papers and Proceedings* 88 (2): 202–06.

Hurd, Michael D. 1990. "The Joint Retirement Decision of Husbands and Wives." In *Issues in the Economics of Aging*, edited by David A. Wise, 231–54. University of Chicago Press.

Lumsdaine, Robin, James Stock, and David Wise. 1992. "Three Models of Retirement: Computational Complexity versus Predictive Validity." In *Topics in the Economics of Aging*, edited by David A. Wise, 19–57. University of Chicago Press.

———. 1996. "Why Are Retirement Rates So High at Age 65?" In *Advances in the Economics of Aging*, edited by David A. Wise, 11–82. University of Chicago Press.

Lundberg, Shelly. 1988. "Labor Supply of Husbands and Wives: A Simultaneous Equations Approach." *Review of Economics and Statistics* 70 (2): 224–35.

Lundberg, Shelly, and Robert A. Pollak. 1993. "Separate Spheres Bargaining and the Marriage Market." *Journal of Political Economy* 101 (6): 988–1010.

———. 1994. "Noncooperative Bargaining Models of Marriage." *American Economic Review Papers and Proceedings* 84 (2): 132–37.

———. 1996. "Bargaining and Distribution in Marriage." *Journal of Economic Perspectives* 10 (Fall): 139–58.

Lundberg, Shelly, Robert A. Pollak, and Terence J. Wales. 1997. "Do Husbands and Wives Pool Their Resources? Evidence from the U.K. Child Benefit." *Journal of Human Resources* 32 (3): 463–80.

Manser, Marilyn, and Murray Brown. 1980. "Marriage and Household Decision Making: A Bargaining Analysis." *International Economic Review* 21 (1): 31–44.

Mariger, Randall P. 1987. "A Life-Cycle Consumption Model with Liquidity Constraints: Theory and Empirical Results." *Econometrica* 55 (3): 533–57.

McElroy, Marjorie B. 1990. "The Empirical Content of Nash-Bargained Household Behavior." *Journal of Human Resources* 25 (4): 559–83.

McElroy, Marjorie B., and Mary Jean Horney. 1981. "Nash Bargained Household Decisions." *International Economic Review* 22 (2): 333–49.

Robb, A. L., and J. B. Burbridge. 1989. "Consumption, Income, and Retirement." *Canadian Journal of Economics* 22 (3): 522–42.

Rose, Elaina. 1999. "Consumption Smoothing and Excess Female Mortality in Rural India." *Review of Economics and Statistics* 81 (1): 41–49.

Stock, James, and David A. Wise. 1990. "The Pension Inducement to Retire: An Option Value Analysis." In *Issues in the Economics of Aging*, edited by David A. Wise, 205–24. University of Chicago Press.

Samuelson, Paul A. 1956. "Social Indifference Curves." *Quarterly Journal of Economics* 70 (1): 1–22.

Thomas, Duncan. 1990. "Intra-Household Resource Allocation: An Inferential Approach." *Journal of Human Resources* 25 (4): 635–64.

———. 1994. "Like Father, Like Son: Like Mother, Like Daughter: Parental Resources and Child Height." *Journal of Human Resources* 29 (4): 950–88.

Wells, Robin, and Maria Maher. 1996. "Time and Surplus Allocation within Marriage." Massachusetts Institute of Technology (February).

COMMENT BY

# B. Douglas Bernheim

Shelly Lundberg's chapter makes a strong case for the view that the retirement of married workers results from joint decisionmaking. For that reason, a serious treatment of intrafamily bargaining has considerable potential to advance our understanding of how people retire. In making this case Lundberg provides an interesting and useful overview of studies on family decisionmaking and suggests some provocative applications to retirement. She has outlined a promising and relatively unexplored line of inquiry, and her paper should prove particularly useful to young economists in search of novel approaches to old problems. Because I am in substantial agreement with the central point of the chapter, my comments are primarily intended as elaborations of some underlying themes, though in a few instances I also have some theoretical quibbles. My comments, grouped into four sections, concern unitary models, cooperative models, noncooperative models, and the interpretation of empirical patterns.

## Unitary Models

Lundberg distinguishes two approaches to modeling joint decisionmaking: unitary models, in which a single utility function is maximized, and collective models, which include cooperative and noncooperative bargaining models. In the archetypal unitary model, a couple maximizes a social welfare function of their individual utilities, subject to a budget constraint that equals the sum of their incomes. Lundberg asserts that this gives rise to family demands with standard properties, that outcomes are necessarily efficient, and that questions of distribution between husbands and wives do not arise in any meaningful way. She then summarizes some empirical findings that contradict a central implication of the unitary framework.

Although I agree that the unitary model is hard pressed to explain the empirical findings that she describes, I think the approach is more interesting than her discussion suggests. I also disagree with her statements on distribution and efficiency. To understand why, consider a unitary model of life-cycle planning by a couple.

Suppose for simplicity that both spouses live for exactly $T$ periods. Let $c_t$ denote household expenditures in period $t$, and let $C_t$ denote the vector $(c_1,...,c_T)$. Assume for the moment that household expenditures are pure public goods from the perspective of the spouses. Suppose that the husband has infinite impatience, so that, in each period $t$, his utility is a function only of current expenditures: $U_t^H(C_t) = u(c_t)$. Suppose that the wife is an altruist, deriving utility directly from consumption according to the utility function $V_t^W(C_t)$ as well as indirectly from the husband's utility function: $U_t^W(C_t) = V_t^W(C_t) + \alpha U_t^H(C_t)$. Assume also that the function $V_t^W$ reflects standard additively separable preferences with constant discounting at the rate $\rho$: $V_t^W(C_t) = \Sigma_{\tau=0}^{T-t} \rho^t u(c_{t+\tau})$. Finally, assume that the wife dictates all household decisions.

This model is unitary in Lundberg's sense in that the household (more specifically, the wife) maximizes a single social welfare function (more specifically, the wife's utility function). There is no bargaining or negotiation. Yet outcomes need not be efficient, and questions of distribution are meaningful. To see this, note that the wife's utility function can be rewritten as

$$(1 + \alpha)^{-1} U_t^W(C_t) = u(c_t) + (1 + \alpha)^{-1}\Sigma_{\tau=0}^{T-t} \rho^t(c_{t+\tau}).$$

These preferences are dynamically inconsistent in the sense that the marginal rate of substitution between consumption in periods $t$ and $t + 1$ change as period $t$ approaches. In particular, the wife becomes less willing to defer consumption between periods $t$ and $t + 1$ when period $t$ arrives. As discussed by David Laibson, who refers to these preferences as a case of "hyperbolic discounting," dynamically inconsistent preferences of this form can give rise to inefficient choices.[1] Though the wife may devise an optimal plan at some point $t$, in general she will be unwilling to follow through on this plan in subsequent periods. Similar conclusions follow even when the husband is patient, provided that the husband and wife discount future utility at different rates.

In this simple model, distributional questions are well posed in the sense that the husband and wife will be affected differently by changes in the environment that induce the dictatorial wife to redistribute consumption between the present and the future. More generally, one could easily extend the model to accommodate situations in which the household makes both private and public expenditures. Changes in the environment that induce the dictatorial wife to alter the composition of consumption between private goods for the wife, private goods for the husband, and public goods plainly have distributional implications.

1. Laibson (1998).

# Cooperative Bargaining Models

The relation between unitary models and cooperative bargaining models, as I see it, is much closer than Lundberg suggests. To understand this point, let $U^i$ and $T^i$ represent, respectively, the utility and threat point of spouse $i$ ($i = H, W$). For the Nash bargaining solution, the household maximizes the expression $\alpha \log (U^H - T^H) + (1 - \alpha) \log(U^W - T^W)$. But, fixing $T^i$, one can always think of the expression $\log (U^i - T^i)$ as the utility of spouse $i$, in which case this corresponds to a standard social welfare function of the sort used in the unitary approach.

In defense of Lundberg's distinction, one might argue that the cooperative model has implications concerning comparative statics that differentiate it from the unitary model. For example, because wage rates do not enter a spouse's utility function directly, changes in wage rates in the unitary model can affect choices only through the household's budget constraint. In contrast, the cooperative model allows for the possibility that the wage rate enters the expression $\log (U^i - T^i)$ directly through the threat point $T^i$.

Although this argument is certainly correct, its practical implications are limited. Unless one already knows a great deal about the extent of substitution or complementarity between consumption and leisure, it is difficult to distinguish empirically between models that allow wage rates to enter the utility function, through the term $\log (U^i - T^i)$, and models that restrict wage rates to enter only through the budget constraint. To put it somewhat differently, if one artificially restricts patterns of substitutability and complementarity between consumption and leisure by adopting a parameterized class of utility function that does not contain the true utility function, the data may falsely reject the unitary model by indicating that the effects of wage rates are not limited to the budget constraint.

Similar observations apply with respect to many, but probably not all, variables that might conceivably enter the bargaining problem through the threat points. In most instances, there is an observationally equivalent unitary model that accounts for the same set of empirical patterns. There are some exceptions, possibly including the transfer of the universal child allowance in the United Kingdom, which Lundberg mentions. But such exceptions are rare and do not provide sufficient information to separately parameterize the utility function and the threat point function with confidence. Moreover, without tight parameterizations of these functions, one cannot use the cooperative bargaining framework to generate reliable predictions about the effects of arbitrary changes in the economic environment.

It is also important to emphasize that the cooperative bargaining framework says nothing about the determination of the threat points. Though the economics of a particular situation may suggest some natural properties (for example, positive dependence of an individual's threat point on his or her own wage rate), one usually cannot say very much beforehand about threat points. For joint decisions by married couples, threat points may correspond to divorce or to the absence of cooperation within a marriage. When threat points correspond to divorce, the economic status of one spouse may not affect the other's threat point (at least in the absence of altruism or envy), but when threat points correspond to the absence of cooperation within the marriage, each threat point will usually depend on the economic outcome for both parties (particularly if the household consumes some public goods). Lundberg mentions these various possibilities but does not explain how in practice one might distinguish between them. I suspect that it would be very difficult to do this in a convincing way.

It is also possible that threat points are determined primarily by noneconomic factors such as emotional distress. When noneconomic factors are sufficiently important relative to economic factors, it may be appropriate to regard the threat points as approximately fixed, in which case one is back in the unitary framework. To put it somewhat differently, the unitary framework is simply a special case of the cooperative bargaining framework wherein threat points are determined by factors outside of the system (possibly emotional reactions).

## Noncooperative Models

In noncooperative models of joint household decisionmaking over the life cycle, behavior corresponds to the equilibrium of a dynamic game. Lundberg emphasizes the fact that this game is nonstationary. Among other things, retirement is a one-shot decision, and the probability of death—hence the likelihood that the game will end—rises with age. I agree with this characterization but would draw somewhat different lessons from it than Lundberg does.

### The One-Shot Nature of Retirement

Lundberg suggests that it may not be possible to sustain an efficient equilibrium if retirement is a one-time decision. She offers two reasons. The first is that, following a premature retirement, the wife would be better off agreeing to restore a period-by-period cooperative outcome under the new postretirement circumstances, rather than maintaining a noncooperative stance as punishment. The second is that the repeated-game folk theorem applies neither in this situation nor to other infrequent decisions that are irreversible and can be made unilaterally by one spouse. I am unconvinced by these arguments and believe that the scope for enforcing the efficient retirement outcome in a life-cycle setting may be substantial.

Lundberg's first argument is familiar to most game theorists.[2] The general problem is as follows. Suppose that players find themselves in some subgame of an extensive form game and that equilibrium strategies prescribe a "punishment" equilibrium in this subgame. If there is a better continuation equilibrium, players should "renegotiate" and agree to continue the game in a way different from originally planned. This observation leads to various equilibrium refinements such as "renegotiation proofness" and "collective dynamic consistency." Thus the problem that Lundberg identifies is generally recognized as an important one. However, it has nothing to do with nonstationarity. The issue is also present in the simplest, stationary repeated games.

Consider, for example, an infinitely repeated prisoners' dilemma game. Players either cooperate or cheat. As long as players place sufficient weight on future outcomes, they can sustain cooperation as an equilibrium outcome by reverting to repetitions of the static Nash outcome (wherein both players cheat) following a deviation. But if players were ever required to enter a punishment phase, they would be better off agreeing to restore a period-by-period cooperative outcome under the new postdeviation circumstances rather than maintaining a noncooperative stance as a punishment.

Contrary to Lundberg's assertion, the potential for renegotiation does not necessarily undermine the feasibility of cooperation. Instead of punishing deviations by moving to an equilibrium that is worse for all players, one can instead move to an equilibrium that is better for one player and worse for another.[3] In that case, at least one party will be unwilling to agree to restore the outcome that would have emerged had the deviation not taken place. More concretely, in the context of the life-cycle problem that Lundberg discusses, one could punish one spouse for retiring earlier (or later) than planned by subsequently shifting to an equilibrium that allo-

---

2. Bernheim and Ray (1989); and Farrell and Maskin (1989).
3. Bernheim and Ray (1989).

cates consumption more favorably from the point of view of the other spouse and less favorably from the point of view of the deviating spouse.

Lundberg's second argument—the repeated-game folk theorem does not apply to nonstationary environments—is technically correct. But the underlying principles of the folk theorem are nevertheless applicable to nonstationary models with infrequent decisions. Generally, perfect cooperation emerges as a feasible equilibrium outcome of a repeated game when the discount factor, $\delta$, exceeds some threshold value, $\delta^*$, where $\delta^*$ is *strictly* less than unity. For $\delta \in [\delta^*, 1]$, the most severe punishments are *more* than sufficient to enforce cooperation, which implies the existence of "slack" enforcement power, which can be applied to other decisions, including infrequent ones.[4] To illustrate, imagine that two parties play the infinitely repeated prisoners' dilemma game, and that one of the parties makes a one-shot decision in the first period. Provided that the discount factor is sufficiently close to unity, punishment equilibria will necessarily be sufficiently severe not only to enforce cooperation within each play of the prisoners' dilemma, but also to ensure a cooperative resolution of the one-shot decision. If one thinks about the one-shot decision as representing retirement and the prisoners' dilemma as representing other household decisions (such as consumption), it is clear that the spirit of the folk theorem applies to Lundberg's life-cycle problem, even if the letter of the theorem does not.

*Declining Survival Probabilities*

Lundberg also discusses the implications of nonstationarity arising from the decline of conditional survival probabilities with age. She reasons that if the probability of terminating marital bargaining increases with age, the effect of the threat of punishment will diminish as death nears and the expected time remaining in the game shortens. As a result, she argues, marital noncooperation becomes more likely and this fact may cause marital cooperation to unravel in previous periods as well.[5] Although these statements contain an element of truth, they require clarification and elaboration. In general, cooperation need not unravel merely because the probability of continuation declines with age.

First, consider the extreme case where the date of death is known, so that the horizon of the game is finite and certain. Cooperation unravels

---

4. See Bernheim and Whinston (1990) for a related discussion.

5. Elsewhere Lundberg argues that the appeal to the repeated game played in marriage to maintain efficient solutions runs into difficulties as the end of life nears. It is important to understand that if cooperation is infeasible in the endgame, cooperation unravels forward from the endgame.

only if the game has a unique equilibrium. Indeed, there is a folk theorem for finite-horizon repeated games, which states in effect that one can get any feasible, individually rational outcome provided that the horizon is sufficiently long and that the stage game has at least two distinct equilibria.[6] Because nonuniqueness of equilibria is common in all but the simplest strategic environments, there is no reason to believe that cooperation in a finite-horizon life-cycle game would necessarily unravel.

Second, even in cases that are not covered by this folk theorem, cooperation does not necessarily unravel unless the continuation probability actually reaches zero at some point. There is also a folk theorem for a general class of repeated games with time-varying continuation probabilities in which the players discount payoffs from period $t + 1$ to period $t$ at the rate $\delta_t$, where $\delta_t$ is always strictly positive but may decline with $t$ and possibly approach zero asymptotically. In these environments one can get any feasible, individually rational outcome, provided that $\delta_t$ stays close enough to unity for sufficiently long periods of time and provided that in the limit, as $t \to \infty$, $\Sigma_{k=1\tau}[2^{-k} \ln \delta_k] > -\infty$. This condition is necessary and sufficient for the existence of cooperative equilibria.[7] The condition is satisfied for the particular case of $\ln \delta_k = \ln a + \alpha^k \ln \lambda$ if and only if $\alpha < 2$. This observation is of interest in the current context because demographers have used this particular functional form to explain the evolution of human survival probabilities and have found that $\alpha$ is indeed less than 2.[8] Consequently, there is no compelling theoretical reason to believe that declining survival probabilities undermine the feasibility of cooperation in life-cycle games (though the extent of cooperation should decline with age once survival probabilities become sufficiently small).

Third, even when individual players are short lived, it is often possible to sustain cooperation if there are overlapping generations of players or if some players are long lived.[9] In the current context, children may extend the life-cycle game, facilitating cooperative agreements among parents by punishing parents who defect from these agreements shortly before a spouse's death, as Lundberg points out.

Fourth, the finiteness of the horizon may not be problematic if players are incompletely informed about each others' preferences. Folk theorems also exist for finite-horizon games of incomplete information.[10] In the

6. Benoit and Krishna (1985).
7. Bernheim and Dasgupta (1995).
8. Gavrilov and Gavrilova (1991).
9. Cremer (1986); and Fudenberg, Kreps, and Maskin (1990).
10. Kreps and others (1982).

current context one might imagine each spouse believing that, with some potentially small probability, the other is "naturally vindictive," that he or she will retaliate against poor treatment irrespective of whether it is in his or her personal interests. In such environments, people have incentives to cultivate reputations for some degree of vindictiveness, and this sustains cooperative outcomes. Though cooperation evaporates probabilistically as the horizon of the game approaches, efficient outcomes are perfectly sustainable when the horizon is sufficiently distant.

Lundberg appears to suggest that altruism may also prevent cooperation from unraveling because mechanisms such as altruism or love for one's partner and a desire to care for the person when he or she is old and disabled, ensure that marital commitments will endure late in life, despite the erosion of threats of retaliation. Although this observation is certainly correct, altruism cannot, by itself, mitigate endgame considerations. Altruism may improve the endgame outcome from a welfare perspective, but it does not necessarily make this outcome conditional on past behavior. Unraveling results from an inability to make endgame outcomes conditional on history, and not from the attractiveness of the endgame outcome per se. Of course, current behavior may affect future preferences. If poor treatment leaves an individual feeling less altruistic toward his or her spouse, current choices may indeed affect future behavior, in which case one can use this dependency to build up cooperative equilibria.

## Empirical Patterns

Lundberg's paper is provocative in part because she speculates on explanations for a variety of interesting empirical patterns. Although these speculations are intriguing, they are preliminary and in many instances incomplete, as the following example illustrates.

Various authors have documented that household consumption declines at retirement and have expressed puzzlement. Lundberg suggests that the phenomenon may be attributable to the decline in bargaining power that occurs with the husband's retirement. She reasons that this would shift the couple's choices in favor of the preferred profile of the wife, who expects to live longer and therefore prefers to maintain savings.

This explanation raises several issues. First, despite their longer lives, single women appear less inclined to save than single men.[11] If these gender-

11. Bernheim (1993).

specific proclivities also characterize married women, any shift toward the preferred profile of the wife would increase consumption, not decrease it. Second, Lundberg's hypothesis implies that single people should not display the consumption discontinuity at retirement. This implication is testable. Third, Lundberg's argument is difficult to justify in a formal model. The husband's bargaining power should decline gradually with the present discounted value of his future earnings, not discontinuously with the cessation of his earnings. One does not observe a gradual tipping of the household's choices in favor of future consumption before retirement.[12]

# References

Benoit, Jean-Pierre, and Vijay Krishna. 1985. "Finitely Repeated Games." *Econometrica* 53 (July): 905–22.

Bernheim, B. Douglas. 1993. *Is the Baby Boom Generation Saving Adequately for Retirement? Summary Report.* New York: Merrill Lynch, Pierce, Fenner & Smith.

Bernheim, B. Douglas, and Aniruddha Dasgupta. 1995. "Repeated Games with Asymptotically Finite Horizons." *Journal of Economic Theory* 67 (October): 129–52.

Bernheim, B. Douglas, and Debraj Ray. 1989. "Collective Dynamic Consistency in Repeated Games." *Games and Economic Behavior* 1 (December): 295–326.

Bernheim, B. Douglas, Jonathan Skinner, and Steven Weinberg. 1997. "What Accounts for the Variation in Retirement Saving Across U.S. Households?" Working Paper 6227. Cambridge, Mass.: National Bureau of Economic Research (October).

Bernheim, B. Douglas, and Michael Whinston. 1990. "Multimarket Contact and Collusive Behavior." *RAND Journal of Economics* 21 (Spring): 1–26.

Cremer, Jacques. 1986. "Cooperation in Ongoing Organizations." *Quarterly Journal of Economics* 101 (February): 33–49.

Farrell, Joseph, and Eric Maskin. 1989. "Renegotiation in Repeated Games." *Games and Economic Behavior* 1 (December): 327–60.

Fudenberg, Drew, David Kreps, and Eric Maskin. 1990. "Repeated Games with Long-Run and Short-Run Players." *Review of Economic Studies* 57 (October): 555–74.

Gavrilov, Leonid Anatolevich, and Natalia Sergeevna Gavrilova. 1991. "The Biology of Life Span: A Quantitative Approach." Reading, United Kingdom: Harwood Academic.

Kreps, David, and others. 1982. "Rational Cooperation in the Finitely Repeated Prisoner's Dilemma." *Journal of Economic Theory* 27 (August): 245–52.

Laibson, David. 1998. "Life-Cycle Consumption and Hyperbolic Discount Functions." *European Economic Review* 42 (May): 861–71.

---

12. Bernheim, Skinner, and Weinberg (1997).

# Contributors

Henry J. Aaron
Brookings Institution

Robert L. Axtell
Brookings Institution

B. Douglas Bernheim
Stanford University

Gary Burtless
Brookings Institution

Peter Diamond
Massachusetts Institute of
    Technology

Joshua M. Epstein
Brookings Institution

David Fetherstonhaugh
Stanford University

William G. Gale
Brookings Institution

Robert E. Hall
Stanford University

Daniel Kahneman
Princeton University

George Loewenstein
Carnegie Mellon University

Shelly Lundberg
University of Washington

283

Annamaria Lusardi
Irving B. Harris School of Public
  Policy Studies
University of Chicago

Ted O'Donoghue
Cornell University

Drazen Prelec
Massachusetts Institute of
  Technology

Matthew Rabin
University of California, Berkeley

Lee Ross
Stanford University

Roberto Weber
California Institute of
  Technology

# Index

285

# THE BROOKINGS INSTITUTION

The Brookings Institution is an independent organization devoted to non-partisan research, education, and publication in economics, government, foreign policy, and the social sciences generally. Its principal purposes are to aid in the development of sound public policies and to promote public understanding of issues of national importance. The Institution was founded on December 8, 1927, to merge the activities of the Institute for Government Research, founded in 1916, the Institute of Economics, founded in 1922, and the Robert Brookings Graduate School of Economics and Government, founded in 1924.

The Institution maintains a position of neutrality on issues of public policy to safeguard the intellectual freedom of the staff. Interpretations or conclusions in Brookings publications should be understood to be solely those of the authors.

# THE RUSSELL SAGE FOUNDATION

The Russell Sage Foundation, one of the oldest of America's general purpose foundations, was established in 1907 by Mrs. Margaret Olivia Sage for "the improvement of social and living conditions in the United States." The Foundation seeks to fulfill this mandate by fostering the development and dissemination of knowledge about the country's political, social, and economic problems. While the Foundation endeavors to assure the accuracy and objectivity of each book it publishes, the conclusions and interpretations in Russell Sage Foundation publications are those of the authors and not of the Foundation, its Trustees, or its staff. Publication by Russell Sage, therefore, does not imply Foundation endorsement.